CHURCH & LEARNING
IN THE
BYZANTINE EMPIRE
867–1185

CHURCH & LEARNING
IN THE
BYZANTINE EMPIRE
867–1185

BY

J. M. HUSSEY, M.A.

NEW YORK
RUSSELL & RUSSELL · INC
1963

FIRST PUBLISHED IN 1937
REISSUED, 1963, BY RUSSELL & RUSSELL, INC.
L. C. CATALOG CARD NO: 63—15164

PRINTED IN THE UNITED STATES OF AMERICA

PREFACE

CHURCH and learning in the Byzantine Empire are linked by more than mere chance. The whole outlook of the East Romans was rooted and grounded in religion, and any reconstruction of their life must recognize that behind the secular everyday education or the state-supported University was the Orthodox Church whose traditions and standards exerted an incalculable influence. This is not to imply that the Church was responsible for the maintenance of a tradition of scholarship. On the contrary, the organization of education and learning in the Byzantine Empire was more independent of the Church than in western Europe. But religion mattered a great deal to the Byzantines: the popular reverence for saints, the place of ecclesiastical ceremonial in public life, the very relation of Church to state—all this helps to show the reality of their belief in their Christian experience as members of the Orthodox Church. As a natural corollary, the Byzantines used all their powers—their reasons as well as their faith—in the service of the Church. However interested a scholar might be in Homer or Aristotle or Proclus, he was equally fired with a passion for theological discussions, applying himself to exegesis of the Scriptures or Patristic works no less than to philology or philosophy. He was, moreover, always conscious that, however wide his dialectical activities might range in private thought, he must guard against presenting them to the public if they were in any way antagonistic to the doctrines of the Orthodox Church; the bounds of orthodoxy were easy to cross, especially as he was free to read what he would, relying on his own common sense to sift the good from the bad, the orthodox from the heretical.

One difficulty in writing of church and learning is the lack of available sources, which in some cases appear to be nonexistent, in others are still unedited. There is, for instance, little evidence concerning schools, and existing matter is almost entirely furnished by the lives of a few individuals. And the position of the Church in this period has to be illustrated largely from the actions of its Patriarchs, because there appears to be insufficient evidence concerning the ordinary life of the bishop

or parish priest. Monasteries were continually founded, and
whenever possible they claimed independence of the secular
ecclesiastical authorities. But again there is often little evidence
other than bare statements of foundation or the record of some
immunity granted by the Emperor. The great contribution to
spiritual development in this period is made by a monk, Symeon
the Young, whose writings equal those of the greatest western
mystics.

An attempt to indicate in so short a space something of the
interest of Byzantine religion and learning during three hundred years can only be inadequate. It is in any case most difficult to describe the work of Byzantine scholars; there are such
manifold activities and interests that a short account tends to
become a meaningless catalogue of names. I have tried to some
extent to avoid this by writing in more detail on the eleventh-
century revival of learning where Michael Psellus and his friends
provide a natural focus for many of the activities of this period.
This has meant that only a brief indication could be given of
the scholarship of the tenth and twelfth centuries. In order to
set a further limit to so wide a subject popular or folk literature
has been omitted. With regard to the Church, issues outside
the life of the ordinary individual have been as far as possible
avoided. Thus little is said about relations with the Roman
Catholic Church as these were largely dominated by political
motives. There were, it is true, certain theological and dis-
ciplinary differences, but these were recognized and regarded
by the Byzantines as unfortunate deviations from the older and
original tradition of the Orthodox Church; the schism of 1054
was not even mentioned by contemporary Byzantine chroniclers.
Both art and liturgy had an intimate place in the Church, but
neither are discussed here, the first for lack of space, the second
because I hope to write of it in connexion with the unedited
Canons of John, the eleventh-century Archbishop of Euchaita.

I should like to thank Professor N. H. Baynes for the unfailing
patience and encouragement which made it possible for this to
be written. I wish also to thank Mr. W. D. Ross for his help
with the Appendix and parts of Chapter IV, and Professor
F. M. Powicke for innumerable kindnesses. I am particularly
indebted to Miss G. Cowan for the assistance which she has

given me in reading the proofs and making the index. My special thanks are due to St. Hugh's College, Oxford, to Westfield College, London, and to Girton College, Cambridge, for financial help and countless other gifts without which I could neither have begun nor continued my work. Finally, I wish to express my gratitude to the Universities of London and Oxford, and to St. Hugh's College, for the generous grants which they have made towards the cost of publishing this book.

J. M. H.

GIRTON COLLEGE,
CAMBRIDGE.
June, 1936.

CONTENTS

MAPS

BYZANTINE EMPERORS, 867-1185.

Macedonian House

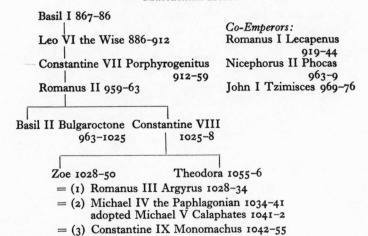

Basil I 867-86
|
Leo VI the Wise 886-912
|
Constantine VII Porphyrogenitus
912-59
|
Romanus II 959-63

Co-Emperors:
Romanus I Lecapenus
919-44
Nicephorus II Phocas
963-9
John I Tzimisces 969-76

Basil II Bulgaroctone   Constantine VIII
963-1025   1025-8

Zoe 1028-50   Theodora 1055-6
= (1) Romanus III Argyrus 1028-34
= (2) Michael IV the Paphlagonian 1034-41
         adopted Michael V Calaphates 1041-2
= (3) Constantine IX Monomachus 1042-55

Interval between the Macedonian and Comnenian Houses 1056-81

Michael VI Stratioticus	1056-7
Isaac Comnenus	1057-9
Constantine X Ducas	1059-67
Romanus IV Diogenes	1067-71
Michael VII Ducas	1071-8
Nicephorus III Botaneiates	1078-81

Comnenian House

Alexius I Comnenus	1081-1118
John II Comnenus	1118-43
Manuel I Comnenus	1143-80
Alexius II Comnenus	1180-3
Andronicus I Comnenus	1183-5

INTRODUCTION

A

THE Byzantine Empire was the medieval Roman Empire, and throughout the middle ages its people usually spoke of themselves as 'Romans'. When the western part of the original Roman Empire was conquered by invasions culminating in the sack of Rome, it was in the eastern half that the Roman Empire continued, until its capital, Constantinople, the New Rome, was sacked in 1204, not by the Turks, but by the Crusaders of western Europe. After this disaster of the Fourth Crusade the Eastern Empire never regained its balance; the Emperors who ruled once more from Constantinople at the end of the thirteenth century were but miserable shadows of their famous predecessors, while the administration and morale of the Empire had been irretrievably shaken.

During the three centuries of the Macedonians and the Comneni both the strength and weakness of the Byzantine Empire are exposed. While western Europe was in the throes of constitutional, ecclesiastical and intellectual development, Constantinople, secure in the possession of an already matured administration and Church and learning, was provided with that stability which enabled it to concentrate on an increasing military vigilance, and thus, not only to preserve its frontiers against the constant aggressions of its neighbours, but to balance loss in one sphere with expansion in another. This is true until the period of the Comneni (1081–1185), when the Empire proved unable effectively either to drive back the Turks from Asia Minor or to control the Crusaders.

A brief survey of the frontier history of the Empire during the years 867–1185 will show the setting in which ecclesiastical and intellectual life must be reconstructed, and will explain something of the difficulty of living at Constantinople. It was, indeed, true to say that the nerves of the Roman Empire were its army,[1] for the story of the foreign policy of the Byzantine Empire at any point in its history was a tale of constant struggle against

[1] Psellus, *Chron.* iv. 19 (i, p. 64).

invasions. Its vast boundaries were always changing, and in its geographical extent it was ambitious; built up on the principles of the old Roman Empire, it included many different races, welding together its heterogeneous subjects by means of a common law and Church and culture.

In 867, on the accession of the founder of the Macedonian house, Basil I, the Empire included the themes of Asia Minor, of Greece and Macedonia, and of south Italy. The chief enemies to be faced were the Slavs and wild tribes on the north and north-east, and, more formidable still, the Arabs on the south, who had already conquered Syria and north Africa and most of Sicily and Crete, all once within the Empire.

When Alexius Comnenus came to the throne in 1081 he found the Empire considerably diminished, for the Italian provinces had been lost to the Normans, who were even dreaming of reaching Constantinople itself, and Syria to the Turks, who had become the masters of the Arabs and were rapidly absorbing the Asiatic themes into what was to become the Sultanate of Rûm. It is true that Bulgaria had been added to the Empire, but the nomadic Patzinak tribes from the northern shores of the Black Sea could still penetrate to the gates of Constantinople. It is, then, remarkable that the Comneni managed to keep some control over the Crusaders, to reconquer part of Asia Minor, and to make a valiant effort to continue the traditions of imperial government. Nevertheless, it was clear that the rule of the Comneni could only postpone, and not prevent, the inevitable downfall. The difficulties introduced by the Latin Christians turned the already uncertain balance, and their perfidy and interference were partly responsible for the final collapse of the Byzantine Empire when the Ottoman Turks captured Constantinople in 1453. Byzantium's more normal existence is to be seen during the period of the Macedonian rulers, for then it was still fighting without the feeling of being foredoomed to failure, and there seemed hope that it might yet preserve its political life.

It was on the northern frontiers that the most successful and permanent advance was made by the Macedonians. The immediate problem was the kingdom of Bulgaria, lying at the doors of Thessalonica and Macedonia, and, at the period of its greatest extent in the beginning of the tenth century, ready both to expand into Greece and to threaten Constantinople. The usual Byzantine policy was that of diplomacy; war it waged, but it always tried to lighten its difficulties by instigating others to embarrass the enemy. The situation in the Balkans afforded ample scope for intrigues and bribery. The Serbians could often be persuaded to attack Bulgaria, while to the north-east were still richer possibilities in the Russians and the savage nomadic tribes of the Patzinaks and Cumans.

The first Bulgarian Empire owed a considerable debt to its highly developed Byzantine neighbours, and for a short time it even hoped to win Constantinople. It took Byzantium more than a hundred years to subdue this ambitious kingdom, but it was finally conquered by Basil II, whose fierce, if effective, methods earned for him the title of 'Slayer of the Bulgarians'. The conquest of Bulgaria may have given some stability and safety to the northern frontiers, but it was never a very serviceable acquisition to the Empire and was constantly unsettled by the inroads of the Patzinaks. Official greed and incapacity, combined with national antagonism, made Byzantine rule a hateful thing, and the rise of the second Bulgarian Empire in 1186 was the logical outcome of such a situation.

Serbia never troubled the Empire as much as Bulgaria, while geography discouraged conquest, and, indeed, rendered it less necessary. The Serbs, who lived in modern Albania and Montenegro, had been converted to the Orthodox Church, and in Basil I's reign were nominally bound to the Empire by ties of suzerainty. During Bulgaria's more prosperous days in the tenth century they were often overrun by this enemy, and expediency forced them frequently to change their allegiance. But once the Bulgarian menace was laid low, the Serbs became more independent. They evidently declared their freedom during the reign of Romanus III, for the chronicler Cedrenus writes that in 1036 they were again forced to submit to the yoke of the Roman Empire. But the mountainous nature of the country did not help the conquerors, and their precarious hold was again shaken towards the end of the eleventh century, when the Serbians defied the Byzantines. It was not, however, until towards the end of the twelfth century that Serbia,

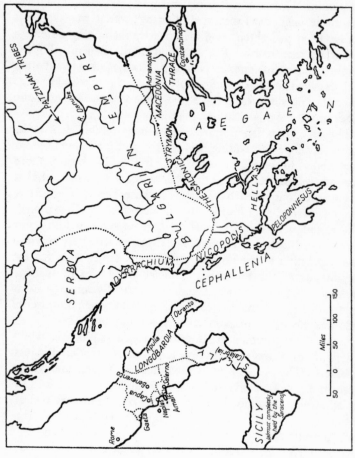

THE WESTERN THEMES AND THE KINGDOM OF BULGARIA. c. 900

like Bulgaria, successfully asserted its freedom from Byzantine interference.

Russia, though too far north of the Empire to cause it such intimate concern as Serbia or Bulgaria, was nevertheless a factor not to be overlooked under the Macedonians. Negotiations with Russia usually aimed at diverting its energies towards the enemies of Constantinople, and thus to prevent their being directed against the Empire. Nor were Byzantine fears an illusion, for not only was Constantinople besieged by the Russians, but the imperial policy of paying tribute was often the only possible course. With the usual judicious management, however, no irremedial harm was done, and gradually the rulers of Kiev, once nomads, became more settled. The last Russian attack against Constantinople was made by sea in 1043.

An important element in the Balkan policy under the early Macedonians was the possibility of stirring up the nomadic Patzinaks to attack Bulgaria, a policy which was equally useful against the Russians or Magyars. But Bulgaria became a Byzantine province; at the same time the Patzinaks were being pushed farther south by the movements of the Cuman tribes behind them. So that what had been a boon, when directed against an enemy, was to become the scourge of the northern provinces. These tribes, who were related to the Seljuq Turks, had by then settled in the area to the north-east of Bulgaria between the Danube and the Dnieper, and from time to time they swept over the frontiers of the Byzantine Empire, pillaging and destroying, even up to the walls of Constantinople.

After Basil II the Emperors had constant trouble with the Patzinaks, and were forced to adopt the usual expedient of buying peace. The difficulty of assimilating such a wild race was beyond the capacity of eleventh-century Emperors, who ruled only for a few years, and who were sometimes neither soldiers nor appreciative of the needs of the army. The power of the Patzinaks reached its highest point at the end of the eleventh century, during the reign of Alexius Comnenus, when, aided by the equally ferocious Cuman tribes, they defeated the Emperor, and reached Constantinople. The danger was increased by the fear that they would ally with a Turkish pirate who was then threatening to unite Patzinaks and Seljuq Turks against the Empire. Alexius tried the policy of bribery, and the Cumans were persuaded to attack the Patzinaks, while similar dissension was created among the Turks. The Patzinaks were so mercilessly defeated by the Cumans that they ceased to be a menace. It was not until John Comnenus's day that they had sufficiently revived to invade the Empire once more, but they were then defeated and never again became the scourge which they had been in the eleventh century.

The northern frontier was the problem of the Macedonians rather than the Comnenian Emperors. They were largely responsible for establishing the Orthodox Church in Serbia, Bulgaria, and Russia; they gave these countries, in varying measure, some knowledge of the heritage of Greece and Rome; and it was their missionary zeal and work of civilization that ultimately made possible the foundation of independent nationalities.

In the west the Macedonians were less successful than in the north, and the Italian provinces were lost, not to the Arabs, but to the Normans. Under the early Macedonians there were two stages in the Byzantine struggle in south Italy: the first, a period of fighting against the Arabs, while Italians, Pope, and western Emperor all played the part they thought most to their advantage, being afraid of Arab aggressions, and yet desiring to undermine Byzantine power in so far as this was consistent with their own safety; the second, in the eleventh century, when the situation changed, and Arabs, Pope, and both eastern and western Emperors were gradually forced to recognize the conquest of south Italy and Sicily by the Norman invaders.

At the beginning of Basil I's reign the imperial possessions in south Italy were the themes which were known in the tenth century as Sicily or Calabria, and Longobardia (Apulia and Otranto); the island of Sicily, which had formed part of the theme of Sicily, was by then almost entirely conquered by the Arabs. It may be wondered what justification Constantinople had for the possession of lands seemingly belonging to the Latin rather than the Greek civilization. But, although Longobardia was Latin in sympathy, and increasingly so as Byzantium unwisely refused any measure of real self-government, Calabria, on the other hand, was very strongly Greek in its outlook. From Basil I to the middle of the tenth century, the Byzantines, with some fluctuation of fortune, kept the Arabs off the Italian themes, while the attitude of the Papacy and the Italian principalities varied with Byzantine success. The Pope was often thankful to encourage any check to the Moslems. Sicily, however, was completely lost to Byzantium by 967. A new phase in the south Italian struggle was introduced by Otto I, the Holy Roman Emperor, who claimed that Italy came under the suzerainty of the Western and not the Eastern Empire. Nicephorus Phocas and John Tzimisces in turn negotiated with Otto, who had successfully invaded Longobardia in 968; finally peace was made, and Otto's son, the future Otto II, was married to a Byzantine princess.

It was not, however, in the Holy Roman Emperors of the Saxon house but in the Normans that the Byzantine provinces were to find their greatest danger. Although the Italian themes had been reorganized at the end of the tenth century, Byzantine control was not very secure, especially in Apulia, and it ultimately proved unable to withstand the combination of the various elements of native discontent, reinforced by the Norman adventurers who were at this time penetrating into every European country. There were three stages in the relations between Norman and Greek: first, the more tentative period when the immigrants tried their fortunes in the service of both Longobard and Byzantine; then the establishment of the Normans as masters of south Italy and Sicily; and, finally, the failure of their ambition to intrude farther into the Byzantine Empire and to conquer Constantinople. By the end of the eleventh century it had become clear that the Byzantine possessions in Italy were irretrievably lost, and, as the Crusades were to reveal, to unpleasantly active foes.

The Crusades of western Europe were only the continuation of a struggle against the Moslems which had been going on for centuries. It was on the eastern frontier that Byzantium had long been fighting for its existence. The Asiatic themes were more important than any others, and once they were lost the strength of the Empire was gone. Moreover, the Arabs were very different foes from the Slavs or Patzinaks; they had their creed and their civilization, and it is understandable that they were often regarded by the Byzantines as preferable not only

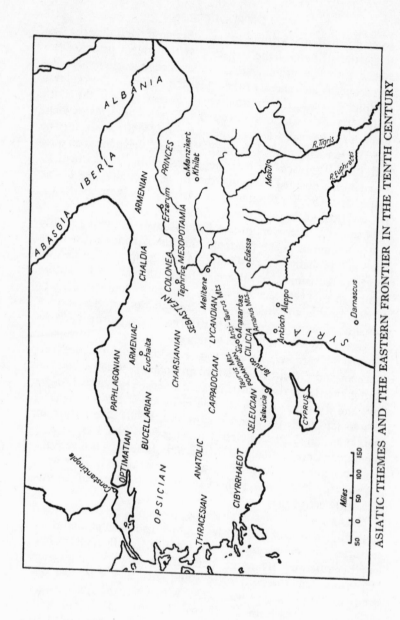

ASIATIC THEMES AND THE EASTERN FRONTIER IN THE TENTH CENTURY

ALBANIA

IBERIA

ABASGIA

ARMENIAN

PRINCES

o Manzikert
o Khilat

R. Tigris

R. Euphrates

CHALDIA

COLONEA

Erzerum

MESOPOTAMIA

Tephrice

Mostllo

SEBASTEA

Edessa

ARMENIAC

Euchaita

CHARSIANIAN

Melitene

LYCANDIAN

Taurus Mts

PAPHLAGONIAN

CAPPADOCIAN

Anti-Taurus Mts

Anazarbas

Amanus Mts

Damascus

BUCELLARIAN

Taurus Mts

Antioch

Aleppo

PODANDUS

CILICIA

ANATOLIC

Tarsus

SYRIA

OPTIMATIAN

SELEUCIAN

Constantinople

OPSICIAN

THRACESIAN

Seleucia

CIBYRRHAEOT

CYPRUS

Miles

50 0   50   100 150

to the enemies on the northern frontier, but even to the Latin 'barbarians' of western Europe.

Beneath a bewildering frequency of border raids and an ever-changing frontier line the struggle under the Macedonians presents some outstanding features. During the course of the tenth century certain factors told in favour of the Byzantines: the Caliphate was slowly weakening, though Byzantium had to face local emirs who were taking advantage of central incapacity to build up their own power; the independent princes of the Caucasus district and Armenia were bribed and forced with increasing success to support Constantinople; and, most important of all, the Empire had a series of great military leaders who changed the annual border raids into an offensive that really pushed back the Moslem frontier.

By the middle of the tenth century Byzantine power had been strengthened all along the eastern frontier, and advances were especially noticeable on the Upper Euphrates and on the borders of the Armenian principalities. In the second half of the tenth century the aim of the great general, Nicephorus Phocas, was to free Cilicia from the border raids of the Emir of Aleppo, and ultimately to reach Jerusalem. His motives were religious as well as political, and in his treatise on warfare he always ended each section with the refrain, 'You will win this victory with the aid of the true God.' Before Nicephorus's murder in 969, Cyprus had been captured, Tarsus taken, and Cilicia reduced, while Antioch and Aleppo had both fallen to Byzantine attack, the former to be garrisoned by the Christians, the latter to become a vassal state.

It was in the middle of the eleventh century that the position on the eastern frontier was changed by the disintegration of the Arabian Caliphates, which finally came under the control of the Seljuq Turks, while the politics of the Byzantine Empire were at once simplified and weakened by the imperial conquest of what remained of Armenia, a kingdom that for more than a century had played the part of buffer state. It was unfortunate that the substitution of weak and unpopular Byzantine rule in Armenia should coincide with a period when a strong military frontier was essential, and when a virile, though independent, kingdom would have better served the imperial needs.

The Seljuq Turks were a nomadic race who had arrived in Turkestan towards the end of the tenth century, and, profiting by the dissensions between the different Arabian Caliphates, established their rule first in Persia, then at Baghdad, whence they penetrated into Syria, Egypt, and Asia Minor. The advance into the Byzantine Empire in the eleventh century was gradual and unorganized, an opportunist policy that was more than invited by the weakness of the imperial defences. The newly acquired Armenia was first conquered, and this was followed by a spasmodic encroachment into Asia Minor. This indefinite position was somewhat stabilized by the foundation of the Sultanate of Rûm with its capital at Iconium; and it was against this that Alexius Comnenus directed his attacks, though necessity had forced him to begin by accepting the Turks as allies.

It was with the coming of the Crusaders rather than the Turks that the history of the Byzantine Empire was irretrievably changed. Hitherto the Empire had fought the Moslem with undivided Christian ranks. Christian subjects had meanwhile managed to live under Moslem rule, the Patriarchs of Jerusalem and Antioch continued to be responsible for the Christians in their patriarchates, and pilgrims, both Greek and Latin, could usually gain access to the holy places. Although political dissension within the Byzantine Empire and innumerable difficulties without had combined to facilitate Turkish advance, it may be surmised that the Comnenian Emperors would have repulsed the Turks more ably had they been unhampered by western interference.

The concern of Alexius Comnenus and his successors was to drive back the Turks in order to recover at least the boundary which the Empire had at the time of the brilliant Macedonian offensive. But the First Crusade, mainly composed of Normans, had little unity either of command or aim. The more spiritually minded, an unarmed host 'more numerous than the sand or stars',[1] desired to liberate Jerusalem from Moslem control; the majority of these died on the way, being unfitted for the inevitable warfare. The more capable had political aims, and they wished to consolidate the deliverance of Jerusalem by the establishment of Christian states in Syria. None considered the

[1] Anna Comnena, *Alexias*, x. 5 (ii, p. 74).

needs and circumstances of the Byzantine Empire, and it was
not unnatural that the Byzantines regarded the devastation of
their lands by uncontrolled hordes and the possibility of small
hostile Christian states in Syria as both an infringement of
imperial rights and a serious impediment to any united attack
on the Turks.

Byzantine fears were realized. The diplomacy of Constantinople was taxed to the utmost to prevent any breach with the
invaders who so discourteously forced their way through the
Eastern Empire; and when later the Latin states of Antioch,
Edessa, Tripoli, and Jerusalem came into being, their rulers
refused to recognize the Emperor as their suzerain, contrary
to the oath of allegiance which had been taken in Constantinople.
It is true that the First Crusade did check the Turks; the very
establishment of the Latin kingdoms was a tribute to its momen-
tary success. But time was to show the impossibility of maintaining the disunited Latin front, while Christian opposition
was lamentably weakened by mutual distrust of Greek and
Latin. The unfortunate Alexius exercised constant vigilance
in his efforts to secure control over the Latin states in Syria,
which he justly regarded as owing suzerainty to the Byzantines,
and it is to his credit that, despite the intricacies of his relations
with the Crusaders, he could still achieve some success against
the Turks in Asia Minor.

Alexius's work was consolidated by his son, John Comnenus
(1118–43). During this reign Byzantium kept what had already
been gained in Asia Minor, while additional security was gained
by John's annexation of Lesser Armenia. This little polity had
been formed in Cilicia by Armenian refugees driven from their
own territory by the Turks. It had inclined towards Antioch
rather than Constantinople, and its reduction by John was the
first step towards the establishment of some control over the
Latins in Syria. This success was followed by further progress
when John forced the Latin ruler of Antioch to take the oath
of fealty to the Eastern Empire.

With Manuel Comnenus (1143–80) the centre of interest
changed. He maintained the Byzantine position in Cilicia and
Antioch, but his real interest was in the west, where he dreamt
of restoring Byzantine rule in the old themes of south Italy,

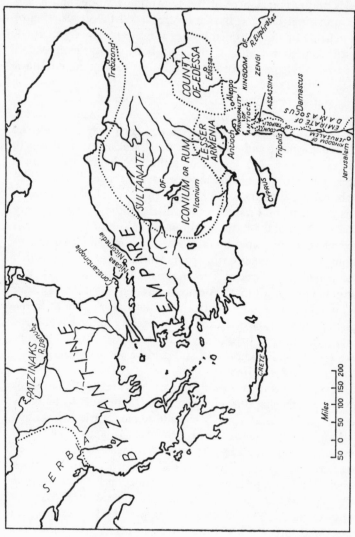

THE EMPIRE AND THE LATIN STATES IN SYRIA. c. 1140

SERBIA

PATZINAKS

R. Danube

BYZANTINE EMPIRE

Constantinople

Nicaea
Nicomedia

CRETE

Miles
50 0 50 100 150 200

SULTANATE OF ICONIUM OR RUM

Iconium

Trebizond

LESSER ARMENIA

COUNTY OF EDESSA

Edessa

Aleppo

ZENGI

KINGDOM OF

R. Euphrates

Antioch

PRINCIPALITY OF ANTIOCH

ASSASSINS

Damascus

EMIRATE OF DAMASCUS

COUNTY OF TRIPOLI

Tripolis

CYPRUS

KINGDOM OF JERUSALEM

Jerusalem

a retrogressive intention, but a natural one for a man who was strongly under the influence of the west, and who encouraged Latins to seek their fortune at Constantinople. Manuel tried to ally in turn with the western Emperor, Venice, the Pope, and other Italian cities, but in the end he failed completely. The reconciliation of Pope, Emperor, and Italian cities at Venice in 1177 was a great blow to Byzantine diplomacy. Manuel suffered an equally crushing reverse in Asia Minor when he was terribly defeated in 1177 by the Sultan of Rûm at Myriocephalon. For Byzantium there was no longer any question of regaining power in Italy or of dislodging the Turks from Asia Minor. The gloomy end of the Comneni was a fitting prelude to the disasters of the thirteenth century.

B

But behind the terrifying array of campaigns and frontier invasions Byzantium lived a life that, if hardly secure, was at least animated with a vitality but inadequately described as 'a preservation of its inheritance'; and beneath the difficult Greek of those authors favoured by an edition there lies a world whose public and private interests were many and vigorous. Its background, its history, its outlook, were all different from those of western Europe, and it had therefore a different approach to political, and educational, and ecclesiastical problems. These were, indeed, not so much 'problems' as 'traditions', remaining, it is true, unaltered in their essential features. The Byzantine polity, with its dual autocracy of Basileus and Patriarch, with its highly efficient administrative and legal system, with its secular education and love of classical learning, with its widespread reverence for the saint and the monastic life, this was rooted and grounded in the developments of the first eight or nine centuries. Despite a sameness of outlook there was nothing that could be described as static about politics at Constantinople, although behind the interest and variety of everyday events there were naturally certain outstanding problems and characteristics during the years 867–1185.

The two hundred years of Macedonian rule saw a tenacious maintenance of the hereditary principle, even to the length of enduring twenty years of an incapable old Empress. But the urgent pressure on not one frontier only, but many, naturally stressed the importance of the army, and it became usual, especially if the heir were a minor or a woman, for a Co-Emperor to emerge and become the real ruler of Constantinople. Romanus I Lecapenus, Nicephorus Phocas, John Tzimisces, all attained this position; the Empress Zoe had successive husbands and an adopted son; Eudoxia married Romanus IV Diogenes, pleading the necessity for a man's control during the minority of her sons; even under the Comneni the same phenomenon appeared, though this time reversed, when Alexius gave control of internal affairs to his able mother, Anna Dalassena. The exigencies of empire demanded some such division as that described by Anna Comnena, who said that while her father was himself responsible for the foreign policy and military operations, 'the whole administration of affairs, the choice of civil officers and the accounts of the income and expenditure of the Empire, he entrusted to his mother'.[1]

This military need had an important corollary: it gave prominence to the great families of Asia Minor. It was from the Asiatic themes that the most experienced generals came, men not only with military talent, but with the backing of considerable possessions. These families, as the Phocae, or Comneni, constituted both a safeguard and a threat during the Macedonian period—a safeguard in that they produced first-class soldiers, a threat in that they resented the control of the civil, or palace, party at Constantinople. The rebellion of some Asiatic rival to the throne was a menace to every Emperor, and sometimes the successful pretender attained to the rank of Co-Emperor, as in the case of Nicephorus Phocas, or even Emperor, as sometimes happened in the eleventh century. The clash between the military and civil parties is seen most clearly in the later years of the Macedonian house (1025–56), and before the rise of the Comneni (1056–81). The nearest approach to a solution came with the establishment of the Comneni, for in addition to their strength and ability as rulers the encroachment of the Seljuq Turks had by then irretrievably crippled the Asiatic themes, a solution that was in the latter respect a curse rather than a blessing.

The difficulty of controlling the great families of Asia Minor

[1] Anna Comnena, *Alexias*, iii. 7 (i, p. 111).

showed itself from time to time in the financial and agrarian policy of the Macedonians and Comneni. The tendency was for the more powerful to absorb the land of the poorer, and hence the continual attempt to grant easy terms of ownership to peasants and to alleviate their burden of taxation. Measures against the rich sometimes, as under Romanus I, included Church property. A measure particularly unpopular among both ecclesiastical and secular landowners was the system of taxation introduced by Nicephorus Phocas, and known as the 'allelengyon', whereby the rich helped those who were too poor to pay their taxes. Finance problems naturally became increasingly acute under the Comneni, and, whereas Basil II could leave a well-filled treasury, Manuel Comnenus was faced with a terrible deficit.

In spite of both internal and external common problems, there is a difference between the two periods. That of the Macedonians is the more varied and interesting, and the more satisfying, with its wholesome indifference to western influence; in Manuel Comnenus's love of the west there is too vivid a reminder of the Crusades and a presage of the disaster of 1204.

The male Macedonians were nearly all outstanding people. The founder of the house, Basil I, formerly a groom, developed in a remarkable manner into a ruler who ably appreciated the traditions of imperial government. Leo VI, who may or may not have been Basil's own son, certainly continued his predecessor's work, especially in the sphere of law and in the establishment of a dynasty, even to incurring the Church's grave displeasure by marrying as many as four times in order to obtain an heir. Constantine VII, although his works show that he had a real feeling for the imperial office, was clearly a scholar rather than an administrator, and for twenty-five years of his reign he had an efficient Co-Emperor in Romanus I Lecapenus, in whom the political interest of the reign centres. Constantine VII's heir, Romanus II, was a vicious and unsatisfactory Emperor, and there was justice in the premature end to his short reign. During the minority of his sons, the Emperors Basil II and Constantine VIII,[1] the government was controlled by two

[1] Although Constantine VIII is usually spoken of as reigning after Basil II, he was in actual fact Co-Emperor with his brother.

Co-Emperors, Nicephorus Phocas, and then John Tzimisces, both of whom were distinguished generals. When John Tzimisces died in 976 the young Macedonian, Basil II, was about eighteen years old. With an energy reminiscent of the founder of his house he suppressed the rebellions of those aspiring to the position of Co-Emperor, making it clear that in future he was to be the customary military Emperor, while his brother, Constantine VIII, by nature indolent and pleasure-loving, was to live a palace life in Constantinople.

During the first hundred and fifty years of Macedonian rule, then, the history of Byzantium, in spite of political vicissitudes, shows in a remarkable way the persistence of an imperial ideal. The work of the founder of the Macedonian house well illustrates this. Basil I, although he had not been born in the purple and had had no training for his high office, showed an unerring appreciation of his duties as Emperor. He emphasized the necessity for religion, and is, indeed, reputed to have told his young son that the imperial virtue above all others was εὐσέβεια, reverence for the Christian principles, a reverence which found its fulfilment in the practical φιλανθρωπία that characterized a Byzantine Emperor. Basil realized, moreover, that if the imperial position was autocratic, its justification was nevertheless the quality of its government; and, as the Emperor was the representative of God on earth, so his rule must be equitable and beneficial, and his first concern the welfare of his people. Basil's attempt to govern wisely is seen most clearly in his legal work, both in the effort to clarify the existing law and in his care for the impartial administration of justice. Education, no less than religion and good government, was the concern of the Emperor, and even though he himself might be absorbed by military cares or unfitted by temperament and upbringing for any pursuit of learning, yet this pursuit was obviously considered an important factor in the normal life of Emperors as well as citizens. It is interesting to note that Leo VI and Constantine VII were men who appreciated this, and they themselves left writings on varied subjects, from military tactics and imperial ceremonial to Church poetry and sermons.

So successfully did Basil surround his family with the aura

of divine right that their disappearance from history was due
not to any political revolution, but to the extinction of the
house with the death of the unmarried Theodora in 1056. The
last thirty years of Macedonian rule (1025–56) and the interreg-
num (1056–81) deserve more attention than they often receive,
and to dismiss these years as 'the decline of the Macedonians
and the troubles before the rise of the Comneni' is to state a
partial truth which does inadequate justice to this period. It is
well to remember the exact nature of the demands upon imperial
resources throughout these years, the rebellions within the
Empire and the constant pressure on every frontier, the com-
plications arising from the lack of any male heir in the Macedonian line, and the constant struggle between the powerful
military families of Asia Minor and the civil party at Constantinople. If the Empire suffered certain grave reverses, especially
in south Italy and Asia Minor, these must be attributed to the
strength of her adversaries as well as to her own military and
financial deficiencies. Imperial extravagance and neglect of the
frontiers are very often undeniable. But it is to the credit of the
administration as well as a tribute to the courage and perseverance of certain of the Emperors, whose sudden elevation
might have had far more disastrous consequences, that the
Empire retained its control over the Bulgarians, imposed some
check on the Patzinaks and Arabs, and made a stubborn, though
fitful, resistance to the Seljuq Turks. Moreover, it was during
these years of great political difficulty that Constantinople was
the centre of a remarkable outburst of interest in learning which
continued to bear fruit long after the Macedonians had been
forgotten.

The last male of the Macedonian house, Basil's brother Constantine VIII (1025–28), was neither soldier nor statesman, but
interested in theatres and horse-racing. He had no son, but
three daughters all unmarried and aged. Zoe, the middle sister,
was the most beautiful and the most adventurous: while her
sisters preferred monastic life, she accepted the husband whom
her father hurriedly selected for her just before his death. For
twenty-two years she enjoyed marriage and a throne and was
extremely popular with the people of Constantinople. Both her
natural inclination and her incapacity for government, as well as

the political need for a leader whose authority would be unquestioned, made masculine support necessary. She had, at various times, three husbands and an adopted son.[1] Zoe died in 1050, and her sister Theodora, nominally Co-Empress since 1042, in 1056. Zoe and Theodora had never been more than pawns in the political game; Zoe's third husband, Constantine IX, was the real ruler until his death in 1055. Throughout the short reigns of Theodora (1055–6) and her nominee, Michael VI (1056–7), the civil element, and more particularly the palace officials, struggled to retain their supremacy. Michael VI, of whom it was aptly said that he was 'simple and harmless',[2] could control neither military nor civil parties, and he precipitated his downfall by his tactless breach with the military nobles from Asia Minor. During the next few years the antagonism between the civil and military parties became acute, and first one and then the other triumphed to the inevitable detriment of any consistent frontier policy. Isaac Comnenus, a distinguished soldier and sound administrator, ruled only for two years (1057–9); the alleged excuse for his abdication was ill health, but there was clearly great opposition to his policy of financial retrenchment. His successor, Constantine X Ducas, showed during the nine years of his reign a disastrous preference for the civil party. Romanus IV, who did lead an army against the Turks, was finally defeated at Manzikert (1071). The interest of the years following Romanus's deposition and death is not so much in the Emperors—first Michael VII, then Nicephorus III Botaneiates—as in the growth of the power of the Comneni. In 1081 Alexius Comnenus was invested as Emperor, and thus the fast-growing palace opposition to the Comneni was forestalled before it could deprive the Empire of the service which was so badly needed.

It is apparent from the internal history of the Empire during the years 1025–81 that the imperial difficulties were enormously increased by the ceaseless attacks on all frontiers. The cry in the struggle for the throne was always for a military leader, but it must not be forgotten that, in spite of the criticism which is levelled against the imperial neglect of the army and which is especially true of Constantine X and Michael VII, generals, and

[1] Romanus III, Michael IV, and Constantine IX; Michael V was the adopted son. [2] Cedrenus, ii. p. 612.

often the Emperor, were always fighting in some part of the Empire.

The military demands of the Empire were fully realized by the Comneni. Alexius spent most of his time on campaign and was an excellent soldier. His immediate difficulties necessitated an efficient army and navy, and these could be neither organized nor maintained without a full treasury. One of the great cares of his home policy was, therefore, to obtain adequate financial supplies, and the empty treasury which he had found was filled by heavy taxation, by confiscations from political offenders, and even by a forced loan from the Church. His concern for orthodoxy and his devoutness did not blind him to the disproportionate wealth of the Church, and it had to suffer with the rest. In spite of Alexius's obvious financial difficulties, he must have managed to command large supplies; he not only found the money for his wars, but he lavishly rewarded his friends and supporters, and he founded orphanages and monasteries.

Alexius has always had an advantage over other Emperors, in that he was the hero of his daughter's history. But even when the eloquence and charm and exaggeration of Anna Comnena's *Alexias* is discounted, he remains a wise Emperor; nor could all the persuasion of his wife convince him that Anna and her husband, Bryennius, would better succeed him than his son, John. According to Zonaras, Alexius died with a smile on his lips, obstinately refusing Irene's last appeal, to her anger and confusion.[1]

John Comnenus, like his father, was a soldier, and his greatest work is to be found in his foreign policy. Anna, who probably hated him, only once mentions him; she says that as a child he was very dark, with 'a broad forehead, lean cheeks, a nose neither snub nor aquiline but something between the two, very black eyes which betokened, as far as one can judge from an infant's face, a quick intelligence'.[2] John married an Hungarian princess, and his court appears to have retained the austerity of atmosphere which Anna Dalassena had introduced. The twenty years of his reign have left little evidence of his home policy, and that which exists concerns religion and learning rather than administration and finance.

[1] Zonaras, xviii. 28 (iii, p. 762).   [2] *Alexias*, vi. 8 (i, pp. 204–5).

Manuel was twenty years old when he succeeded his father, John. The apparent charm of his personality was misleading; his courage was reckless and he never acquired the seasoned wisdom of a general; his excessive love of theological discussion was often as superficial as was his pleasure-loving court; his wide plans for the restoration of Byzantine boundaries and prestige were founded upon a misunderstanding of contemporary politics and practical possibilities. Like Alexius and John, he had to give thought to military need, and the constant problem was to find men and money for the army. But he roused considerable opposition. His taxation of ecclesiastical wealth and his insistence on his theological knowledge alienated many of the clergy, and his partiality for westerners provoked the anger of the people.

After his death Manuel's unwise policy was at first continued by his Latin wife, the Regent, Mary of Antioch, but she had to face a fast-growing antagonism. Gradually Andronicus Comnenus, Manuel's cousin, gained control of the government. Manuel's young son, the Emperor Alexius II, was murdered in 1183, but Andronicus only ruled for three years; he was in turn murdered in 1185, to be succeeded by the incompetent Isaac Angelus.

Without detracting from the fame of the Comneni, it may be suggested that they had several advantages over other Byzantine Emperors. They were men who reigned for a substantial time; they, and especially Alexius and John, ruled on the whole efficiently under difficult circumstances; they shone in comparison with their immediate predecessors; they reaped the benefit of the intellectual enthusiasm of the eleventh century; and, finally, by reason of the course which history took, they have always been better known in western Europe, although it is true that until recently they were too often made the scapegoats of the crusading failures. But the twelfth century was a period of compromise, unfortunate for east and west alike, and resulting not in mutual enrichment and defence, but in mutual suspicion and envy.

A comparison of the Macedonian and Comnenian periods only emphasizes the difficulties introduced by increasing western interference. It may be true that the Byzantine Empire was not destined to be an end in itself, but that like the Roman Empire in western Europe, was eventually to give place to separate national polities; nevertheless, there might have been a gentler evolution had it been unharassed by the Crusaders and the increasing intricacy of its foreign policy. It is, however, remarkable that, in spite of constant external pressure, the Byzantines maintained their heritage, an administrative system, a secular education, an Orthodox Church. Western Europe owes Byzantium a threefold debt: protection from the Asiatic invaders who moved westwards throughout the Middle Ages, the preservation of the tradition of classical learning, and the development of art and mysticism wherein medieval Byzantium showed its creativeness.

CHAPTER I

LEARNING UNDER THE MACEDONIANS IN THE NINTH AND TENTH CENTURIES

Like a bee, I shall gather all that conforms to the truth, even extracting help from the writings of our enemies. . . . So, as I would emphasize, I am not offering you my own conclusions, but those which were laboriously arrived at by the most eminent teachers, while I have only collected them, and summarized them, as far as was possible, into one treatise.

John of Damascus, Prologue to *Fons scientiae*, PG, xciv, cols. 524–5.

WITH the notable exceptions of art and mysticism, it must be admitted that Byzantine history records preservation rather than creation; but without genuine appreciation it would have been impossible to preserve a tradition of learning. Byzantium produced no one who can compare with the best western medieval thinkers, but its people were, on the other hand, better educated. They studied classical authors who were for centuries unknown in the west, and a knowledge of these was considered as essential as it was to become in western Europe of the sixteenth century. This is especially the case in the period of the Macedonians and Comneni, and evidence points to some continuity of Byzantine education, despite the difficulties which beset men of letters amid the uncertainties of political life. Byzantine standards were not lowered by the vicissitudes of constant invasion from which scarcely any part of the Empire was spared.

Byzantine education and scholarship did not depend so much on ecclesiastical schools as in western Europe. There was an unbroken tradition of secular learning, while the aim of its monasteries was to produce saints rather than statesmen or teachers. The ecclesiastical schools which existed were something apart from ordinary public education, and this cleavage between theological and secular instruction was, as Fuchs shows, from the earliest times a feature of Byzantine life. There is no evidence for a theological faculty in Theodosius's original foundation of 425, and Junilius mentions as a contrast to the custom of the City, 'Syrorum schola in Nisibi urbe . . . ubi divina lex per

magistros publicos, sicut apud nos in mundanis studiis gram-
matica et rhetorica, ordine ac regulariter traditur.'[1] Nor did
the ninth-century revival of the University offer any theology
among the subjects taught; and later the interest and importance
of outstanding monastic figures, such as Symeon the Young or
Nicetas Stethatus, is found in their contribution to the development of mysticism. Most Byzantine monks had little opportunity for increasing their knowledge of secular authorities
within the monastery, and their libraries, as in the cases of
Attaleiates' and Christodoulus's foundations, would probably be
theological. There is not much evidence of any interpenetration
between secular learning and Church schools although the latter
certainly did exist.[2] Byzantine public education was, at least
until the end of the eleventh century, predominantly secular,
and one of the functions of the University of Constantinople
was to provide the Empire with well-trained civil servants.

The difficulties of Byzantine politics cannot be alleged as an
excuse for the lack of intellectual creativeness, but they do
explain why there appears to be some uncertainty in the life of
the University at Constantinople.[3] As in every department, it
was the Emperor who controlled the University, and, harassed
by foreign wars or civil struggles, he obviously had little time for
affairs of a less urgent nature. It was unfortunate that so much
depended on the personal initiative of the Emperor and that
an institution which was of value alike to administrative and
academic life could therefore have little assurance of continuity.
In the ninth century the Amorians, zealous for the reputation
of Constantinople, and stimulated by the growing reputation of
Baghdad, had shown an interest in learning which had manifested
itself in Caesar Bardas's establishment of the University in the
Magnaura Palace, presided over by Leo the Mathematician,
who himself taught philosophy.

[1] *Iunilii Africani instituta regularia divinae legis*, ed. H. Kihn, Freiburg,
1880, p. 468, quoted by Fuchs, p. 5.
[2] Cf. Christopher of Mytilene, To the school of S. Theodore of the
Sphoracius (ed. Kurtz, pp. 5–6), To the master of the school of the Chalcopratia (ibid., p. 7); Psellus, From the master of the Diaconissa school asking
for the school of S. Peter.(Sathas, v, *Ep.* 162), To the master of the school
of the Chalcopratia (ibid., *Ep.* 168).
[3] The University was organized as early as A.D. 425 by Theodosius II;
see Fuchs, *Die höheren Schulen* . . .

Under the early Macedonians this official interest continued. The *Kephalaia*, which Basil I may or may not have written for his son Leo's instruction,[1] begin with a restatement of that which had long been the conviction and practice of the Byzantines: 'Education is a vital necessity and most desirable for private people as well as for Emperors, and to those who have acquired this, there is great reward both in body and soul.'[2] Basil I, if circumstances had left him comparatively uneducated, was certainly determined that this should not be the case with his sons. Leo's literary and legal activities show him to have been a man of liberal education, and more than average ability, and his brother Alexander is also mentioned for his interest in learning.[3] It is improbable that either Basil I or Leo VI would have refused their support to the University in the Magnaura Palace. But when Leo VI died in 912, his brother in 913, the Emperor Constantine VII, whose name was to become famous in the history of learning, was still a child. For about twenty years he could obviously do little, and during that time the regency, and then the Co-Emperor Romanus I, were apparently too pre-occupied to subsidize scholarship.

Circumstance and inclination, however, eventually gave to Constantine VII an outlet for his activities. Consumed with a passion for knowledge of all kinds, he was equally solicitous for the promotion of learning.

'The sciences, that is arithmetic, music, astronomy, geometry, stereometry, and philosophy, the mistress of all, for a long time dead through the neglect and ignorance of those in power, he restored by his personal activity. He searched for the most famous masters and the most distinguished, and when he had found them he appointed them teachers, and reassembled[4] around them those who were eager for knowledge.'[5]

There is probably some exaggeration in Cedrenus's words 'for a long time dead through the neglect and ignorance of those in

---

[1] See A. Vogt, 'La jeunesse de Léon VI le sage', RH, 174 (1934), pp. 408 ff.   [2] PG, cvii, col. xxi.

[3] *Vita Sae Theophano*, ed. E. Kurtz [*Mémoires de l'Académie impériale des sciences de S. Pétersbourg*, VIII série (Classe historico-philologique, vol. iii, no. 2 (1898), p. 14, 16)], quoted by Fuchs, p. 20, note 4. But Kurtz in his introduction (p. iii) suggests that this is only judicious flattery of Alexander.

[4] συγκροτέω is the word used.

[5] Cedrenus, ii. p. 326; cf. Theophanes Continuatus, vi. 14 (p. 446).

power'. This may refer to the apathy of the imperial authority, possibly to the closing of the University due to the withdrawal of financial help; but learning itself could have been in no sense dead, for otherwise Constantine VII would never have been able to find the famous and distinguished teachers whom he is reputed to have reassembled. It was not merely academic learning in which Constantine was interested. He loved music and art, and encouraged all kinds of writing. The introduction to the *Geoponica*, a treatise on agriculture, emphasizes this, and says that after Constantine VII had retrieved philosophy and rhetoric from the vast depths of oblivion (a rhetorical exaggeration) he turned to the other and more practical branches of science.[1]

After Constantine VIII's death in 959 there is a long gap, until the reopening of the University in 1045 and the organization of the faculties of law and philosophy. But this does not necessarily imply the complete disappearance of scholars, although there seems to be no evidence of official support, unless John Tzimisces' words can be interpreted as such, when, writing to an Armenian scholar, he invited him to confer with 'our scholars and philosophers'.[2] There can, however, be no doubt that, whatever may have been the dearth of scholars in the opening decades of the eleventh century, there was every sign of intellectual life in the tenth and second half of the ninth.

The legal work of Basil I and his son Leo VI is one of many symptoms indicative of the activity of the period, even if the excellence of the reform was not equalled by the use made of it in legal training and practice, to judge from the scathing comments in the constitution of the Law faculty of 1045.[3]

Byzantine prose found its most living form in historical writings, for, where its sermons and philosophical works are often only quotation and compilation, its chronicles and histories are far more alive and human, reflecting the opinions of the writer. Krumbacher[4] divides the works of historical writers into two classes, chronicles and histories, the first being encyclopaedic in character and often anonymous, the second being drawn from the author's personal experience and therefore often of

---

[1] *Geoponica sive Cassiani Bassi scholastici de re rustica eclogae*, ed. H. Beckh, Leipzig, 1895, pp. 1–2.   [2] Matthew of Edessa, p. 380 (quoted Fuchs, p. 22).
[3] See Chapter III, pp. 52 ff.   [4] GBL, p. 219.

greater value as contemporary history. Into the class of chronicles go all those world histories, begun by one, continued by another, and presenting complicated problems to the modern historian. Chronicles made unacknowledged use of all available sources, and their work would in turn form material for later compilations. In the chronicles certain idiosyncrasies of outlook or style do from time to time emerge, but although it is possible to see where one man left off and another took up the thread, it is often difficult to make any positive identification of the author.

In the tenth century there are two outstanding problems connected with the continuations of George the Monk (or George Harmatolus) and Theophanes. It is perhaps useful to summarize these difficulties, not only because they are at least evidence for historical interest and activity, but because they well illustrate the uncertainties and limitations of Byzantine historical evidence.

George the Monk lived in Michael III's reign, and he began his story with the Garden of Eden and ended with Theophilus's death in 842. His chronicle appears to be continued by one Symeon the Logothete and Magister, a contemporary of Romanus I Lecapenus, for whom he had a great affection. Symeon stopped with the year 948, and it is considered possible that he may be Symeon Metaphrastes, the compiler of the lives of the saints. The original continuation of Symeon does not exist, but there are five copies of varying value, one of which is a Slavonic translation; the Greek versions appear under the names of Georgius Monachus Continuatus, Leo Grammaticus, Theodosius of Melitene, and Symeon Magister (not the original chronicler Symeon).[1]

The chronicle known as the *Continuation* of Theophanes was really the work of a group of men who continued the chronicle of Theophanes at the request of Constantine VII, covering the years 813–961 in six books. The sixth book contains the long period of 886–961 (Leo VI–Romanus II). The last part of this compressed sixth book uses the Logothetes' continuation of George the Monk, and it may have been compiled by Theodorus Daphnopates.

Histories were written in the tenth century by Joseph Genesius

[1] See GBL, pp. 358 ff.

and Leo the Deacon. Genesius, working at the command of Constantine VII, wrote of the period 813 to the death of Basil I (886), which can hardly be called contemporary history. Leo the Deacon, writing after 992 in the reign of Basil II, produced an account of the years 959–75, thus providing an important contemporary history of Nicephorus Phocas and John Tzimisces, which stops abruptly by reason of the author's death. Leo's story of the tenth century is almost as delightful as Psellus's of the eleventh, although quite different in style and outlook. Less sophisticated, less personal than Psellus, he has a vividness and simplicity of description well suited to the dramatic events of which he tells. His account, for instance, of the December night when the Emperor Nicephorus was murdered presents the facts in such a way that they give his readers both drama and interpretation. He tells of the tension of the fruitless search in the women's apartments where the conspirators were already concealed in 'a small and unlit room' by the Empress, and the contrasting peace of the Emperor's last hours; 'throughout the watches of the night the Emperor prayed to God as was his wont, and meditated on the holy writings, and when at last he was overcome by sleep, he lay at rest upon the floor on his leopard skin and scarlet pallet, in front of the sacred icons of the divine yet human form of Christ, and the Mother of God, and John the Baptist'.[1]

Another piece of graphic historical writing is John Cameniates' account of the Ethiopian sack of Thessalonica in 904. He himself, 'a priest from the imperial household',[2] was taken captive, but finally escaped and wrote his story. The peaceful and unsuspecting city, the sudden attack of the pirate fleet, the Ethiopians, naked, with drawn swords and grinning teeth,[3] especially one who leaps on to the altar in a church, 'crossing his legs under him in barbarian fashion, exulting in his mad pride',[4] all this is described, to be followed by a still more harrowing tale of the defeated Greek population, packed into incredibly congested quarters on the ships, and taken to Crete or Tripoli, where such as survived the sufferings of the voyage were sold as slaves.

[1] Leo Diaconus, v. 6 (p. 86).
[2] Cameniates, p. 563 (ed. CB, with Theophanes Continuatus).
[3] Ibid., p. 550.   [4] Ibid., p. 558.

The historical poem of Theodosius, a deacon of Constantinople, describing Nicephorus Phocas's capture of Crete from the Saracens, is less valuable as a source than John Cameniates, but even its digressions and bombast give some indication of the trend of Byzantine education, with its knowledge of classical authors and preference for Christian interpretation. The poem is full of the contrast between the exaggerated valour of the old heroes, especially Homer's, and the true worth of the Byzantines whose help is in Christ:

> Demosthenes, Philip's power was nil,
> Plutarch, Caesar's boldness was nothing,
> Dion, in vain was Sulla a dictator,
> Cease, O Xenophon, to write of your invincibles,
> Admire the Roman, and tell only of him,[1]

the 'Roman' being, of course, Nicephorus Phocas, for the Byzantines were the heirs of the elder Rome.

The most monumental, and certainly the most interesting, historical works of the tenth century were those of the Emperor Constantine VII. Besides a short life of his grandfather Basil I, he preserved invaluable information concerning Byzantine administration in the widest sense of the word. The *De administrando imperio* contains instructions to his son about the neighbours of the Empire and the appropriate diplomacy to be observed towards them, ranging from the Italians and Venetians to the Patzinaks and Russians. Still more detail, especially on the Empire itself, is provided by his *De thematibus*. In the *De cerimoniis aulae* there is an account of the whole life of the Byzantine polity, with its hierarchy of lay and ecclesiastical officials, and the traditional ceremonies which had long been associated with the various functions. Beginning, as was natural to a Byzantine, with the more important Church festivals, it described the processions to S. Sophia and the services there, even giving the different responses for each occasion. Then follow the imperial festivals, from the coronation and burial of an Emperor to the baptism of his son; after this come other important events, such as the election or burial of a Patriarch. Throughout minute regulations are given, often affording

---

[1] Theodosius, p. 273 (ed. CB with Leo the Deacon).

evidence for much other than purely ceremonial detail.[1] But the *De cerimoniis* was not compiled in a purely antiquarian spirit; it was written in order to safeguard and preserve the dignity of Byzantine public life. In his introduction Constantine VII wrote, 'Perhaps some, failing to appreciate its necessity, will consider this work superfluous. But to us it seems most dear, most essential, and, indeed, the most intimate of all our interests, since it is through its glorious ceremonial that the imperial majesty is increased in splendour, and raised to greater glory, thereby becoming the wonder of other people and of our own subjects.'[2] It is, then, clear that it was the maintenance of a right tradition with which Constantine VII's writings were concerned; the Byzantines never forgot their inheritance.

This feeling for continuity is even more apparent in their theological writings, especially commentaries or attempts to convert those outside the Orthodox Church. The least conventional writings are found among the lives of the saints, though hagiography often tended to become artificial. But at their best the lives of the saints reproduced many characteristics of the Byzantine religious outlook, its reverence for the monastic life and the saint, and its belief in miracles and signs; moreover, there is in them both simplicity and humour of a kind found in no other branch of Byzantine writing, except occasionally in the chronicles or histories. At their worst, as in the case of Symeon Metaphrastes' work in the second half of the tenth century, they were fruitless and injudicious compilations of false as well as genuine evidence.[3] The years 867–1025 contain an abundance of hagiographical writings, which would be a study in themselves,[4] and can only be mentioned as important political, social, and religious sources presented in the most animated and least artificial form of Byzantine religious writings.

Polemic, of necessity and inclination a primary concern in the earlier centuries of the Byzantine Empire, had somewhat

[1] In his edition Vogt attempts to distinguish between the original composition of Constantine VII and later additions (*Commentaire*, pp. xviii ff.).

[2] *De cerimoniis*, i. pp. 3–4.

[3] See Delehaye, *Les légendes hagiographiques* (*Subsidia hagiographica*, 18), 3rd ed., Brussels, 1927, for an excellent analysis of the historical approach to the lives of the saints.

[4] See GBL, pp. 197 ff., for a preliminary list of the lives of this period.

subsided by 867, although it could never completely die, as the twelfth-century controversies showed.[1] The Orthodox Church accepted as its duty the conversion of pagans or heretics or Christians in schism, and not only did scholars write treatises and letters, but important missionary work was achieved, notably among the Slavs in Moravia and Russia. But here the primary concern is with the literary productions within the Empire. Many of these can hardly be called creative; they are often monotonous and stereotyped, consisting of endless quotations from the Bible and the Church Fathers; after all, there was little for a Byzantine to do except make a skilful use of his predecessors of the patristic period. Photius wrote a series of four long sermons, or rather, small treatises, against the Manichaean heresy and its later development, the Paulician heresy. Himself vitally concerned with the relation of Constantinople to Rome, he wrote his *De S. Spiritus mystagogia*, defending the procession of the Holy Spirit from the Father alone, and attacking the *Filioque* addition to the Latin creed. Photius is one of the more convincing authors of this period, writing in a clear and unexaggerated style. In contrast to him, Nicetas of Byzantium, called φιλόσοφος and διδάσκαλος, produced justifications of orthodoxy so dull that they could scarcely have lured any one into the fold. Nicetas, living in the days of Michael III and Basil I, attacked the usual enemies of the Greek Church, the Armenians,[2] the Moslems, and the Latins.

Closely allied to polemic, and, indeed, its foundation, was a right exegesis, whereby the faithful might be enabled to understand more clearly and the heretics to realize their errors. A favourite method with the Byzantine was the presentation of material in the form of answers to difficult questions. Like Psellus's *De omnifaria doctrina* of the eleventh century, Photius's *Amphilochia* consists of answers to questions of various kinds, in Photius's case mostly theological. Arethas, an important scholar and exegesist, produced in 895 a commentary on the Revelations of S. John the Divine. Like many Byzantine writings,

[1] See Chapter V.

[2] See also Demetrius of Cyzicus, *Liber de rebus Armeniae* (GBL, p. 81, says it is wrongly attributed to Philippus Solitarius, PG, cxxvii, cols. 880–901). Against the Jacobites or Syrian monophysites there is a fragment by Athanasius, Archbishop of Corinth, PG, ċvi, col. 1024.

this bristles with difficulties because of the free, and often un-acknowledged, use of earlier sources. The basis of this particular commentary is an earlier one by Andreas of Caesarea (c. the first half of the sixth century), which Arethas sometimes alters and sometimes quotes almost word for word. Again, the natural basis of any explanation is the patristic literature. In one place Arethas sheds an interesting light on the Constantinople of his day; the Babylon, he says, mentioned in Revelation, xvi. 19, is no other than Constantinople, where once justice reigned, while now there is only murder and strife, and laity struggling to become the equals of ecclesiastics.[1] But such diversions as this are rare.

It is a relief to turn to the sermon, an art in which the Byzantine often excelled. Many of these are not yet edited, but of those in print the largest collections belong to Nicetas David, Bishop of Dadybra in Paphlagonia (†c. 890), the Emperor Leo VI, and Symeon the Young. Of occasional sermons there are many writers, as Theodorus Daphnopates, Cosmas Vestitor, John Geometres, or even the Emperor Constantine VII. But the larger collections of Nicetas, Leo, and Symeon may be taken as illustrating the faults and merits of the Byzantine sermon.

Ehrhard remarked with justice that Nicetas was the forerunner of Symeon Metaphrastes.[2] His sermons were rhetorical, full of long quotations, and often consisting of page after page of adjectival phrases. When preaching on the Cross his "$\tau\acute{\iota} \,\delta\epsilon\hat{\iota} \,\mu\alpha\kappa\rho\eta\gamma o\rho\epsilon\hat{\iota}\nu$"; after he already seems to have exhausted every possible epithet only raises a false hope in his readers, who have to listen to a further demonstration of the artificial fertility of the preacher's imagination.[3] However, he goes from bad to worse, and the extravagant imagery of his sermon on the Apostles Peter and Paul[4] is only outdone by the exaggerated enthusiasm of his panegyric on S. Andrew.[5] In comparison with the sermons of Xiphilinus or Cerularius in the eleventh century, Nicetas's are marked by an entire absence of moral bite; they could have done little but awaken in their listeners a false emotion.

The Emperor Leo's sermons are of a higher order than

---

[1] PG, cvi, col. 713.   [2] GBL, p. 168.   [3] PG, cv, col. 33 (Or. 2).
[4] Ibid., cols. 37 ff. (Or. 3).   [5] Ibid., cols. 53 ff. (Or. 4).

Nicetas's, but even they are not particularly outstanding. They show the same rhetorical and laudatory characteristics as most Byzantine sermons; in parts they are even pedestrian, as, for instance, in the opening sermon on the birth of Our Lady.[1] Another trait which they share with Nicetas's sermons is that they are either panegyrical or else a statement of the Christian inheritance of the Byzantines, and there is little attempt to relate this to the moral difficulties of everyday human life.

Perhaps the truth is that all sermons of this period suffer in comparison with those of Symeon the Young. Writing at the end of the tenth century and beginning of the eleventh, he was one of the greatest of the Byzantines. His clarity of outlook and unusual spiritual knowledge found a perfect expression in his sermons.[2] The restraint and forcefulness and austerity of his exhortations, relieved by the contrasting and almost lyrical beauty of the passages[3] describing the divine love, is a perfect demonstration of the flexibility of the Greek language as a medium for the expression of spiritual experience.

Although Symeon's sermons contained his teaching on the ascetic rule of life, he wrote a further and more systematic exposition of this in a series of short paragraphs or *capita*. In his case there is a thread running through these *capita practica et moralia*; but often this summarized form of presentation was only a judicious use of older pagan and Christian authors, suiting the Byzantine love of compilation. John Geometres' *Paradisus*, written in the second half of the tenth century, is a series of ninety-nine epigrammatic hints and comments on the ascetic life, each consisting of two elegiacs, with no connexion save their unity of outlook.

There are two distinct forms of poetry in this period. The first is rhythmical, the scheme depending on the *number* of syllables in each line. This class consists of religious writings, chiefly Church hymns or canons, and such writings are much freer and less stiff than a good deal of the Byzantine poetry which is in a quantitative metre. They represent a break with tradition,

---

[1] PG, cvii, cols. 1 ff. (*Or.* 1).

[2] See Chapters X and XI for a detailed discussion of Symeon and his writings.

[3] Especially ὦ ἀγάπη παυπόθητε (*Cod. monac. gr.* 177, f. 108ʳ = PG, cxx, 422 C, *Or.* 22, *o desideratissima caritas* . . .).

resulting in the discovery of a medium of expression whose spontaneity and elasticity was well suited to the lengthy hymns which formed an increasingly important part in the Church service. Symeon the Young's mystical writings or *Divine Hymns of Love*[1] are written in this free verse form, though there is occasionally a line reminiscent of some classical metre, as, for instance, in Nos. 11[2] or 26;[3] where the fifteen syllables sometimes fall into an iambic or trochaic tetrameter catalectic, perhaps an unconscious reminiscence of the Saint's early education at which he would have been horrified.

The second class of poetry is the short poem in some classical metre, representing that continuity of tradition upon which the Byzantines prided themselves. Both religious and secular poems are written in this form; the favourite metres are elegiacs and iambics. John Geometres used both, and his poems are the most delightful of this period. They are very similar in style and subject-matter to those of the eleventh century written by John of Euchaita and Christopher of Mytilene; but they do not show the same strong human sympathy as John of Euchaita's and are sometimes spoilt by an overpowering insistence on secular learning that is in contrast to the author's strong religious convictions and asceticism.

The longest of John Geometres' religious poems are those written in elegiacs to the Virgin, whose virtues he praises in a long list of epithets. Almost each elegiac begins with χαῖρε,

> Hail! lily and roselike bud and dewy anemone
> Pure narcissus, gleaming whiter than snow,[4]

and in spite of the length of these descriptions the author achieves a freshness and spontaneity which is often missing in Byzantine poetry.

Geometres' epigrammatic style is more suited to secular than religious verse. He was fond of playing with his words; "τὸν χρυσὸν φιλέων, φιλέειν ἔραμαι καὶ Χριστόν,"[5] is a characteristic beginning of one of his short poems. Sometimes he overdoes this play on words, making the poem seem artificial,

---

[1] The Latin version given in PG, cxx, is printed as prose, but the original Greek in MS. is usually written in lines, each having the same number of syllables.   [2] *Cod. monac. gr.* 177, f. 223ᵛ ff.   [3] Ibid., f. 270ᵛ ff.
[4] PG, cvi, col. 857 (Hymn 2).   [5] Ibid., col. 873 (Poem 21).

while many of his short poems lose their point in translation.
The following 'To the philosophers' is a characteristic couple
of elegiacs:

Τρεῖς σοφίης πολυΐστορος ἔκκριτοι ἀστέρες οἷοι
'Ενθέμενοι βίβλοις ὄλβον ἀπειρέσιον.
'Αρχύτας ἦρξε, Πλάτων πλάτυνε, τέλος δ' ἐπὶ πᾶσι
'Ως ἔτυχε κληθεὶς θῆκεν 'Αριστοτέλης.[1]

In spite of John's obvious bias towards the ascetic way of
life and his frequent protests against the snares of the world, he
cannot forget, and never despises, the best things of secular
life; he speaks of pagan Greek writers as often as of Christian
saints, and he loved everything that was beautiful. His poem on
The Spring is a great contrast to the sternness of many monastically minded Christians:

The soft narcissus springs joyful from the earth,
And the gracious golden-flowered crocus and the anemone, . . .
The swallow pours forth its untiring song,
And in its nest at dawn chatters like a maiden.[2]

John could not be silent about the beauty of the world around
him, even though he goes on to speak of failing strength and
approaching old age and the mutability of all except belief in
Christ.

There are others of this period, but they are versifiers rather
than poets and their writings have less charm and distinctiveness
than those of John Geometres. Leo the philosopher, a pupil of
Photius, Constantine Sicelus, one of Leo's pupils, Constantine
the Rhodian, and others have left poems. There is, too, the
Anthologia Palatina, a tenth-century collection of epigrams of
all ages, edited at the beginning of the tenth century by Constantine Cephalas.

Byzantine secular prose of this period, as far as it is possible
to judge at present, contains little individual or constructive
contribution to knowledge.

Letters[3] stand in a class by themselves. Those of the Patriarchs
Nicholas and Photius are interesting, but they are nearly all
concerned with politics or religion. Compared, for instance, with

[1] PG, cvi, col. 919 (Poem 20).   [2] Ibid., col. 984 (Poem 161).
[3] Arethas of Caesarea's letters are still unedited. See GBL, pp. 524–5.

those of the fifth-century western Sidonius they are disappointing in the absence of any reflection of the normal events of
family and secular life.

There are many indications of interest in classical authors,
but there appear to be practically no original productions.
Arethas of Caesarea, one of the most famous scholars of the
tenth century, must have been a learned man. He had all kinds
of manuscripts copied, including Euclid, Plato, Lucian, and
Aristides; he also commented on classical writers and left glosses
in some of his manuscripts.[1] But much more work needs to be
done on the question of the exact depth of tenth-century scholarship before it is possible to analyse the extent of its contribution
to knowledge.

One of the achievements of the tenth century was the compilation known as Suidas's lexicon, a fitting symbol of the attitude and achievement of Byzantine scholarship in this period.
It is more of an encyclopaedia than a dictionary, and contains a
vast amount of information on all kinds of subjects.

But whatever may be the difficulties in describing this period
there is one point on which there can be no doubt, and that is
the general interest in learning; Photius's *Myriobiblion* is striking
evidence of this. A collection of notes on various books read by
Photius and a circle of friends, it was written for the benefit of
an absent brother. It occupies more than one of the large
Patrologia volumes, and its long list of secular and theological
authors, some of which have since been lost, as well as the
actual comments, indicates the wide literary background of the
educated Byzantine, as well as the private activities of men
whose primary concern had become not scholarship but the
administration of Church and State. Byzantine education and
scholarship shows not so much originality as enjoyment of the
accumulated intellectual wealth of centuries. Men such as
Photius and his friends must have had a real appreciation and a
literary background that would have been impossible without
a tradition of education and learning. It is the same with John
Geometres, whose poems are full of references to classical
authors, Xenophon, Sophocles, Homer, Aeschylus, Euripides,
to mention only a few. The difficulty is that it is often little else

[1] GBL, pp. 524 ff.

but names that are mentioned, and that apart from reading of Plato 'the teacher of immortality',[1] or Aristotle 'the definer of the bounds of mind and nature',[2] there is often no means of probing the depths, or otherwise, of the author's knowledge of these writers.

[1] PG, cvi, col. 917 (Poem 14).   [2] Ibid., col. 917 (Poem 13).

CHAPTER II

THE BACKGROUND OF THE ELEVENTH-CENTURY REVIVAL OF LEARNING

In you I have spent the whole day in my task of lecturing, setting some right, forcing others to retrace their steps, judging disputes between teachers and pupils, ready to make answer to all, and toiling over letters and books. In you I have increased my knowledge by studying, in you I imparted this knowledge to those who were anxious to learn, and made many young men wise without asking for any fee.

> John of Euchaita, *To his own house when he sold and left it*, Lagarde, p. 25 (Poem 47).

We helped each other into the country of knowledge.

> Psellus, *Funeral oration on Xiphilinus*, Sathas, iv, p. 427.

IT would be interesting to know exactly how far the imperial attitude influenced the private outlook towards literature and philosophy. Probably not very much, for even if it is true that the Emperors after Constantine VII Porphyrogenitus, being soldiers by nature and necessity, took little thought for education, yet the existing evidence suggests that there was no lacuna in intellectual life between the end of the tenth century and the reopening of the University in 1045. In Anna Comnena's words: 'From the time of the Emperor Basil the Porphyrogenitus down to the Emperor Monomachus the study of letters, although neglected by the majority, had nevertheless not entirely died out.'[1] Psellus is inclined to the opposite opinion, but probably from ulterior motives.[2]

With Basil II the imperial anxiety to stimulate knowledge certainly disappeared. 'He did not rule the state according to the written laws but according to the unwritten laws of his own well endowed soul, with the result that he paid no attention to learned men, but he completely despised this class of people.'[3] Romanus III Argyrus, whom Psellus had seen and once spoken to,[4] was admittedly interested in learning, but is bitingly condemned for his superficiality. 'And one saw the royal

---

[1] Anna Comnena, v. 8 (i, pp. 177–8).
[2] Psellus, *Chron.* iii. 3 (i, p. 33) and vi. 43 (i, p. 138).
[3] Ibid., i. 29 (i, p. 18).   [4] Ibid., iii. 1 (i, p. 32).

presence clothed as a philosopher, but this a mere mask and pretence and in no way a touchstone and searching out of the truth.'[1] Romanus's ardour was the result of personal vanity, and found its outlet in barren theological discussions rather than in care for public education. Michael IV, if he had the self-control of a philosopher, was a stranger to Hellenic culture;[2] Michael V's short and disastrous reign left little time for interest in learning, even had he so desired, and it is not until the accession of Constantine IX Monomachus that there is evidence of imperial consideration for scholarship.

Although admittedly much depended on the Emperor's attitude, there was nothing to prevent the existence of private schools, but unfortunately there is little evidence about these. On the other hand, the existence of men of outstanding scholarship shows that Anna's words—'had nevertheless not entirely died out'—are based upon inadequate appreciation of the vitality of learning previous to Psellus's work at the reopened University. By reason of inconclusive evidence it is still difficult to estimate the fluctuations in the fortunes of Byzantine scholarship, but it is probable that they were less pronounced than is often supposed. 'N'attache-t-on pas trop d'importance aux imprécises expressions des historiens et d'autres écrivains qui nous parlent périodiquement d'une décadence ou d'une éclipse de bonnes études?'[3] In spite of remarks made by Psellus or Anna Comnena, and in spite of certain lapses, such as the inadequate provision for the study of law in the first half of the eleventh century, the Macedonian period had no serious breach in the continuity of scholarship.

In the first half of the eleventh century it was not always easy to pursue a course of higher studies, largely owing to the paucity of teachers, but it would be a mistake to imagine that the closing of the University with the death of Constantine VII dealt any final blow to learning in Constantinople. It is contemporary evidence that throws the most convincing light on this point. Here the chroniclers are of little help, for they make no mention of eleventh-century scholars and learning previous to 1045. The

---

[1] Psellus, *Chron.* iii. 3 (i, p. 33).   [2] Ibid., iv. 7 (i, p. 56).
[3] H. Grégoire's review of H. Fuchs, *Die höheren Schulen* . . ., in B, 4 (1927–8, published 1929), p. 773.

most notable evidence is that of Michael Psellus, himself a distinguished scholar, who praises his friends and teachers in his funeral orations and panegyrics. But his tendency to exaggeration makes evidence with which to supplement or check his statements particularly valuable. Psellus's teachers were John Mauropous[1] and Nicetas of Byzantium, and of these only John has left any writings. John's works are, indeed, invaluable as showing both the scholarship and the teaching available at Constantinople at the beginning of the eleventh century; they indicate, moreover, that there is some exaggeration in Psellus's statement that he himself roused philosophy from its death-bed, and that neither Athens, Nicomedia, Alexandria, Phoenicia, nor the two Romes gloried in the pursuit of learning.[2]

The interesting points in connexion with John are, first, the extent of his knowledge as far as can be gathered from his own writings and contemporary references, unfortunately mainly in Psellus's works,[3] and secondly, a point that is often insufficiently emphasized, the debt owed to him by Psellus. John's own writings consist of poems, letters, sermons, and a short life of S. Dorotheus the Younger, as well as unedited canons. He was a man who came to Constantinople early in the eleventh century and, like Psellus and Xiphilinus, was at the same time both teacher and student. In one of his poems he describes his life in his house, his 'faithful corner', which circumstances unfortunately compelled him to leave. The poem addresses the house itself: 'You are my nourisher and nurse most dear, tutor and only teacher. In you I have borne lasting pains and toils, in you I have passed whole sleepless nights.' John must evidently have had a considerable number of pupils for he not only taught himself, but he speaks of supervising masters and students, adding that he demanded no fee from those who could not afford this.[4] And he sadly concludes his farewell to his house with these words: 'Now you will have others to teach and to care for, you will give to others opportunity for knowledge if they love learning, but to me no longer.'[5]

[1] Also known as John of Euchaita; see Chapter III, p. 68.
[2] Psellus, *Chron.* vi. 43 (i, p. 138).
[3] Sathas, v, Funeral oration and letters.
[4] Cf. Psellus, *Chron.* vi, 43 (i, p. 138).   [5] Lagarde, pp. 24–6 (Poem 47).

John makes no direct reference to the contents of his studies, but his writings mention the Bible, the Church fathers, Epicurus, Pindar, and Plutarch, and certainly point to some knowledge of Plato, especially the poem in which he stresses the affinity between the ethics of Plato and Christ, claiming that Plato was a Christian in all essentials. 'If, my Christ, Thou shouldst wish to exempt any of the pagans from Thy threats, choose for me Plato and Plutarch. For both these in thought and deed showed how very near they were to Thy laws. They may not have known that Thou art the God of all, but this is only a further claim on Thy mercy, the gift through which Thou desirest to save all men.'[1] That John had an unusual reverence for knowledge is apparent not only from his own works, but from Psellus's panegyric, where he praises John's scholarship in all the various branches of learning—dialectic, logic, physics, astronomy, philosophy.[2] John was no doubt thinking of his own experience when he wrote, 'Life is short but the arts are many.'[3] He must have been a singularly attractive man, quiet, reserved, observant, and a lover of nature, with a very real religious sense.[4] He characteristically reflects the felicity of his spiritual life when he says:

'And thus, O Logos, mayest Thou guide and bear me, constant, unshaken, unmoved, remaining within the bounds of moderation, living among books like a bee among flowers, nourishing myself on words like a grasshopper in the dew, content to live only in the present, demanding nothing save salvation, to which mayest Thou, O Saviour, swiftly bring me, lest I grow very weary of the present. For the longed for haven far excels the easy labour of even a fair voyage, and is the consummation of all toils. May I quickly reach this, O my Christ.'[5]

John's sincerity is all the more marked in contrast with Psellus; he gives the impression that he is thinking of the meaning that lay behind whatever he is describing, while Psellus is often led

---

[1] Lagarde, p. 24 (Poem 43).   [2] Sathas, v, pp. 142–67.
[3] Lagarde, p. 93 (No. 173).
[4] His simple devoutness is nowhere better illustrated than by his poems. It is interesting to compare them with those of Christopher of Mytilene (especially their respective poems on the Nativity: Lagarde, pp. 2–3 (Poem 2), and Kurtz, p. 86 (Poem 123).   [5] Lagarde, p. 43 (Poem 89).

astray by his love of rhetoric. John has, moreover, a faith that it
would be difficult to attribute to Psellus. He is above all a scholar
of serene outlook, without the failings and inconsistencies of his
famous pupil, although his modesty and shyness in no way
deterred an outspokenness that was unusual in the imperial
circle.

In comparison with Psellus John has left few writings, and
one of the most interesting aspects of his work, his contribution
to hymnology, has been comparatively neglected. His canons
form the greater part of his writings, and these are still unedited.[1]
Pitra, who had read them in manuscript, considered them to be
important evidence for the political events of the eleventh
century,[2] but this statement is supported more by the inscriptions[3] than the contents. Nevertheless, the canons, in spite of
their length, are as interesting as John's other writings; as Psellus
says, he has a style which 'bursts into flower as unexpectedly as
a rose in winter'.[4]

The very paucity of John's work adds to the difficulty of
estimating the nature of his influence on Psellus, and most of the
evidence, both direct and indirect, must be found in Psellus's
writings.[5] It is interesting to find that he speaks of John's use
of the corporeal as a means of approaching the incorporeal, a
very marked characteristic of his own philosophy, which, if his
words are to be believed, he owed to the teaching of John.
Again Psellus is found attributing to John one of the funda-
mentals of his own learning, that is, an insistence on the necessity of combining rhetoric and philosophy, and of clothing ideas
in beautiful language.[6] But although Psellus frankly stresses
this as the foundation of John's teaching, it is a quality which

[1] One of the most important collections is in *Vindob. cod. theol. gr. 78*
(*Nessel*). This contains 106 Church canons, each canon usually having eight
odes, and each ode being composed of a varying number of verses. I hope
shortly to publish a life of John and an edition of these canons.

[2] Pitra, p. 61.

[3] e.g. f. 205ᵛ, κανὼν παρακλητικὸς εἰς τὴν ὑπεραγίαν θεότοκον ἐπὶ προσδοκίᾳ βαρέος
πολέμου κατὰ τὴν μεγάλην πόλιν ἐκ διαφόρων ἐθνῶν τῆς Ἰταλῶν γλώσσης συγκροτη-
θησομένου.

[4] Sathas, v, p. 149. Cf. Lagarde, pp. 51–2 (No. 100), which might almost
be the draft of a poem.

[5] Especially Sathas, v.

[6] Cf. Lagarde, p. 19 (Poem 34), which is directed against misplaced ver-
sifying, and also John's preface, ibid., pp. 1–2 (Poem 1).

Psellus's biographers often attribute to him without any reference to the probability of his debt to John,[1] and, indeed, it is possible that Psellus may owe more to his teacher than is often recognized.

Nicetas, who was Psellus's other teacher, is only once mentioned by Ehrhard.[2] If he did write anything, it does not appear to have survived, and Psellus's funeral eulogy seems to be the only source of information concerning him.[3] Psellus speaks as though Nicetas were not much older than himself, and he stresses the depth of their personal friendship. He describes how he sought for a teacher of rhetoric and how he found in Nicetas one who, 'the more he outstripped the others, the more he turned back to those behind'.[4] And even though he was victor in the race, he still had thought for those who brought up the rear. Psellus continues the metaphor by saying that Nicetas helped him to run abreast of him, 'he encouraged me to run the race of wisdom'.[5] This formed the starting-point of a friendship based on common interests and a common temperament, which grew more and more intimate. Psellus points out that they each stressed different aspects of learning, for, while he loved philosophy, 'the other half of learning',[6] Nicetas was devoted to orthography,[7] although he nevertheless made philosophy his basis in character and action. Nicetas must have been an eager student, not as quiet and retiring as John Mauropous, but with a keen, alert[8] brain which made him a ready dialectician. The information which Psellus gives supplies none of the facts of his life, and in many respects he remains an enigmatical figure. Psellus is obviously only interested in Nicetas's life as a teacher and student, and especially in those aspects of it which bore some relation to his own mental development.

Thus John and Nicetas show the scholarship and private teaching which was available in Constantinople in the first decades of the eleventh century. Their evidence can be sup-

---

[1] Cf. C. Zervos, *Michel Psellos*, pp. 112 ff. and E. Renauld's Introduction to his edition of the *Chronographia*.

[2] GBL, p. 438.

[3] Sathas, v. pp. 87–96.

[4] Ibid., p. 89.   [5] Ibid.   [6] Ibid., p. 90.

[7] Psellus speaks at some length of Nicetas's scholarship and method of teaching. See Chapter III, pp. 61 ff.

[8] ὀξύτης is the word Psellus uses (Sathas, v, p. 89).

plemented by examining the education and attitude not only of their most famous pupil Michael Psellus, but also of John Xiphilinus and Constantine Leichudes. To do so is to approach life in Constantinople from varying angles since Psellus was a philosopher, Xiphilinus a lawyer, Leichudes a statesman; the lights and shades in their respective temperaments, as well as their relations to each other, help to explain not only the outlook of the scholars who induced Constantine IX Monomachus to reopen the University, but the enmity which they roused and which caused them temporarily to retreat to the monastic seclusion of Mt. Olympus, a retreat which produced, moreover, characteristically different results.

Scholarship in the eleventh century is often unconsciously considered in terms of Michael Psellus, and indeed, when all due respect is paid to his contemporaries, he still remains the most prominent figure of the revival of learning in the eleventh century. Psellus was born in 1018 near the monastery of Narses in Constantinople,[1] and in his funeral oration on his mother[2] he gives the details of his early life, mentioning among other things that he found no difficulty in learning, and that while he was still a boy he knew by heart the whole *Iliad*.[3] He stresses his desire for knowledge, which was encouraged by his mother, even though family fortunes were always low. It was, indeed, these financial difficulties which largely accounted for his versatility, for from his childhood onwards he had never been able to devote himself exclusively to the learning which he longed to pursue. At the age of sixteen he was collecting taxes in the western provinces, but on his return to Constantinople he resumed the life of a student, finding his masters in John Mauropous and Nicetas of Byzantium, his friends in the future Patriarchs Xiphilinus and Leichudes, and Constantine Ducas, later Constantine X.

Krumbacher judged him harshly and found in him all the disagreeable traits of Byzantine life. 'Es ist über allen Zweifel erhaben, dass kriechender Servilismus und Rücksichtslosigkeit in der Wahl der Mittel, unersättlicher Ehrgeiz und masslose

---

[1] See Zervos, pp. 61 ff., for a discussion of his birthplace and the date of his death.

[2] Sathas, v, pp. 3–61.   [3] Ibid., p. 14.

Eitelkeit die hervorstechenden Züge seines Charakters bilden.'[1]
Nobody will deny the truth of this condemnation, but the unpleasant aspects of Psellus's character are partly the result of the
age in which he lived, since the position of the last of the Macedonians, the long-lived Empresses Zoe and Theodora, afforded
endless opportunity for intrigue. For a man such as Psellus,
who had no estates in Asia Minor or in Europe, and who could
rely only on a precarious professional career, imperial patronage
was often the only alternative to obscurity. Where John of
Euchaita would have preferred the latter, Psellus chose the
former, hence the inevitable inconsistencies of his life. By
nature he was neither a mystic nor an ascetic, but a man of
secular disposition with a many-sided appreciation of learning.
His best work is the *Chronographia*, in which his capacity for
using words finds its characteristic expression in prose descriptions of people; he is never a poet. As far as he had any creative
outlet it was in his love of philosophy and in his dialectical
attitude of mind, but even here his writings owe their virtue
rather to appreciative imitation than to original thought.

Psellus is never consistent, and the unevenness of his character
and the weakness of his moral sense ill accord with his love of
Plato. His work as a philosopher is treated below,[2] and it is
sufficient to say here that, having studied rhetoric and philosophy under John Mauropous, he applied himself to legal
studies with the aid of his friend Xiphilinus, who in return was
instructed in philosophy. Psellus pursued his legal course so
successfully that he practised as a lawyer until he entered upon
his career as a court official under Michael IV. From this time
onwards Psellus was employed at court, except for short in-
tervals when he was in disgrace; but in spite of his official duties
he must have found considerable time for his studies, and was
the centre of intellectual life at Constantinople.

Xiphilinus, the great friend of Psellus's youth, is an equally
interesting figure,[3] and his career throws considerable light on
the condition of law before 1045. He came from Trebizond,[4]
and was older than Psellus, and born probably about 1010–13,

[1] GBL, p. 435.   [2] See Chapter IV.
[3] See W. Fischer, *Studien*, for a more detailed account of Xiphilinus.
[4] Sathas, iv, p. 424.

for Psellus says that he was only growing his beard when Xiphilinus already had his,[1] and he was certainly over thirty at the reopening of the University.[2] Like Psellus, Xiphilinus owed much to his mother's upbringing. The difficulty of obtaining higher education in his own city combined with his desire for knowledge to induce him to go to Constantinople, and it was here that he formed with Psellus the friendship which resulted in their mutual instruction; it was through Psellus's influence that he devoted considerable time to the study of rhetoric, which was obviously of first importance for a barrister. The fact that they taught each other is sometimes used to support the theory that there were no available teachers, but it should be remembered that Psellus says that it was partly lack of money which hindered them. Certainly John Mauropous was a first-rate teacher of rhetoric had Xiphilinus wished to go to him. But possibly, after they had both not only attained a foremost position among scholars, but reached the highest rank in imperial life, Psellus may have been tempted to heighten the difficulties of their youth by suggesting scarcity of teachers as well as lack of funds.

Nevertheless, there is no need to underestimate the obstacles in Xiphilinus's path; he undoubtedly found Byzantine law suffering from years of continuous ill treatment at the hands of badly instructed judges. The root of the evil was, as he realized, the absence of any school of law, for this deficiency of definite legal training meant that men intending to enter the profession had a general education, followed by a course of rhetoric. After this they went straight to a συμβολαιογράφος (notary) or συνήγορος (advocate) and, having no thorough knowledge of the sources of Byzantine law, they relied on the interpretations of their teachers. Hence the law tended to resolve itself into faction fights between the various parties, to the detriment of equity, and with the still more disastrous result that there was no efficient body of servants for the administrative and judicial affairs of government. Xiphilinus saw the ignorance of his contemporaries, and when he studied law his acutely logical mind remedied the evil by going straight to the great codes of Justinian and Basil, and having mastered these he worked down through the different

[1] Sathas, iv, p. 427.   [2] Ibid., v, p. 195.

interpretations until he came to his own day. He worked his-
torically, 'as a stream from its source',[1] a method the reverse
of that he saw around him. His own writings help both to check,
and in this case to confirm, Psellus's picture of the great lawyer
who was to prove himself an equally great Patriarch, and fortunately some of his works are extant. They mostly belong
to Xiphilinus's ecclesiastical period, and hence demand some
explanation of the manner and reason for his transition from
the legal to the monastic life.

When Psellus and his friends fell into disfavour in the later
period of Constantine IX's reign they went to the monasteries
on Mt. Olympus in search of the stability and contemplative
peace which court life had denied them.[2] The results of this
were not surprising. Psellus, who entered last, left first, having
made the discovery that a monastery was something more than
a scholarly retreat for a court official—*otium cum dignitate*. But
Xiphilinus stayed for the nine years which were to form the most
important transitional period of his life. Scylitzes mentions his
departure from public affairs. 'He was a wise man of high
learning, looked up to in public matters, and cheerfully practising virtue, so that he welcomed monastic life at the outset of his
fame and in the prime of life, and for a considerable time chose
to lead the retired life of Mt. Olympus.'[3] The cloister developed
in Xiphilinus latent qualities of asceticism, which combined
with the natural vigour of his mind to make him an important,
if sometimes an unpleasant, member of the community. Always
a reformer, Xiphilinus became a fanatic, and was intolerant in
his strenuous efforts to apply discipline both to himself and
to others. His philosophic training showed itself in his concern
for theory as well as practice, and, in contrast to Psellus, he
became almost exclusively Aristotelian, a development which
was to widen the growing divergence of their paths. In the
monastery Xiphilinus vigorously studied the writings of the
Church Fathers and became the master of his subject as he had
previously done in the sphere of law. The climax of his sojourn

[1] Sathas, iv, p. 453.
[2] See Chapter III for a more detailed discussion of this episode.
[3] Scylitzes, ii, p. 658; Attaleiates, pp. 92–3, uses practically the same
words.

in Mt. Olympus came with his election to the office of Patriarch. His uncompromising integrity, and perhaps the knowledge that he had been a lawyer, drew to the Patriarch's house throngs of unfortunate people who had been disappointed of justice and who implored his aid, nor did Xiphilinus hesitate to condemn the deficiencies of legal administration.

Xiphilinus's reforming zeal was not confined to purely ecclesiastical matters; he openly accused Psellus of loving Plato to the detriment of his spiritual life as a Christian. Needless to say, Psellus ably defended himself from the charge.[1] Xiphilinus's philosophical attitude is interesting, and it is unfortunate that the writings apparently philosophical in content which Psellus mentions[2] have been lost. Psellus asserts in the funeral oration that these so emphasize the Aristotelian point of view that they show an unjustifiable bias against Platonism.

The works of Xiphilinus which exist fall into two classes—his legal works[3] and his sermons.[4] It is from the latter that his character lies self-portrayed: they were written for the different canonical feasts and they are a distinct contrast to the sermons of John Mauropous or Symeon the Young. Xiphilinus was evidently an intense and severe man, striking no note of mysticism, but in plain prose, unendowed by metaphor or poetry, hammering in his emphasis on the evils of sin, rather after the manner of S. Paul, uncompromisingly driving home his point and strengthening it by countless quotations from the Bible. There are no references to secular writers, no indication of his own erudition, but only an exhortation to follow the ascetic way of life, presented with a ruthless directness that is reminiscent of his legal training. Psellus, in spite of his complete antithesis of outlook, evidently retained a genuine appreciation of Xiphilinus, as he shows in the funeral oration,[5] which is very different from that which he wrote for Cerularius or John

---

[1] See Chapter IV, pp. 86 ff.
[2] Sathas, iv, pp. 461–2.
[3] Mainly marginal notes on the Basilica (GBL, p. 171).
[4] PG, cxx, cols. 1201–92. Ehrhard says that this is the earliest collection of Sunday sermons extending throughout the whole year which we have (GBL, p. 163). Migne only published a few of these and the rest are still in manuscript (GBL, p. 171), but are in process of being edited. Ehrhard also mentions his hagiographical writings, and on this point see BZ, ii (1893), p. 631.
[5] Sathas, iv, pp. 421–62 (this ends abruptly in Sathas's edition).

Mauropous. The tone is simple and straightforward, evidently born of a sincere respect, and unusually severe, with an absence of those rhetorical passages which so frequently occur in his other orations. Psellus appears, moreover, to be genuinely interested in the problems which he is discussing, and this again makes the atmosphere less artificial, though this is perhaps only natural, as Xiphilinus was far more bound up with Psellus's life than Cerularius or even John Mauropous.

The other prominent figure in Psellus's circle of friends is Leichudes, of whom little is known. He unfortunately left no writings and his character can only be deduced from Psellus's works,[1] supplemented by the very bare references in contemporary historians, Attaleiates and Scylitzes. He is a very perplexing person, appearing occasionally in a context which makes it clear that he was an important figure. The fullest description of him is found in the *Chronographia* when Psellus recounts how much Monomachus depended upon him when he first came to the throne.

'He was a man of noble birth, possessed of great eloquence, which was ready and prepared for every shade of meaning, and moreover was accurately versed in affairs of state. And with his rhetorical powers which he expanded to perfect their persuasiveness, he mingled his knowledge of the laws of politics, thus linking them both together as members of one whole, so that he embellished the law with which he was dealing with more artistic work. He had also been endowed from above with a most practical mind, and his perfect understanding of public affairs was heightened by his logical faculty and natural ability. And, loving beautiful speech of every kind, he suited it to the practical form of the matter under discussion, and if it was a question of a rhetorical speech he excelled in elegant Attic style, if of practical politics a style that was simple, familiar and clear. He was distinguished by his athletic build, and the beauty of his diction, and had moreover something harmonious and distinctive about him, especially when he was proclaiming the imperial decrees from on high.'[2]

Psellus here lays characteristic emphasis on Leichudes' powers of oratory, his appreciation of Attic Greek, and his pleasing personal appearance, qualities which specially appealed to him.

[1] The funeral oration, letters, and the *Chronographia*.
[2] Psellus, *Chron.* vi. 178 (ii, pp. 58–9).

Not that these were of any avail against the intrigues of the court, for Leichudes, like his friends, fell into disgrace in 1050,[1] and retreated to monastic life. But he evidently reappeared as Psellus did when a favourable opportunity arose, for he was the 'third person' mentioned by Psellus in the embassy sent by Michael VI to Isaac Comnenus and there described as 'one of the most prominent among the Romans, the leader of the Senate, in whom intellect and eloquence vied with each other. He had in the first place toiled for the Emperor Monomachus and later graced the office of Patriarch, and then having dedicated himself to the Word, he in turn dedicated the Emperor [Isaac Comnenus] to the Father.'[2] It was in 1059 that he became Patriarch. He was equal in dignity to his predecessor, Cerularius, and his successor, Xiphilinus. At this point he again emerges from the mists as Psellus describes his accession to the office of Patriarch, especially when he says, 'For this renowned Constantine who had earlier brought the Empire safely to shore through a tempestuous sea, had been completely secured[3] for the service of many of the Emperors.'[4] But as to the nature of the tempests Psellus is silent, though it may be surmised that they belong to the sphere of politics and not learning. Scylitzes mentions Leichudes' election to this office—his only reference to him except for a brief mention of his death,[5] and he corroborates Psellus's description. These are his words:

'The office of Patriarch was undertaken by Constantine Leichudes, the president and protovestiarius,[6] who had earlier been elected by the vote of the metropolitans, clergy and laity. He was a man who from the reign of Constantine Monomachus to the time of the election had won great distinction in the conduct of imperial affairs. And he

[1] Psellus, *Chron.* vi. 181 (ii, p. 60).
[2] Ibid. vii. 18 (ii, p. 93), referring to Isaac's abdication and monastic vows.
[3] περιάρπακτος (completely hooked) is the word used.
[4] Psellus, *Chron.* vii. 66 (ii, pp. 123–4).
[5] Scylitzes, ii, p. 658.
[6] πρόεδρος καὶ πρωτοβεστιάριος.   See Bury, *The Imperial Administrative System in the Ninth Century*, p. 125; Ebersolt, *Sur les fonctions et les dignités du Vestiarium byzantin*; and E. Stein, *Untersuchungen zur spätbyzantinischen Verfassungs- und Wirtschaftsgeschichte*, pp. 32 ff. In the eleventh century this signified rank and office of considerable importance, but see J. E. Dunlap, on the rival importance of the παρακοιμώμενος, pp. 228 ff. For the office of πρόεδρος see also C. Diehl, *De la signification du titre de 'proèdre' à Byzance*.

gained for himself great fame in the administration of the whole government and the care of the Mangana[1] and the guardianship of equity was transferred to him by the Emperor we have mentioned.'[2]

Attaleiates' only brief mention of Leichudes is almost the same as that of Scylitzes, except that he adds that he was famed for his generosity among the clergy[3] and the people.[4] His conduct in his ecclesiastical office was such as befitted Psellus's description of him as a minister of Constantine IX. He was a man who was not open to every outside influence, but pursued his own course.

'He conducted matters of administration in the spirit not of a mere rhetorician but of a philosopher. . . . If he was considered as a statesman he appeared to be adorned with ecclesiastical majesty, if he was approached as a Patriarch, who was ordinarily regarded with fear and trembling, then there shone forth the graces of a statesman with decision of character and smiling dignity, and throughout his life he inspired confidence, whether earlier in his military career and his political life, or now by his generosity and tact.'[5]

Nevertheless the implication is that he was a man of action rather than a scholar, and although he is described as directing affairs "$\phi\iota\lambda o\sigma\delta\phi\omega s$" there is no suggestion that this meant any more than a capacity for statesmanship which was equally successful in serving both Church and state.

Such were the friends of Michael Psellus—Mauropous, Nicetas, Xiphilinus, Leichudes. There were other equally outstanding and interesting figures, Cerularius, the first of three great Patriarchs, Christopher of Mytilene, both poet and man of the world, Cecaumenus, the soldier who stressed practice rather than theory; but these were not directly concerned with the eleventh-century revival of learning. It was Psellus and his friends who inspired the reopening of the University, and their interests form the background of a movement which gave new impetus to a tradition of scholarship which Byzantium had always valued.

---

[1] This was probably the office of $\kappa o\nu\rho\acute{a}\tau\omega\rho$ $\tau\hat{\omega}\nu$ $M\alpha\gamma\gamma\acute{a}\nu\omega\nu$. See Bury, op. cit., pp. 101–2.

[2] Scylitzes, ii, pp. 644–5.

[3] $\acute{\iota}\epsilon\rho o\kappa\hat{\eta}\rho\nu\xi$, 'a word applied to sacred writers, also priests and readers in the Christian churches' (Sophocles). Here it must mean the clergy in general.   [4] Attaleiates, p. 66.   [5] Psellus, *Chron.* vii. 66 (ii, p. 124).

CHAPTER III

THE REOPENING OF THE UNIVERSITY OF CONSTANTINOPLE IN 1045

He made an end to foreign wars and civil strife, and now the balance is redressed and his subject peoples pacified, so that a great calm is settled upon the Roman Empire, and nothing now disturbs our minds, so, with the gracious assent of the imperial will, we turn all our thoughts towards the restoration of our constitution.

> John of Euchaita, *The Constitution of the Law School*, ed. Cozza-Luzi, pp. 299–300 (ch. 4).

The knowledge which I acquired with so much pain I imparted to all, not selling my words for money, but even aiding with financial help those who were willing to receive it.

> Psellus, *Chron.* vi. 43 (i, p. 138).

THE reopening of the long-closed University of Constantinople in 1045 may be attributed to various causes: there were men interested in scholarship, there was an Emperor ready to give imperial consent and financial support, and finally there was urgent public need for the establishment of at least a School of Law. Unfortunately it is difficult to find any detailed evidence concerning this event. Psellus says in the *Chronographia* remarkably little and nothing definitely about the opening of the University. After a few lines he passes rapidly to a long and interesting digression on a subject to which he was always partial, that is himself and his own attitude to learning. All he says about Constantine IX in this context is one short and vague sentence, giving none of the fullness of detail which might reasonably be expected—'He was not exactly well versed in letters nor had he reached any proficiency in philosophy, but he admired this type of man, and from all parts he gathered into the palace the more learned men, and most of them seemed to be in extreme old age.'[1] Cedrenus makes no mention of Constantine's partiality for men of letters nor of the reopening of the University. Attaleiates, however, gives a brief but important reference.[2]

[1] Psellus, *Chron.* vi. 35 (i, p. 134).
[2] Attaleiates, p. 21.

'So when the Emperor had successfully concluded the struggle[1] he lived in peace and gladly devoted himself to civil administration. He stimulated a school of law-givers and appointed a "guardian of the laws." But he also paid attention to the teaching of heavenly philosophy, and appointed as head of the philosophers a man excelling any of us in knowledge. He exhorted young men to pursue training in philosophy and mathematics and to take advantage of the teachers offered them, and he rewarded with imperial honours those who were public orators. And, moreover, he introduced a secretariat[2] for private sentences and he called the man who presided over this "ἐπὶ τῶν κρίσεων".'[3]

It is evident that the reopened University consisted of two Faculties, the one of Law and the other of Philosophy, but there is some doubt whether one was constituted before the other, and, if so, which one. Zervos maintains that the School of Philosophy was the first to be reopened.[4] He bases his statement upon certain passages in the constitution of the Law School, which was drawn up by John Mauropous. The first passage in question deals with the neglect of law in contrast to the other sciences:

'For it is really a terrible and disgraceful state of affairs when the other sciences and arts, both liberal and even some illiberal, have their own chairs and professors, possess a definite standing, are provided with stipends, and everything possible is done for the benefit of the students, while the most necessary of all sciences, the most vitally useful of all studies, apart from which all else is superfluous and of no avail (for what is the use of these things when lawlessness prevails?), this science, I say, is, as it were, pushed outside the state, and left without form or shape as if it were a worthless little subject, utterly useless for human life. . . .'[5]

The second passage is much shorter and states that the head of the Law School is to have the same holidays as the Philosophy professors; his work is only to cease 'on those days on which the

---

[1] i.e. the Russian war.

[2] Reading σέκρετον instead of δέκρετον, as Fischer suggests, Studien, p. 19, note 5 (beginning on p. 18).

[3] i.e. supreme judge. C. Zervos, Michel Psellos, p. 66, says that this office was conferred on Xiphilinus, following Sathas, iv, p. 431. See W. Fischer, Studien, p. 18 (note 5), for discussion of this.

[4] C. Zervos, Michel Psellos, p. 90.

[5] Cozza-Luzi, pp. 300–1 (ch. 4).

school of letters is accustomed to have a holiday'.[1] With regard to the precedence of the schools Schlumberger takes the opposite view to Zervos; although he does not give his reference, he appears to be relying on Attaleiates, who mentions law and then philosophy.[2] He speaks first of the disastrous effect which the neglect of legal studies has had on the civil government, and he implies that this was the chief reason why Constantine was interested in the reopening of the University. 'Le premier soin de Constantin Monomaque et de ses conseillers fut de restituer ainsi à l'enseignement juridique la situation prépondérante qu'il devait avoir dans l'État.'[3] This may well have been Constantine's real attitude, but in the actual question of precedence the evidence found in the constitution of the Law School makes it probable that Schlumberger is wrong.

If this problem cannot be conclusively settled, it remains that there were two Faculties, that of Philosophy, and that of Law. The influences at work were obviously Psellus and Xiphilinus, the one a philosopher, the other a lawyer. 'For I, on the one hand, championed the sciences and arts, and he, on the other, legal studies. And the whole body of eminent learning was evenly divided in its support of us.'[4] Nor would either party yield, since to each the establishment of its own faculty seemed all-important. Psellus would no doubt have liked to see the predominance of philosophy, possibly with a subordinate school of law. Xiphilinus was equally determined and had reason on his side in urging the necessity for emphasizing legal training. The dispute was evidently pointed and bitter, and the matter was finally settled by the imperial establishment of the two faculties.[5]

Unfortunately only the text of the constitution of the Law Faculty remains. It was drawn up by John Mauropous, who was at that time regarded with considerable admiration not only by the Emperor but by the scholars of either party. Among John's writings there is the following poem:

[1] Cozza-Luzi p. 305 (ch. 8).
[2] Attaleiates, pp. 21-2. There is no indication that law was thought of before philosophy; the implication is that *both* were considered.
[3] G. Schlumberger, *L'épopée byzantine*, iii, p. 534.
[4] Sathas, iv, p. 433.
[5] Ibid., iv, p. 434.

'On the Novel concerning the guardian of law.'

This man it was who considered the general value of the plan,
He it was who unfolded it to the Emperor,
He it was who convinced him, he it is who is writing this.[1]

John would no doubt draw up the constitution of the Law School
subject to the imperial approval. It was customary for important
documents to be signed by the Emperor, and this occasion was
no exception; John wrote a poem under the title of 'On the
signature of the document in purple colour', which says, 'The
hand of the wise Emperor Monomachus implants intelligence
in young men, adorning the glorious sign of the imperial dignity
with flowers of purple.'[2]

The text is an interesting document: it shows the condition
of legal studies, the improvements aimed at, and the means by
which these were to be achieved. Xiphilinus's experience as a
young man seeking legal training has already shown the condition of law in the first half of the eleventh century[3] and there
is no doubt that the situation was urgent. One of the first things
that the constitution states is that 'young men are anxious to
seek somebody to give them legal instruction, but since they
can find nobody appointed by the profession and furnished with
imperial approval, for lack of any better teacher they each take
as master whomsoever they can find'.[4] Formerly notaries and
advocates belonged to separate corporations under the control
of the city eparch, having a school of law with recognized
teachers. They had evidently gradually slipped from public
control and had lowered their standard; hence the chaos in legal
training.[5] Constantine IX meant to re-establish the state control
over the teaching of law, and the constitution shows that both
the school and its head were bound by the imperial regulations.

The School of Law was situated within the newly founded
monastery of S. George. This was the S. George of the Man-

---

[1] Lagarde, p. 50 (Poem 94). This is wrongly cited by Cozza-Luzi, p. 292,
as PG, cxx, col. 1194, Poem 94: he confuses Migne's numbering with that of
Lagarde.
[2] Lagarde, p. 37 (Poem 70).
[3] See Chapter II, pp. 45 ff.
[4] Cozza-Luzi, p. 298 (ch. 3).
[5] See Laborde, pp. 146 ff.

gana, which was on the west slope of the Acropolis, and was known in the Middle Ages as 'angulus Sancti Georgii in Manganis'.[1] It had formerly been the θέατρον κυνηγετικόν. The word 'cynegion' was familiar from its connexion with the Sclerena whom Constantine IX visited with such frequency that it was said that he built the church in order to provide himself with an excuse for lingering in those quarters. The site as well as the monastery certainly justified the enthusiasm with which it is described as "κάλλιστον καὶ τερπνότατον".[2] Behind the building rose a wooded slope, in front of it were the walls of the city, beyond these the precipitous shore and the sea. To-day no trace of the church and monastery of S. George in Mangana exists: nothing of the Mangana district of Constantine Monomachus's day remains, except part of the palace foundations.[3] It was in these pleasant surroundings that the Law School was established and given the formal name of 'διδασκαλεῖον νόμων'.

The constitution gives considerable prominence to the duties and position of its head, whose functions and privileges it defines at length. His title was νομοφύλαξ. The first to be thus named was John Xiphilinus, who was eminently suited for this office both in character and experience;[4] he is thus described in the text as

'the illustrious and most learned John, a judge in the Hippodrome and exactor, by surname Xiphilinus. He used his vast store of learning, not secretly or unworthily or obscurely, but he shone forth publicly and openly in treatment of case law (πεῖρα).[5] He was equally well versed both in the art of letters and of law, nor did he ever neglect our commands.'[6]

The privileges which pertained to this office of 'guardian of

[1] See Du Cange, lib. iv, p. 124.
[2] Cozza-Luzi, p. 302 (ch. 6).
[3] Mordtmann, p. 51.
[4] In his funeral oration Psellus gives an account of Xiphilinus's powers of oratory and astounding memory.
[5] See Mortreuil, ii, pp. 467–9, for a discussion of the word πεῖρα, i.e. 'ce que la pratique du droit avait de réel et de positif par opposition aux spéculations théoriques de la science'. See also W. Fischer, *Studien*, pp. 55–6, on the πεῖρα.
[6] Cozza-Luzi, pp. 301–2 (ch. 5).

the laws' show that it was considered to be of great importance.

'And he shall enjoy these rights and privileges:—he shall be counted
among the senators of highest rank; he shall have his seat next to that
of the chief judge; he shall have access to our powerful majesty on
the same days as he has; he shall be honoured in like manner to him
with our speech and glance—and all this that excess of honour may
stimulate his zeal. And every year he shall receive a gift from us of
four litrai, and a purple silk cloth,[1] and a palm.'[2]

The appointment was made for life, but was naturally dependent upon the conduct of the Nomophylax, a condition inserted
with more regard to the future than the present, as there seems
to be no doubt of Xiphilinus's willingness and ability to reach
the exacting standard required. 'And let him devote his whole
life to this, by night pursuing those things which pertain to an
interpretation, and by day unfolding the truth and giving un-
stinted instruction to his followers.'[3] It is interesting to note
that among his duties as a teacher he was required to teach
Latin as well as Greek. 'And he shall have an accurate knowledge of both languages, by this I mean Greek and Latin.'[4] So
that if his honours were great they were not out of proportion
to his duties, while the position accorded to him makes it quite
clear that he is an important public official.

The aim of the School of Law was to provide a thorough
legal knowledge, so that those who were to be the judges and
administrators and lawyers of the future might base their prac-

[1] βλαττίον (Sophocles).
[2] Cozza-Luzi, p. 304 (ch. 7).
[3] Ibid., p. 305 (ch. 8).
[4] Ibid., p. 307 (ch. 9). As early as the middle of the tenth century in his
De Thematibus, i, p. 13 (CB, iii), Constantine VII wrote 'καὶ ἑλληνίζοντες καὶ
τὴν πάτριον καὶ ῾Ρωμαϊκὴν γλῶτταν ἀποβαλόντες'. By the eleventh century
knowledge of Latin was unusual. Psellus mentions it as one of the acquire-
ments of John Mauropous (Sathas, v, p. 148) and he himself had, he says,
given some time to its study (Sathas, v, p. 492). E. Renauld, Étude de la
langue et du style de Michel Psellos, pp. 417–19, shows that while the evidence
of Psellus's writings indicated a knowledge of legal terms, he was certainly
unacquainted with Latin literature; for instance, when speaking of the warlike
character of the Romans, he could talk of the Κικέρωνες ... ἄνδρες οὐδὲν ἄλλο ἢ
θεράποντες ῎Αρηος (Εἰς τὸν Λογγοβάρδον ᾿Ιωάννην). (Ed. Boissonade, p. 169.)
The constitution of the Law School probably spoke of Latin as well as Greek
in order to emphasize the erudition of the Nomophylax. But cf. Anna
Comnena's scorn of any association with the 'barbarians'.

tice on sound theory. The purpose manifested throughout the text of the constitution was to remedy the difficulties which Xiphilinus had to face when he was a young man, and which must have been well known to Mauropous as well as to Psellus. Hence Constantine endowed the school not only with their pleasant buildings and competent staff, but with a library. 'And he [i.e. the Nomophylax] shall have charge of the books of the law, which he shall receive from the library from the most devout librarian for his free use, to administer as seems good to him: these books will be, of course, those which are most useful and necessary for the teaching of law.'[1] Unfortunately there is no indication of the titles of these books, but they would presumably be exclusively legal works, especially the Code of Justinian and the Basilics. Xiphilinus certainly considered them necessary for any legal training, and they had formed the foundation of his own studies and practice.

The students thus trained would have some definite standard on which to base their sentences; they would no longer disagree among each other, thinking of their own reputations rather than of the administration of justice.[2] To ensure as far as possible that a high standard was maintained, the constitution determined that no student could proceed to legal practice unless he had pursued the required course of studies and had obtained from the Nomophylax a certificate to this effect.

'And they are not only to employ every means towards making a thorough study of the law with the most learned guardian of the law, but neither may they be registered as members of any legal body until he himself, their teacher, testifies with both tongue and pen to their proficiency, with reference to their knowledge both of the laws and of other sciences.'[3]

The constitution states further that no one is to follow the calling of notary or advocate without the duly written qualification, so that the imperial foundation had almost a monopoly of legal training. One wonders what was to happen to those who were already practising without this training and written qualification; there must have been considerable rivalry between the old and new school of lawyer.

---

[1] Cozza-Luzi, p. 303 (ch. 6).
[2] Ibid., p. 299 (ch. 3).   [3] Ibid., pp. 309–10 (ch. 11).

The foundation of the School of Law was essentially democratic. Its aim was to admit the best, exclusive of the claims of
birth or money, teaching all free of charge.

'And you shall not make unfair discriminations between those
who come to study the law, nor in electing to the rank of a chair shall
you take any account of wealth, but, as is right, only of merit. And
indeed, without any invidious distinctions you shall admit all to the
curriculum. You shall teach all gratuitously and without payment.
And with pure hand, with pure voice and mind you shall expound
the laws, which attack with the utmost severity those in other
positions of authority who degrade themselves by taking bribes, as
you, the interpreter of the law, know better than anyone else.'[1]

Unfortunately an inconsistent corollary is added to permit gifts
from rich pupils, a possible loop-hole for evading the spirit of the
constitution. The text ends with an exhortation to the youth of
the day to take every advantage of the facilities afforded them,
and John inserts a vivid picture of the difficulties which formerly
beset law students, contrasting these with the present opportunities. Not that he wishes to imply that these favourable
conditions can ever eliminate the need for patience and hard
work. So he adds, with a characteristic touch,

'You must imitate those who are good and prudent farmers, who
deem the land they cultivate worthy of the utmost care. And they
do not strip it of fruit once and for all, and allow it to bear thorns and
run to wood, but they take care that it may be perpetually fruitful
and may remain equally productive for themselves and be no less so
for posterity.'[2]

The constitution clearly emphasizes two points—the pressing
need for reform, and the means by which this was to be achieved.
The actual text is characterized by the general nature of its
clauses; for example, when it describes the duties of the Nomophylax it gives no details concerning the academic teaching which
it was his place to provide. The document gives the impression
that it was drafted by a man who was unacquainted with the
technicalities of legal training, and this would probably be the
case with John Mauropous. The School of Law seems to have
had little connexion with the School of Philosophy, and the

[1] Cozza-Luzi, pp. 305–6 (ch. 8).   [2] Ibid., p. 312 (ch. 13).

text of its constitution makes only two references to other branches of learning.

It is unfortunate that no text of the constitution of the Philosophy School exists. This would not only have contributed considerably to the problem of precedence, but would have given valuable information concerning the nature of the foundation. Other sources which might be expected to mention the University are disappointing, and, apart from Psellus, Attaleiates is the only historian who has even a reference to the School of Philosophy. But he only mentions it in passing, and the words "φιλοσοφίας οὐρανοβάμονος"[1] give none of the detail which would be valuable. The only evidence of any importance is that which Psellus himself gives. The faculty was organized on lines similar to those of the Law School, or perhaps it would be more accurate to say that the constitution of the Law School was framed after the plan of the already established School of Philosophy. It was to be situated in the church of S. Peter, and was called "ἡ σχολὴ τοῦ ἁγίου Πέτρου".[2] The 'church of S. Peter' may have been on the hill known as the Petrion, which took its name from this church and was the site of several monasteries and churches; its significance was similar to that of Mt. Athos or Mt. Olympus, and it played an important role in the life of Constantinople.[3] Although the majority of Byzantine scholars agree that Psellus is referring to the School of Philosophy when he writes 'ἡ σχολὴ τοῦ ἁγίου Πέτρου', it has been asserted by Fuchs, following Giakoumakes, that this is not so.[4] He explains that Nicetas was a teacher first at the Patriarch's School of S. Peter and afterwards at the University, though it seems odd that Psellus should in this case refer to him when he died as 'master of the School of S. Peter'.[5] But Fuchs, having disposed of the difficulty of the title of the funeral oration, brings forward more positive evidence to show that the school

---

[1] Attaleiates, p. 21.
[2] Psellus in his funeral oration on Nicetas describes him as μαΐστωρ τῆς σχολῆς τοῦ ἁγίου Πέτρου, Sathas, v, p. 87.
[3] Mordtmann, p. 41.
[4] Fuchs, p. 28.
[5] Fuchs might have supported his argument by the title of the Vatican MS. of Psellus's oration on Nicetas which only gives "ἐπιτάφιος εἴς τινα φίλον αὐτοῦ καὶ συμμαθητήν". Cod. vat. 672, f. 209, quoted Bezobrazov, Materials, ii, p. 75.

was located in a completely different place. This he finds in two sources: first, Matthew of Edessa, who says, 'Tous les philosophes qui siégeaient dans l'Académie admirèrent la solidité des raisonnements de Kakig';[1] secondly, Gregorius Magister, a philosopher,[2] who went to Constantinople about 1044, and who speaks both of reading a certain work in 'l'Académie d'Achille',[3] and of 'les philosophes du sénat'.[4] Fuchs concludes that these 'philosophers' are the teachers of the School of Philosophy and that this was situated 'im Mittelpunkt der Stadt, gegenüber dem Senat, im Bereich des Portikus des Achilles, in der antiken Umgebung von Säulen, Statuen und περίπατοι'. It may be suggested that Fuchs's citation from Matthew of Edessa only stands if it is assumed that the University continued after 1054, and also its context is such that the 'philosophers' might have been collected for the occasicn. For Matthew of Edessa has just spoken of learned men and scholars who were gathered together at Constantinople, the purpose of the meeting being the reunion of the Armenian and Orthodox Churches, under the auspices of the Patriarch Xiphilinus, a thought prompted by the devil according to this chronicler.[5] It seems improbable that Xiphilinus would have wished for the co-operation of the secular School of Philosophy, led by a man of whom he was already suspicious,[6] although on the other hand it should be remembered that Psellus stood high in the favour of Constantine Ducas. If Fuchs's evidence for the 'Portikus des Achilles' is inconclusive, his suggestion that the school was not that of S. Peter rests on firmer ground. There is evidence that S. Peter's was associated with an ecclesiastical school,[7] in answer to which it may be replied that there was more than one church of S. Peter.[8] So, as is often the case, it is only possible to state the evidence, without reaching any definite conclusion.

[1] Ed. and trans. E. Dulaurier, p. 151. This is in Constantine Ducas's reign and Fuchs takes the passage out of its context.
[2] Ed. and trans. V. Langlois, p. 52 (Ep. 46): 'Quant à moi, je n'ai jamais cessé de traduire beaucoup de livres que je n'ai pas trouvés dans notre langue: les deux livres de Platon, intitulés dialogues du Timée et du Phédon ... et d'autres philosophes encore.'
[3] Ibid., p. 46 (Ep. 27), quoted by Fuchs, p. 29.
[4] Ibid., p. 51 (Ep. 44).   [5] Ed. and trans. E. Dulaurier, p. 133.
[6] See Chapter IV for the breach between Psellus and Xiphilinus.
[7] Sathas, v, p. 420 (Ep. 162); Fuchs, p. 49.   [8] See Du Cange, iv, p. 115.

The head of the school was Psellus, who had the title of ὕπατος τῶν φιλοσόφων.[1] The members of his staff were called μαΐστορες. There is no information concerning the number of subordinate chairs, and all that is known is that two of them were held by Psellus's friends, Nicetas of Byzantium and John Mauropous. Psellus wrote funeral orations for both these men, but he does not give any formal information about the constitution of the foundation; on the other hand, he speaks about the aspect of their lives which really interested him, namely, the nature of their teaching. Thus it is possible to reconstruct from his evidence the scope of the lectures and the spirit which inspired them. Psellus, as befitted his position, was evidently the predominant personality of the staff, and his teaching, the climax of the curriculum, was only imparted to those who had attended a preparatory course of instruction given by other masters. There was some similarity between the curriculum of the University at Constantinople and that found in the schools of western Europe. Psellus, in speaking of John Mauropous's education, describes what was evidently the usual process: 'When he had learnt the elementary rudiments, and had thence arrived at the summit of the art of grammar, he then obtained a complete understanding of the greater sciences.'[2] The first stage was that which was known as the Trivium in the west, comprising Grammar, Rhetoric, and Dialectic.

Nicetas held the Chair of Grammar until his death. In the funeral oration written on this occasion, Psellus speaks in some detail of the scope and method of Nicetas's teaching. The study of Grammar involved a detailed knowledge of orthography and philology, subjects in which Nicetas was well versed.[3] It was only when this background had been mastered that he turned to the more literary aspects, studying Greek authors with the aid of the philological technique which had already been acquired. From Psellus's words it is evident that Nicetas took care that his students were not so immersed in the technical side that they lost all sense of perspective or appreciation; for Nicetas himself did not study grammar as many did, who were content with

---

[1] Scylitzes, ii, p. 688. See Fuchs, pp. 29 ff., on this title.
[2] Sathas, v, p. 147. Cf. the *colloquium scholasticum*, ed. M. Treu, BZ, ii (1893), pp. 96–105.   [3] Ibid., pp. 90 ff.

discussing the metre and appearance of words, but he sought a beauty beyond the mere content of the passage, and 'with the aid of reason and contemplation he passed beyond the corporeal and penetrated within the shrine'.[1]

In the teaching of rhetoric Psellus must have received considerable help from John Mauropous, whose capacity as scholar and teacher has already been discussed.[2] He held the Chair of Rhetoric and must have been an important member of the staff. The study of rhetoric was wide and comprehensive. It was an aspect of learning which appealed to the Byzantines, and Krumbacher stresses the continuity of its history.[3] The necessity for an adequate study of rhetoric was one of Psellus's favourite themes, and one which he may have owed to John Mauropous. While maintaining that the highest stage of knowledge was philosophy, he openly despised the philosopher who neglected to present his thoughts in the most beautiful language; therefore rhetoric formed an important feature of his curriculum. 'Learning is divided into two parts, the one is composed of rhetoric, the other is concerned with philosophy' he wrote in the *Chronographia*.[4] In the same passage he defined rhetoric, and proceeded to argue for a balance between the two, rhetoric and philosophy. He said that most men failed to realize that the one was the complement of the other; and therefore they either concentrated on rhetoric and neglected philosophy, or else studying only to enrich their knowledge they forgot the flowers of speech. It was an attitude which had its disadvantages. Psellus's own works sometimes suggest that he himself was led astray by thinking too much about style, and his writings often show undue elaboration; for, as he exhorted his students to follow the industry and example of Plato or Pythagoras, so he himself deliberately attempted, often without success, to revive the style of Demosthenes or Thucydides.

When they had finished their training in grammar and

---

[1] Sathas, v, p. 92, λόγῳ καὶ θεωρίᾳ διασχὼν τὴν ὕλην καὶ εἴσω τῶν ἀδύτων γενόμενος. A passage reminiscent of the debt which Psellus owed to the Neoplatonists. [2] See Chapter II.
[3] GBL, p. 450; see E. Renauld, *Étude de la langue et du style de Michel Psellos*, pp. 410–11, on the favoured books of rhetorical technique, and especially Hermogenes of Tarsus of the second century A.D.
[4] Psellus, *Chron.* vi. 41 (i, p. 137).

rhetoric students proceeded to the higher course of lectures, which included arithmetic, geometry, music, and astronomy, and culminated in philosophy. The aim of this course was clearly set forth by Psellus in the *Chronographia* where he gives a long description of his own intellectual development. For it may be assumed that when he was in charge of his students he would naturally wish to put into practice the fruits of his own experience, gathered only at the expense of much painful effort. After speaking of his own longing for philosophical knowledge, he then said that this could only be acquired if the right foundations were already laid.

'For this reason I used arithmetical methods; I adopted geometrical proofs, which some call necessary laws; I paid attention to the study of music and astronomy, and any other knowledge on which these subjects are based. I neglected none of these, but first of all went through them singly, and then linked them all together, since they all harmonized to the same end, as the Epinomis claims. And by this process I was thus able to attack higher knowledge (τὰ ὑψηλότερα).'[1]

The recognition of the importance of grappling with these intermediary sciences influenced Psellus's whole approach to learning. It was only when these had been mastered that it was possible to turn to philosophy:

'I strove to attain to the higher philosophy, and to become versed in pure knowledge. I first studied the theory of things incorporeal in the branch of science known as mathematics, which held an intermediate place, that is to say, on the one hand it concerned the nature of bodies and the unfettered understanding of these, and on the other it concerned the essences themselves which appertain to pure understanding. My aim was to find something that was beyond this in knowledge, and beyond this in essence.'[2]

Thus it would be a mistake to regard Psellus as a philosopher in any narrow sense of the word, nor did he wish to give his pupils a limited or superficial education. Their knowledge of philosophy, for this was undoubtedly the end which he had in view for those who were capable of attaining it, was to be based on a wide and thorough understanding of those branches of knowledge which, if regarded by Psellus as subordinate, were nevertheless recognized as essential in the initial stages of learning.

[1] Psellus, *Chron.* vi. 39 (i, p. 136).   [2] Ibid., 38 (i, p. 136).

Only the very best could ever expect to reach the summit of knowledge and apply themselves to those higher studies of which Psellus speaks. In his system of education Psellus was certainly working in concert with John Mauropous, his old teacher, and it is possible that the theories which he was putting into practice had been first instilled into him by John.

Psellus, as a teacher, must have been famed not only for the content of his lectures, but also for his method of presentation. The charm of his personality, the magnetism of his enthusiasm, must have given to his lectures the same fascination which students found in those of Abelard. There is, no doubt, considerable truth in his exaggerated words to Cerularius:

'the Celts and Arabs came under our sway, men from the other continent journeyed here because of the report of our fame. And as the Nile watered the land of Egypt, so our discourses refreshed the soul. And if you happen to talk with Persians or Ethiopians, they will say that they know and admire me, and have come in pursuit of me; and now one from the borders of Babylon has arrived, with untamed zeal, to drink at my springs.'[1]

Psellus has left several short addresses to his students, and these show the spirit which animated his teaching. He must have been a strangely versatile man; there is nothing in his political career to suggest his singular capacity for scholarship in the truest sense, scholarship that was, moreover, so alive with enthusiasm that it could impart its vitality to others, inspiring them with a love of knowledge, and, above all, of philosophy. He pleads for more courageous persistence in the pursuit of learning, 'For you do not rouse your souls, neither do you devour the fire of my zeal, but you lay hold of knowledge as though you were one of those in the market place.'[2] He then proceeds to contrast, as he was so fond of doing, the present with the past, finding in ancient Greece all the virtues he would wish to see in his own pupils, and especially courage in the face of difficulties and determination to seek knowledge even at the cost of journeying to a foreign land. In another address[3] he gives an impassioned picture of classical scholars, who did not require to be goaded to continue that which their masters had begun. The very earnestness of

[1] Sathas, v, p. 508 (*Ep*. 207).
[2] Boissonade, p. 137.   [3] Ibid., pp. 147–53.

Psellus's appeal to his students seems to suggest that there was no general enthusiasm for learning; otherwise he would surely not have made such efforts to rouse this, even though he was unusually serious in his devotion to his subject.

Unfortunately the work of Psellus and his friends as masters in the Faculty of Philosophy was distinguished not only by its quality but by its brevity. The reason is not far to seek, and is found in the opposition which they stirred up and which was equally directed against Xiphilinus and the Faculty of Law. In order to understand how this arose, it is necessary to give some indication of the underlying currents of Byzantine politics. An outstanding feature of the University was its democratic foundation, and Psellus and Xiphilinus themselves were not members of the older and more important families; their rise to power was due to their own efforts[1] and their natural ability, and many, especially those of the military party, probably regarded them with dislike and contempt. Suspicion of the new schools would only be heightened by the fact that the men who inaugurated them remained, moreover, among the most important of the court officials; it was with the definite intent of placating those who attacked him for his pluralism that Psellus actually took a lower place at court. The attack was therefore provoked by antagonism to the political activities of the professors as well as by dislike of the new schools. The story of the downfall of Psellus and his friends is short, and it unfortunately appears to involve the downfall of the University. In the *Chronographia* Psellus does not say much concerning the history of the intrigue and his subsequent disgrace. The account given is misleading, because he was too vain to admit that the real cause of his leaving Constantinople was the successful opposition of an aristocracy to a self-made man. But it is not difficult to imagine the antagonism which would be roused by such a measure as that described in Xiphilinus's funeral oration,[2] where Constantine admitted men to the senate and to office on a basis of intellectual qualification rather than birth or hereditary right. It is easy to condemn the servility and self-seeking of Psellus's politics, but

---

[1] Cf. the independent attitude of Attaleiates, who was a contemporary of Psellus, and who made no attempt at gaining himself a place at court by means of flattery and intrigue.   [2] Sathas, iv, pp. 430-1.

an analysis of his gradual fall from favour shows both the constant opposition which he had to face and the instability of the Emperor's character. The government of Byzantium was a despotism, the success of which depended on a masterly control of circumstances, mainly to be interpreted as the army and Constantinople; within the smaller circle of court life the will of the Emperor was supreme, and it was because they offended Constantine IX that Psellus, Xiphilinus, Leichudes, and John Mauropous fell from favour.

Psellus writes quite frankly in the *Chronographia* concerning Leichudes' disgrace. Constantine IX became infatuated with a eunuch, John by name,[1] and he entrusted the control of the imperial administration to him, having previously listened to those who were jealous of Leichudes.[2] He was, no doubt, all the more inclined to believe scandal against a man whose control he must have found irksome; for Leichudes consistently refused to condone the Emperor's wanton extravagance—'he did not give rein to him, saying philosophically that he would not voluntarily bring the Emperor to ruin'.[3]

But behind this attack against Psellus and his friends stood more than the intrigues of a eunuch or the whim of an Emperor. Fischer says, 'Es ging damit eine von den in Byzanz so üblichen Parteiumwälzungen vor sich; das Gelehrten- und Bürgerelement ward entfernt, das adelige trat wieder an seine Stelle.'[4] This aristocratic party was represented by the dominating figure of Michael Cerularius. Born of a noble family, he was evidently a child of marked personality, silent and reserved; he grew into a man of ambitions, filled with a secret desire to control others. In the reign of Michael IV he became implicated in a conspiracy and was forced to become a monk, and it was not until 1041 that he was recalled from exile by Constantine IX. His relations with Constantine IX are difficult to determine because Psellus's evidence is so contradictory, and, moreover, the political motives behind the *Accusation* and *Panegyric* make it almost impossible to tell how far Psellus was then writing in obedience to imperial command.[5] In the *Panegyric* Psellus speaks of Cerularius's in-

---

[1] Psellus, *Chron.* vi. 177 (ii, p. 58); see Cedrenus, ii, p. 610.
[2] Ibid., 179 (ii, p. 59).   [3] Ibid., 180 (ii, p. 60).
[4] W. Fischer, *Studien*, p. 20.   [5] See Chapter VIII.

fluence with Constantine, who consulted him in both divine and human affairs and called him "ὁμωρόφιος καὶ ὁμοδίαιτος",[1] and in the spring of 1042 he was elected to the office of Patriarch.[2] The security which this position afforded gave his opposition a constancy which made it all the more dangerous, though it may have seemed at the time that it was safer for the Emperor to have him as Patriarch rather than as a possible rival to the imperial throne. Cerularius sent his nephews to study under Psellus, but this is no evidence for the continuity of their good relations; in any case, Psellus's outlook was different from Cerularius's who therefore regarded with suspicion both his philosophical position and his political activities. While Psellus held the most influential place among Constantine's advisers there was no room for Cerularius.

With the knowledge of this powerful opposition, Psellus and Xiphilinus must have felt extremely insecure, especially as soon after Leichudes' departure they began to be exposed to attacks both direct and indirect.[3] Xiphilinus was attacked by a man called Ophrydas, and Psellus defended him; since the matter did not go into the courts, Psellus's defence must have been primarily for the benefit of the University.[4] Although Ophrydas died soon after, the attacks continued, and it is evident that Constantine IX made no definite attempt to defend his favourites. The logical corollary was an attack on Psellus himself.[5] Psellus's account of the reasons for his passage to the 'better life' is very amusing.

'The majority of people were astonished that I swept everything aside in order to undertake the heavenly life just as my star was gradually ascending and was overcoming the intrigues of many. The reason for this change was a kind of implanted longing which since childhood had taken root in my soul. It was also the complete reversal of circumstances and I feared when I saw the instability of the Emperor's disposition.'[6]

The real reason is obviously to be found in the weakness of his position at court, as he admits, not only in the passage just quoted, but again when he speaks of the actual course of events.[7]

[1] Sathas, iv, p. 324.
[2] See Chapter VIII.
[3] Psellus, *Chron.* vi. 191 ff. (ii, pp. 65 ff.); Sathas, iv, pp. 435–6; v, pp. 181 ff. *passim.*
[4] Sathas, v, pp. 181–96.
[5] Ibid., pp. 168 ff.
[6] Psellus, *Chron.* vi. 191 (ii, p. 65).
[7] Ibid., 194 (ii, p. 66).

There is certainly nothing in Psellus's character or actions to suggest that he had always longed for monastic life, and his very reactions to it show that it was the last thing for which he was suited. The truth is that the uncertainty of conditions under so changeable an Emperor as Constantine IX compelled Psellus and his friends to seek a monastic retreat. At this point the narrative of the *Chronographia* shows some inconsistency. Psellus speaks first of the common pact made by the three friends,[1] and the context supports the conclusion that these were Psellus, Xiphilinus, and John Mauropous.[2] Then he says that the first to go was Xiphilinus, and that he himself followed some time after, making no mention of the third friend. Xiphilinus did not go until 1054, because he became Patriarch in 1063, having spent nine years in a monastery. The difficulty is to discover what happened to John Mauropous.

This is an old problem. Dreves, Draeseke, and Gudeman[3] do not agree on the sequence of events in John's life, but the available evidence is so inconsistent and inconclusive that it is impossible to speak with any certainty. Some of the inscriptions of his canons refer to John as 'the monk John, afterwards consecrated Archbishop of Euchaita',[4] and he was, in the course of his life, both monk and Archbishop. He was clearly made Archbishop very much against his will,[5] but there does not seem to be sufficient evidence for saying that his appointment was in the nature of a punishment because he had displeased the Emperor by writing a history that was too outspoken.[6] He must have been elected Archbishop some time before September 1047.[7]

---

[1] Psellus, *Chron.* vi. 194 (ii, p. 66).

[2] In this passage Psellus does not refer to the third friend by name. But we learn that he was an older man than Psellus, a lover of philosophy and learning, while he was not anxious to follow Psellus and Xiphilinus to court and came some time after them.

[3] Pauly-Wissowa, ix. 2, cols. 1751 ff.

[4] e.g. *Vindob. cod. theol. gr.* 78 (*Nessel*), f. 315ʳ.

[5] Lagarde, pp. 42 ff. (Poems 89–93).

[6] This is maintained by Draeseke, BZ, ii, pp. 476 ff.

[7] W. Fischer, *Studien*, p. 20, and E. Renauld, *Chron.* ii, p. 60, note 1, say that John left the court soon after Leichudes, who went in 1050. But J. Draeseke gives the year 1046 and says that John was then appointed to the see of Euchaita, since he seems to have returned to Constantinople as Archbishop in the year of Leo Tornicius's rebellion (this took place in September 1047). See John's speech on the condition of Constantinople at this time, Lagarde, pp. 178 ff., no. 186.

Whatever its reason, this appointment to the see of Euchaita in Asia Minor was more than exile to a man whose meditative and scholarly nature had already sunk its roots deep into the soil of Constantinople, and his correspondence with Psellus shows how he longed to return.[1] But according to the *Chronographia*, it would appear that John was one of the three who were driven by growing opposition at court to seek the refuge of monastic life. An explanation that takes all the available evidence into account is that John, already a monk, went to court at Psellus's instigation and taught at the reopened University; then for some reason he was appointed to the see of Euchaita. He returned to Constantinople from time to time, but he naturally fell under the shadow that threatened his friends towards the end of the reign. Whether he went, like Psellus and Xiphilinus, to a monastery, or whether he returned to his see, it is difficult to say. If Psellus is referring to John in the *Chronographia* he certainly implies the former, though he does not explicitly say so; on the other hand, it would seem more normal for John to retire to Asia Minor, especially as there is some evidence that he was still Archbishop there in Alexius Comnenus's reign.[2]

If Psellus is obscure in the *Chronographia* concerning the fate of John, he speaks at length about his own actions and motives. He was characteristically the last to go, and he lingered in Constantinople until he was sure that there was no opportunity of regaining his position at court. Finally, fearing lest the death of Constantine should imperil his life, he entered a monastery in Constantinople, nor did he actually leave the city until he was convinced that the accession of Theodora offered him no opportunities. Her first minister, Leo Strabospondylus, hated him. Therefore, thinking discretion to be the better part, Psellus left for Mt. Olympus.[3] Bezobrazov says that the unpublished "Ἐνκώμιον εἰς Νικόλαον μοναχὸν γενόμενον ἡγούμενον τῆς ἐν Ὀλυμπῷ μονῆς τῆς ὡραίας πηγῆς"[4] shows that Psellus went to the monastery of

---

[1] See especially Sathas, v, *Ep*. 80, 173, 202, 203.

[2] This is, of course, only a very tentative suggestion; I hope to deal at greater length with this problem in my book on John of Euchaita.

[3] Psellus's letters to Xiphilinus and to various monks show his hesitation and the extent to which he considered the step he was about to take. Sathas, v, *Ep*. 36, 37 (to Xiphilinus), and 27, 166 (to a monk at Mt. Olympus).

[4] *Cod. vat.* 672, f. 77, quoted by Bezobrazov, *Materials*, ii, p. 74.

the Beautiful Source, built by this Nicholas, a relation of Constantine Monomachus. Psellus was evidently impressed by Mt. Olympus, though rather by its natural beauty than its spiritual life. He was, as a rule, more interested in human beings than in the country, but his descriptions of Mt. Olympus form a notable exception, and he gives it the highest praise he can when he says that only the tongue of Plato is worthy to describe the meditative calm of its valleys and mountains.[1] The most interesting aspect of the Mt. Olympus episode is the extent to which it brings out the difference between the characters of Psellus and Xiphilinus; Psellus's longing for 'the better life' faded away when he fathomed its real meaning. He found it impossible to appreciate the outlook of a medieval monk, although, as far as Christian dogma was concerned, he never had any difficulty in making profession of his faith. In the asceticism of the monks there was something completely at variance with his many-sided appreciation of the things of the world and his insatiable desire for intellectual knowledge and understanding. It is difficult to comprehend the dualism of Psellus's nature: yet it is only this that can account for the extent to which his scholarship was interwoven with his work as a politician. He had no regret for his sudden return from his better life, and when Theodora recalled him[2] he was in no way reluctant once more to risk his fortune in the uncertain fluctuations of court patronage.

It is clear that the disgrace of Psellus and his friends must have seriously affected the recently opened University. The absence of Psellus, Xiphilinus, and John Mauropous, combined with the death of Nicetas, could only mean that the inspiration of the movement was gone. It is extremely difficult to decide exactly when the University was shut, and whether this would include both faculties and mean the complete cessation of public teaching. Schlumberger merely states, 'Monomaque ferma de nouveau l'Université',[3] nor does he give any evidence for this statement. Zervos writes, 'après la fermeture de l'Université de Constantinople, les professeurs furent rappelés au palais',[4] but

---

[1] Sathas, iv, p. 443.　　　　[2] Psellus, *Chron.* vi. a. 13 (ii, p. 78).
[3] G. Schlumberger, *L'épopée byzantine*, iii, p. 675.
[4] C. Zervos, *Michel Psellos*, p. 66.

again he gives no evidence for this, nor does he suggest any date. But as he says in the same passage that Psellus and his friends, with the exception of Leichudes, taught for nine years, the earliest possible date is 1054. This agrees with Fischer's statement that Xiphilinus was Nomophylax for nine years (1045–54). Therefore both the Law School and the Philosophy School must have been open until 1054, the year in which Constantine IX Monomachus died. Schlumberger and Zervos both affirm that the University was closed, but they bring no positive evidence in support of their statement. It seems impossible to believe that the University could have exerted any important influence if it had been shut after so short a period as nine years. Zervos says that Psellus's success as head of the Philosophy School bore fruit in the form of 'une école brillante, pleine de vie et forte de la science de ses maîtres, qui eut pour tâche de conserver la civilization hellénique dans le monde byzantin. L'humanisme de la Renaissance lui-même eut plus tard sa source dans l'école de Constantinople du XIᵉ siècle.'[1] Nine years is a short time for one man and his friends to accomplish so much. In the *Chronographia* Psellus himself makes no reference to the reopening of the University after Constantine's death, nor does he give any indication that it was shut, nor does he even mention the revival of 1045. If Fuchs is right in his belief that Matthew of Edessa's 'philosophers who sat in the Academy' are teachers of the University, then this is evidence that it was open during the time when Xiphilinus was Patriarch (1064–75). Even in the absence of more positive evidence it would seem that possibly the University was shut temporarily; but to judge from results this could not have been final.[2] For why, if it were otherwise, should John Italus succeed to Psellus's title? 'Later, after Psellus had taken the tonsure and left Byzantium, Italus became the foremost teacher of all philosophy, and was given the title of ὕπατος τῶν φιλοσόφων and he gave lectures explaining the books of Aristotle and Plato.'[3]

It is, then, difficult to estimate the effects of this revival of learning. Zervos finds a resemblance between the School of

---

[1] C. Zervos, *Michel Psellos*, p. 108.

[2] This is assumed by Fuchs in his discussion of learning in the eleventh century.   [3] Anna Comnena, *Alexias*, v. 8 (i, p. 179).

Law at Constantinople and that at Bologna,[1] and whether the School was or was not closed after nine years, an impetus had certainly been given to legal studies. Scylitzes could write that in the reign of Constantine X Ducas soldiers put away their arms in favour of a legal profession.[2] It remains to mention a certain document in this connexion. It is given by Treu under the title of 'ein byzantinisches Schulgespräch', although it is not strictly accurate to refer to it as a *colloquium scholasticum* since only the teacher speaks and there is consequently no dialogue. The purpose of the writer is to show the branches of learning necessary for the education of a cultured man—grammar, rhetoric, philosophy, and law. It is the emphasis on the study of law that forms Treu's argument for placing the document in the later part of the eleventh century; he points out that it was then that the importance of legal knowledge was especially stressed, this being the result of the newly opened Law School.[3]

There is, on the other hand, no doubt that there was a continued interest in philosophical studies. Psellus's influence certainly did not cease with the closing of the University, and he was a prominent figure in the reigns of Monomachus's successors, especially that of his pupil Michael VII. The influence of Psellus, especially through his philosophical writings, falls into its place after the discussion of him as a philosopher;[4] nor is it possible to speak here of the evidence afforded by the philosophical studies of later Byzantine scholars. With regard to the effect of the University on interest in education as a whole, no generalization can be made. The University must have owed its prosperity to the personalities of its professors, and it would naturally attract younger men rather than older scholars; it probably stimulated learning indirectly as well as directly, for the private school could not fail to be touched by the current of enthusiasm. More than this it is impossible to say.

[1] C. Zervos, pp. 104–5.
[2] Scylitzes, ii, p. 652. See Psellus, *Chron.* vii a. 16 (ii, p. 146).
[3] M. Treu, *Ein byzantinisches Schulgespräch*, pp. 102 ff.
[4] See Chapter IV.

MICHAEL PSELLUS

At that time there were few learned men, and such as there were stopped short at the portals of the Aristotelian philosophy and repeated only the symbols of the Platonic teaching.

Psellus, *Chron.* iii. 3 (i, p. 33).

The process of reasoning, my friend, is neither contrary to the dogma of the Church nor alien to philosophy, but it is indeed the only instrument of truth and the only means of finding that which we seek.

Psellus, *Letter to the Patriarch Xiphilinus*, ed. Sathas, v, p. 447.

PSELLUS'S teaching in the University shows the extent to which his intellectual outlook was dominated by his love of philosophy. But it must not be imagined that his teaching was exclusively Platonic. He wished to revive a spirit of interest in classical learning, and the receptivity of his own mind found an outlet both in his own studies and in his teaching. Philosophy, which was the goal of a long and varied course, began with the logic of Aristotle, but, after reaching metaphysics, Aristotle was left and the consummation of philosophical learning was found in Plato. In the *Chronographia* he often digresses, as we have seen, to speak of his own intellectual outlook, and to discuss the condition of learning in his own day; after the paucity of detail concerning earlier Byzantine Platonists, it is interesting to find a full account of both mental development and the available sources.

Psellus says that in his twenty-fifth year he had two objects, to perfect himself in the art of rhetoric, and to purify his soul by means of philosophy.[1] He found a scarcity of teachers, and fewer still who went to the very springs of philosophy, for, in Psellus's words, they 'stopped short at the portals (πρόθυρα)'.[2] He himself sought to study Aristotle and Plato; he then completed the round by studying Plotinus, Porphyry, and Iamblichus, finally arriving at Proclus, εἰς τὸν θαυμασιώτατον Πρόκλον ὡς ἐπὶ λιμένα μέγιστον κατασχών, πᾶσαν ἐκεῖθεν ἐπιστήμην τε καὶ νοήσεων ἀκρίβειαν ἔσπασα.[3] After this he studied mathematics, which he considered an essential step towards any knowledge of things

[1] Psellus, *Chron.* vi. 36 (i, pp. 134–5).   [2] Ibid., iii. 3 (i, p. 33).
[3] Ibid., vi. 38 (i, p. 136).

incorporeal: thus he carefully applied himself to arithmetic, geometry, music, and astronomy, studying each branch separately, yet not forgetting that each was related to the other, and that all were stages in the path which led towards the same goal. The straightforward outline of the *Chronographia* is supplemented by the detail of one of his addresses to a man called Andronicus. This is written in a style unlike the *Chronographia*; it is more conversational, as befits the occasion, and Psellus mingles earnest enthusiasm with light-hearted gaiety.[1] In it he says that natural sciences, though important, are only the very beginning of knowledge. On the other hand, mathematical sciences, since they are connected both with the corporeal and the incorporeal, form a link between the two, and at the same time bring the learner to some conception of abstract knowledge.

'For Plato, putting within hidden doors the highest philosophy, as being incorporeal and real energy (οὐσιώδης ἐνέργεια), has prevented him who would enter from so doing without the science of geometry. . . . Therefore urge on your love of mathematical learning, and, when you have stolen from intelligence the incorporeal quality in these things, and have realised the light within the body of the sun, then you will turn with the keenest vision to the incorporeal itself. So concentrate not on those matters which are table talk, mingled with laughter and wit, and handled with a certain mirth and delight, but on those which must be expounded and revealed beneath drawn brow and intent countenance.'[2]

It was, then, only after he had concentrated on the mathematical sciences that he turned to philosophy, the highest form of knowledge.

It is evident, from Psellus's own words, that his attitude was the complete antithesis of the ecclesiastical ideals of the Greek Church. It is only necessary to compare his more characteristic works with those of Symeon the Young or Nicetas Stethatus, to realize the gulf between the secular and monastic outlooks. Psellus's enthusiasms are not for the ascetic way of life, but for the processes connected with the use of the rational powers of the mind. When he speaks of the knowledge that transcended all intelligent demonstration, probably mystical

[1] Boissonade, *Psellus*, pp. 159–63.   [2] Ibid., pp. 162–3.

experience, he confesses that he himself has never experienced
this, nor, he spitefully adds, does he believe that anybody else
has.[1] It must not be inferred that he ignored ecclesiastical
writings, although it is certainly true that he never gave them
any position of exclusive predominance. He had a great admiration for certain of the Church Fathers,[2] especially Gregory
of Nazianzus,[3] but it may be suspected that this admiration
was due not so much to Gregory's teaching as to his powers
of oratory. Nevertheless, he justly claimed that he had studied
both profane *and* divine philosophy,[4] and his *Oratio in salutationem* can bear comparison with the sermons of his ecclesiastical
contemporaries.[5]

In attempting to put into practice his theory of knowledge,
Psellus had, as he himself says, read 'many books'.[6] He had
amassed a vast store of learning, and his writings, some of which
remain unedited, show the encyclopaedic nature of his scholarship. Those treatises which are concerned entirely with philosophical problems[7] are few in comparison with his other writings,
a considerable number of which are occupied with the occult
practices which were so common in the eleventh century.
Psellus was obviously extremely well versed in the theory and
practice of the Chaldaean mysteries.

Psellus did not claim to be an original thinker, as indeed he
was not. He says with unusual modesty:

'For indeed I am not deceived by self admiration, nor am I ignorant
of my own capacity, which is most limited in comparison with those
who are above me in their powers of sophistry and philosophising.
I have no merit save that I drank my measure of learning, not from
a pure running spring, but from one whose outlets I found choked
so that I could not easily make the hidden knowledge gush forth
until I had opened and purified them.'[8]

Upon every possible occasion he eulogized the name of Plato.
Nor did he hesitate to emphasize, like Arethas of Caesarea, the

---

[1] Psellus, *Chron.* vi. 40 (i, p. 136).
[2] See PG, cxxii, cols. 901 ff.
[3] See περὶ τοῦ θεολογικοῦ χαρακτῆρος, ed. A. Mayer, BZ, xx (1911), pp. 27–100.
[4] Psellus, *Chron.* vi. 42 (i, pp. 137–8).
[5] Ed. M. Jugie, PO, xvi (1922), pp. 515–25.
[6] Psellus, *Chron.* vi. 42 (i, p. 138).
[7] See Bibliography.   [8] Psellus, *Chron.* vi. 42 (i, p. 138).

extent to which the intellectual foundations of Christianity
rested upon Platonism. He maintained, not that classical learning was made up of a number of different schools of thought,
but that these differing schools found their completion in the
teaching of Plato. It was not that Psellus neglected other philosophers for Plato. His philosophical writings were based, not
only on a knowledge of Plato's own works, but on a study of
other schools of Greek thought, especially the Platonism of
Plotinus and his followers. It is, therefore, necessary to digress
at this point in order to give a brief indication of that development in the early centuries A.D. which resulted in what is usually
known as Neoplatonism; whether we speak of Platonism or
Neoplatonism, it provokes the problem of how far this was a
continuation of the teaching of Plato and the result of the direct
study of his writings.

It was inevitable that between the fourth century B.C. and the
fourth century A.D. there should be considerable development
of the philosophy of Plato. The academy existed from 387 B.C.
to A.D. 529, and during this time professed to continue the
teaching of its founder. But it naturally became modified by
its contact with Stoicism and Scepticism, while it always had
to face difficulties resulting from the inconsistency on certain
points of Plato's own thought. In spite of this Philo of Larissa,
in the first century B.C., definitely maintained that the doctrine
of the School had not changed.[1] Philo was not strictly accurate,
although it was not until the third century A.D. that Platonism
underwent that important development which was to form a
landmark in its history. This was the result of Plotinus's teaching at Rome. He not only eliminated certain inconsistencies in
Plato, but he attempted to supplement the incompleteness of
his doctrines. He made a tripartite division of $\tau\grave{o}$ $\H{\epsilon}\nu$, $\nu o\hat{v}s$, and
$\psi v \chi \acute{\eta}$, and said that, although $\tau\grave{o}$ $\H{\epsilon}\nu$ or $\tau\grave{o}$ $\mathring{a}\gamma a\theta\acute{o}\nu$ was Perfect
or Absolute, yet it pervaded all the varying degrees of life;
the Universe was an endless hierarchy, each grade of intelligence
being connected with the next. Plotinus himself was anxious to
emphasize his debt to ancient philosophers, and especially to

[1] Cicero, *Academica Priora*, 13, 'Antiochi magister Philo, magnus vir . . .
negat . . . duas esse Academias, erroremque eorum qui ita putarunt coarguit,'
quoted by A. E. Taylor, *Platonism*, p. 135, note 2.

Plato, and he declares that his own doctrines are not new.[1] But, even though Augustine could write that it was especially in Plotinus that Plato came to life again,[2] the Platonism which the first centuries A.D. knew was not the original teaching of Plato. By the end of the fifth century Neoplatonism had been systematized by Proclus (†485), who completed the work of Porphyry († *c.* 300) and Iamblichus († *c.* 330), the other important disciples of Plotinus.[3] In common with later Greek religion, this Neoplatonism recognized one God (τὸ ἕν), but placed a hierarchy of intermediary beings between God and man; it found its authority for this in Plato,[4] as Plutarch asserted when he wrote: 'Those who refuse to acknowledge the daemon-kind, do away with the possibility of intercourse between gods and men, abolishing, as Plato said, the beings whose office it is to act as interpreters and ministers.'[5] This was an important part of Neoplatonic doctrine, and it gave an opening for demonology and magic, which crept in from the East, and which were characteristics of later Greek thought. How far it was an integral part of Neoplatonism remains a disputed question, which will arise for discussion in connexion with Psellus's quarrel with Cerularius and Xiphilinus. Neoplatonism certainly had, largely by reason of Porphyry's strong peripatetic tendencies, absorbed much that was strictly outside its own province. It not only became the source of late hellenic philosophy, but exerted considerable influence on late hellenic culture.

In his philosophical writings Psellus reveals his debt to the Neoplatonists, especially Plotinus and Proclus. Nothing shows this more clearly than the διδασκαλία παντοδαπή, in which Christian dogmas and philosophical teaching are inextricably interwoven. This work is composed of a number of short paragraphs on various religious, philosophical, and even scientific problems. Zervos claims to find in it something more than a collection of ideas and says that it is the synthesis of Psellus's thoughts, gathered from the many sources of his knowledge;

[1] Plotinus, *Enn.* v. 1. 8 (ii, p. 171).   [2] Augustine, *Contra Acad.* 3. 18.
[3] Important as the writings of these Neoplatonists are for the understanding of Psellus's philosophy, it is beyond the scope of this book to describe them in any detail. See T. Whittaker, W. R. Inge, J. Bidez, and E. Bréhier.
[4] *Symposium*, 202 E, 203 A.
[5] Plutarch, *On the Cessation of Oracles*, quoted by E. Bevan, p. 124.

but although he occasionally quotes from Ruelle's additions to
the *Omnifaria doctrina* he does not emphasize the extent to
which Migne's edition[1] is far from being complete. This was
noticed some years ago by Ruelle,[2] who points out that Leo
Allatius, at the end of his *Diatriba de Psello*, refers to 194[3]
chapters of the *Omnifaria doctrina*,[4] but gives no reference to the
manuscript containing these which Ruelle thinks is probably
at Rome. Fabricius only published 157 chapters in the *Bibliotheca Graeca*,[5] following the manuscript of Hamburg, and he
treats these as though they were the whole 194. This error
was noted by Harles in the second edition of the *Bibliotheca Graeca*,[6] but Migne unfortunately used the first edition.
Ruelle gives an account of manuscripts in which he has found
more complete versions of the *Omnifaria doctrina*,[7] and he then
prints certain chapters which are not included in Migne.
These are mainly concerned with the Soul (ψυχή) and Virtue
(ἀρετή).

If it is an exaggeration to claim to find in the *Omnifaria
doctrina* the synthesis of Psellus's knowledge, it remains, nevertheless, an interesting document. The order in which Psellus
treats his problems, as well as the conclusions he reaches, show
a strong Neoplatonic influence. The divisions which he makes
are identical with those of Plotinus, namely, God or the Unity,
Mind (νοῦς), the Soul (ψυχή), and the Sensible World. The
opening paragraph is a statement of the author's belief in the
Christian Trinity, an orthodox opening that was perhaps due
to the fact that this work was written for the young Michael VII

---

[1] PG, cxxii, cols. 687–784.

[2] Ruelle, 'XLII chapitres inédits et complémentaires du recueil de Michael
Psellus intitulé διδασκαλία παντοδαπή ou notions variées', AEG, xiii (1879),
pp. 230–78.

[3] i.e. 193+the *Credo*, which Migne and Fabricius number as the first
chapter, thus making 194 chapters altogether.

[4] PG, cxxii, cols. 524–7.   [5] Vol. v, Hamburg, 1712, pp. 70 ff.

[6] Vol. x, Hamburg, 1807, pp. 83 ff.

[7] Ruelle mentions manuscripts at Paris and Madrid, and the chapters are
found under various headings. He thinks it is possible that 201 chapters
(the total number found in MS. 2087, *Bib. Nat.*) and the 29 chapters found
under the heading of 'Ἐπιλύσεις σύντομοι φυσικῶν ζητημάτων πρὸς Μιχαὴλ τὸν
Δούκαν ἐν βιβλίοις δυσί (= *Solutiones quaedam*, PG, cxxii, cols. 783–810)
may all have been included in the original *Omnifaria doctrina*; Bezobrazov
challenges the authenticity of the 'Ἐπιλύσεις, *Materials*, ii, p. 73.

Ducas, who was Psellus's pupil. This is followed by a discussion of the interpretation of certain difficult words in connexion with the Christian faith, such as ὑπόστασις and ὁμοούσιος. Then he tries to fathom what God is (τίς ὁ θεός), and, like Plotinus, he first of all uses the negative method, and shows what God is not. 'God is not the sky, nor the sun, nor anything that can be perceived, nor the best possible mind, nor a Platonic Form, apart from matter, . . . nor is He visible to the senses, or the intellect, but is of an unfathomable nature.'[1] Human knowledge of God comes only through a perception of the order of the Universe.[2] After God Psellus speaks of Mind (νοῦς—a word difficult to translate), and he distinguished between Mind-participating, Mind-non-participating, and Mind in the World.[3] The essence and potentiality of Mind are contained in Eternity, and this Mind is self-sufficing, a complete unity, filled with divine Ideas. After Mind comes Soul, in which Psellus is evidently specially interested. He devotes considerable time to its study, examining its characteristics and its birth: it is incorporeal, coming between the world of νοῦς and the Sensible World; it is of divine origin, and on the question of the Soul's descent Psellus follows Iamblichus, who 'brings down the rational soul (ἡ λογικὴ ψυχή) from God to earth'.[4] The soul radiates from the body, just as the rising sun shows abroad its light; it uses the body as though it were its instrument, which is reminiscent of Plotinus. It is capable of three stages of development, νόησις, διάνοια, and δόξα (intuitive thought, discursive thought, and opinion); the extent to which the Soul has advanced along the upward path is shown by the stage it has reached. But, like Plotinus, Psellus did not despise the body, and the emphasis is laid on the word 'instrument'; the body itself helps the Soul to perceive objects of the Sensible World, which are reflections of higher forms, and a reminder, therefore, of those things to which the Soul should aspire. Zervos says that Psellus's theories of the Soul are further developed in his δόξαι περὶ ψυχῆς, but Bezobrazov affirms that this is wrongly attributed to Psellus.[5] Psellus not only reproduces Plotinus's

---

[1] PG, cxxii, col. 697 (ch. 15).
[2] Ibid., col. 700 (ch. 18).
[3] Ibid., cols. 701 ff. (chs. 20 ff.).
[4] Ibid., col. 709 (ch. 34).
[5] Bezobrazov, *Materials*, ii, p. 73.

division of the Universe, but he discusses the problems of evil
and free will in a characteristically Neoplatonic manner, more
or less repeating the conclusions of Plotinus and his followers.
Evil is only relative, a want of good, and man is free to choose,
not bound by a predetermined fate. And then, again following
Plotinus and Proclus, Psellus discourses on the virtues which
help the Soul to become reunited to God.

To anyone who has read the Enneads the debt which the
Omnifaria doctrina owes to Plotinus is obvious. Zervos rightly
maintains that Psellus, much as he stressed the actual writings
of Plato, was essentially a Neoplatonist. It would, indeed, have
been impossible for him to escape this influence. He was in no
way an original thinker, and, even were it within the scope of
this book, a detailed analysis of his philosophical works would
in all probability reveal nothing that he did not owe to some
predecessor. But there is one aspect of his philosophy that may
be taken to show how he interwove the teaching of Plato with
that of the Neoplatonists. In his περὶ τῶν ἰδεῶν ἃς ὁ Πλάτων
λέγει is found an example of the way in which he interpreted
Platonism through the eyes of the Neoplatonists. This is not
included in Migne, but is edited by Linder.[1] There is nothing
original in it, nor is it a particularly good exposition of the
Platonic theory of ideas, but it does show the extent to which
Psellus was versed in the writings of both Plato and Aristotle
as well as their followers. It certainly could not be said with any
justice, as Gibbon asserts of the minds of the Byzantines, that
Psellus's taste had been vitiated by the homilies of monks.[2]

It is not only in his treatment of purely philosophical problems
that Psellus shows his debt to the Platonists. His περὶ ἀριθμῶν
stresses the importance of numbers, and is obviously due to
Iamblichus's *De theologica arithmetica*; his theology, too, reflects
his enthusiasm for Greek philosophy, and his favourite Church
Fathers are those who were influenced by Platonism, such as
the Alexandrine school, or Gregory of Nyssa. In his interpretations or commentaries upon the Bible he spontaneously avails

[1] Ed. Linder, C.G, xvi (1860), pp. 523–6. See Appendix for a translation
of this.
[2] Gibbon, vi, p. 108, nor, it may be added, were these homilies 'an absurd
medley of declamation and scripture'. Cf. Nicetas Stethatus or Symeon the
Young. Neither of these monks had anything in common with Psellus.

himself of Platonism. He is far from regarding philosophy as the *ancilla theologiae*, it is rather 'the mistress of all'; not that he denies the importance of theology, but he insists that it should be regarded in its relation to other branches of knowledge.

It would, however, be a mistake to define philosophical interests in any narrow sense or to speak of Psellus's Platonism without realizing what he himself would have meant by this. Psellus was influenced almost more by the Neoplatonists than by Plato; he made no distinction between the two for he evidently considered that the latter was a legitimate development of the earlier teaching. Very closely allied to his purely philosophical discussions were his writings on the natural and occult sciences, and although it may seem inappropriate to mention these in connexion with philosophy, yet to make too sharp a division would be to misunderstand the thought of the eleventh century. It is, moreover, well to realize the very indefinite barrier between the discussion of abstract principles and the application of rational thought to any branch of learning. This is shown both by Proclus's additions to Platonism, and by Psellus's use of Proclus. Psellus himself says that Proclus was his favourite philosopher,[1] a statement which is supported by M. Bidez's analysis of the sources of Psellus's writings, especially those concerning demonology and alchemy.[2]

Psellus was certainly scientific in his outlook, and despised indifference which often sheltered beneath the cloak of orthodoxy; he thought it was wrong to regard some such event as a thunderbolt or an earthquake as a just punishment coming from the will of God. When he wrote about natural phenomena such as thunder and lightning, heat and cold, or similar subjects, he always tried to give reasonable and not irrational explanations, and M. Bidez finds the source of his statements on these occasions in Aristotle's scientific writings as interpreted by Olympiodorus.[3] Psellus, moreover, had at some time in his life been engaged in the occupation of the transmutation of

[1] Psellus, *Chron.* vi. 38 (i, p. 136).

[2] In this and the following paragraphs I am greatly indebted to J. Bidez, *Catalogue des manuscrits alchimiques grecs*, vi, where there is a full analysis of the sources and manuscript tradition of Psellus's writings on alchemy, demonology, and other subjects, some of which have hitherto been unedited.

[3] Bidez, *Catalogue*, pp. 51 ff.

baser metals into gold. His exposition, the Chrysopee, has been
pronounced worthless by modern alchemists,[1] but it is at least
interesting for its statement of his method of approach. He
writes to Cerularius[2] that even though the Patriarch is bringing
him from the heights of philosophy to the baser art of fire, to
transmute matter and transform its nature, yet when, after a
long time, he did consider the obligation which had been imposed upon him, to bring the apples of the Hesperides, to change
lead into gold, he then withdrew to take counsel of his reason
and to investigate the causes of things in order that, when he
had found a rational starting-point, he might succeed in obtaining his object by strictly scientific methods.[3]

Nor did Psellus's rational outlook prevent him from sharing
the interest of his contemporaries in the occult sciences which
were based on Chaldaean teaching. It has already been noted
that oriental influences appeared in Neoplatonism in the
third century A.D. before Plotinus died, becoming a recognized
feature of later Greek thought. Porphyry wrote a treatise which
went under the name of *De philosophia ex oraculis haurienda*,
while both Porphyry and Iamblichus were of Asiatic origin.
Moreover, the Byzantine Empire included many non-hellenic
elements; it was specially the eastern provinces which came into
contact with such influences, notably in Syria, where Platonism
was tinged with the occult and tended to resolve itself into the
study of magic and demonology. Chaldaean knowledge concentrated on astronomy, astrology, and divination, and its worst
side was reflected in its pursuit of magic and the occult.[4] This
was, then, originally not inherent in Platonism, but it was an
aspect of knowledge the influence of which Psellus could not
altogether escape.

So Psellus was well acquainted with Chaldaean knowledge,
and he despised this only when it degenerated into an absorption
in magic to the exclusion of those scientific methods of thought
of which he approved. He defended his own interest in astrology,
and said that this study was only to be condemned if it led to
practices forbidden by the Church,[5] but he never abandoned

[1] Bidez, *Catalogue*, p. 93.   [2] Ibid., p. 26.   [3] Ibid.
[4] Cf. Eunapius, *Vitae sophistarum* (esp. Maximus in the reign of Julian).
[5] Psellus, *Chron.* vi a. 11–12 (ii, pp. 77–8).

his belief that knowledge proceeded from the intellect, and he therefore opposed any cult of a debased and degrading theurgy. Psellus prided himself on what he considered his hellenic spirit, and, as in the problems of natural science, he argued that belief in the supernatural arose from ignorance of those laws of nature which rule the universe, adding that surely the rational course was to study them still further.[1] It was this attitude which dominated Psellus's exposition of the popular demonology which is found in Neoplatonism. In his *De operatione daemonorum*[2] he showed not only how a complete science of demonology existed, but that it had been adopted by many Christians of his own day. This cult was based on magical rites, the end aimed at being the vision of God ($\theta\epsilon o\phi\acute{a}\nu\epsilon\iota a$), though this was regarded as a supreme climax rather than a frequent occurrence; there were elaborate ceremonies in order to procure intercourse between human beings and demons, and the latter were given a defined existence in the universe, and analysed into classes and species.[3]

The most interesting practical example of both Psellus's erudition and the extent to which his contemporaries were absorbed in occult sciences is found in the *Accusation* which he drew up as evidence for the Patriarch Cerularius's deposition. The first and most important charge was that of $\dot{a}\sigma\acute{\epsilon}\beta\epsilon\iota a$, in itself a more than sufficient reason for so grave a step as the degradation of a Patriarch, and indeed, Psellus begins the long speech, which he never delivered by reason of the sudden death of Cerularius, by saying that his main concern is the preservation of orthodoxy. 'A man is not pious who believes some of the dogmas which the Church Fathers have handed down and rejects others which he doubts,' he must believe the whole teaching of the Church and avoid all heresies 'and above all the Chaldaean philosophy with its inventions and tales about oracles, different kinds of spirits, spells, and the differentiation

[1] Cf. Gibbon, vi, p. 108. 'The minds of the Greeks were bound in the fetters of a base and imperious superstition . . . in the belief of visions and miracles they had lost all principles of moral evidence.'

[2] PG, cxxii, cols. 819–82; French translation given by Renauld, REG, xxxiii (1920), pp. 56–95.

[3] For the details of Psellus's demonology see Bidez, *Catalogue*, pp. 97 ff., and Svoboda.

of gods '.[1] It is this last heresy which is the main ground for the accusation of ἀσέβεια.

Psellus's evidence, elaborately set forth and carefully arranged to give an unfavourable impression, is based on one episode in Cerularius's life, and, as the *Accusation* seems to be the only evidence concerning this, it is difficult to pass any judgement upon the orthodoxy of the Patriarch's conduct. The story which Psellus tells[2] is that Cerularius gave ear and hospitality to two monks from Chios, John and Nicetas, 'of whom most of you have often heard'. With them was a woman, Dosithea, who had once been an actress, and who claimed to be a prophetess and sooth-sayer. She could, so Psellus says, turn herself into a man, and she pretended to be filled with the godhead. Cerularius saw in their claims and teaching 'a great and shining windfall, and he embraced the complete error and was straightway cap-tured by pagan modes of evoking God (ἑλληνικαὶ θεαγωγίαι)'.[3] These people were taken everywhere by Cerularius and given the freedom of his house and of S. Sophia, while 'he who was the priest of things divine, simply practised the pagan (hellenic) rites, and pursued the Chaldaean oracles'.[4] Even after allowing for Psellus's prejudice, it is difficult to know whether the monks and Dosithea were genuine; the partition between Christian mysticism and pagan frenzy is but slender and not to be lightly judged by externals. Some of Dosithea's experiences can be paralleled by those of Symeon the Young,[5] though on the other hand contemporary verdict had condemned the prophetess some time before the *Accusation* was written. If Psellus is to be trusted the prophesies had made considerable stir in Theodora's reign, 'the sayings of the oracle spread through-

---

[1] *Accusation*, ed. Bréhier, p. 385.   [2] Ibid., pp. 386 ff.
[3] Ibid., p. 387.   [4] Ibid., p. 388.
[5] Cf. ibid., p. 388. 'But when all the preparations were completed she shuddered throughout her body, perhaps because she could not bear the weight of the spirit, and immediately became dumb, as they say who announce such things, and was raised aloft. And now indeed her tongue moved, but with what foolish talk! For she spoke falsely of the moving of everything, of the hidden future, of the signs of the heavenly ranks. Some prophets and martyrs were present, and a crowd of holy women, and above all John the Baptist . . . and the Mother of God whom she, as if pitying her, called "the great sufferer", her blasphemous tongue wrongfully attributing woe and pain to her at the birth of the Logos.' Cf. *Vita Symeonis*, pp. 8–10 (ch. 5).

out the city, the poison was assimilated, and the majority
swallowed this evil to which impetus had been given by the
Patriarch's foolish patronage'.[1] The monks and the woman
were expelled from the city, not by a council of State and
Church presided over by the Patriarch, but by the Empress.[2]
When Isaac Comnenus obtained the throne, Cerularius successfully petitioned for the return of his friends, whose teaching
had not been formally condemned.[3] Psellus's statement that
Cerularius's example contaminated the flock entrusted to him[4]
probably means that there was a widespread interest in these
exponents of the Chaldaean teaching, and indeed, his assumption throughout the *Accusation* that everybody knows about the
affair is probably more than a rhetorical device.

The *Accusation* is valuable not only as evidence for Cerularius's
life and ambitions and for the occult interests of the eleventh
century, but it is a document which illustrates more than any
other the extent of Psellus's knowledge. After all criticism of
partial representation and rhetorical exaggeration has been
justly brought forward, it remains an interesting statement of an
eleventh-century attitude. Beneath the essential orthodoxy
Psellus shows that he has an acute and well-informed mind. To
avoid heresy was indeed necessary, but it could best be avoided
by a discriminating knowledge of what heresy might be. There
were those such as Plato and Aristotle, the Stoics and the
Pythagoreans, and many others, all of whose writings contained much that had been anathematized by the Church, and
much that was not alien to its teaching. It is true, wrote
Psellus, that matter and ideas have nothing in common according to our dogma. 'But', he continued, 'when Aristotle explains
that matter has no beginning, then we indeed dissociate the
Church from such.'[5] As Aquinas found, it was possible to
distinguish between truth and error in pagan authors, and in
such circumstances even Aristotle could become 'the master of

---

[1] *Accusation*, ed. Bréhier, p. 392.   [2] Ibid., pp. 392 ff.
[3] Cf. ibid., p. 395, 'since these men were not condemned by a synod', but
he says farther down, 'there were archbishops present who censured their
words and condemned their teaching as false and untrue'. Psellus is trying
to show that they had really been expelled for their doctrines. This may,
or may not, be special pleading; Cerularius was certainly out of favour with
Theodora and her ministers, who may therefore have wished to annoy him.
[4] Ibid., p. 408.   [5] Ibid., p. 404.

them who know'; while in the *Accusation* Psellus had the courage to say,

'All the false opinions which we are now attacking, have taken part of their teaching from the Catholic doctrine. Since I speak to those who know I will not expand, except in so far as I reasonably must. For example, the famous Origen, the contemporary of the philosopher Porphyry, was the pioneer of all our theology and laid its foundations, but on the other hand all heresies find their origin in him.'[1]

If Psellus was as outspoken as this in the *Accusation*, which was written for an ecclesiastical gathering, it is not difficult to understand that he at least twice incurred the displeasure of the Church. There is little evidence about the first occasion, but Psellus had to make a profession of faith in Constantine IX's reign.[2] He was later reproached by his old friend, the Patriarch Xiphilinus, for spending too much time on Platonism. The quarrel between Xiphilinus and Psellus can be traced in Psellus's correspondence[3] and in the funeral oration which he pronounced on the dead Patriarch.[4] Xiphilinus was interested in Aristotle rather than Plato; in one of his letters to Xiphilinus Psellus complains that he has been asked by his friends to perform a most burdensome task, 'namely a restatement of the Aristotelian corpus of logic into a clearer form'.[5] The difference between the two men is most plainly shown by the letter in which Psellus emphatically denies that his love of Plato is in any way detrimental to his orthodoxy. "'Ἐμὸς ὁ Πλάτων, ἁγιώτατε καὶ σοφώτατε, ἐμός …" he begins in indignation—mine, indeed, but after the manner of the great Fathers who used such philosophy with which to refute heresy. 'My Plato! I do not know how to bear the weight of such a word. Have I not long honoured the divine Cross above everything else, and now the spiritual yoke as well?'[6] The argument of the letter is that Psellus sees no reason why he should cease to study Plato or any other philosopher, 'but as for their opinions,' he adds, 'some I at once put aside, others,

---

[1] *Accusation*, ed. Bréhier, pp. 403–4. Αὐτίκα γοῦν Ὠριγένης ἐκεῖνος, ὁ συνακμάσας Πορφυρίῳ τῷ φιλοσόφῳ, καὶ τῇ καθ᾽ ἡμᾶς θεολογίᾳ προβέβηκε, καὶ τὴν οἰκονομίαν ἐδέξατο, ἀλλὰ ταῖς αἱρέσεσι πάσαις τὰς ἀρχὰς ἐκεῖνος ἐνδέδωκε.

[2] Bandini, vol. ii (1768), cols. 547–8; Coxe, col. 729 (Misc. 179, No. 44).
[3] Especially Sathas, v, pp. 444 ff. (*Ep.* 175).   [4] Ibid., iv, pp. 421–62.
[5] Ibid., v, p. 499.   [6] Ibid., p. 444.

which helped me, I willingly kept, comparing them with the holy words, as was the habit of the great lights of the Church, Basil and Gregory.[1] . . . I may belong entirely to Christ, but I will not deny the wiser of our writers, nor the knowledge of reality, both intelligible and sensible. But, according to my capacity, I will intercede with God through prayer, and I will eagerly take whatever may be granted me; then descending from such heights, by reason of the restlessness of nature, I will traverse the meadows of learning.'[2]

It is perhaps impossible to do more than quote such letters as proof of the integrity of Psellus's intentions of orthodoxy, nor was it easy for a man who was interested in so many branches of knowledge to avoid the charge of heresy. Psellus escaped any condemnation, which may, of course, be a tribute to his agility of mind rather than his consistency of belief. It was easy to read many authors, heretics or otherwise, but to do this and yet to teach students, to argue with friends, to lead a public life at court, and still to escape any charge of heresy was no inconsiderable achievement in the eleventh century. There is no reason to suppose that Psellus sacrificed his intellectual independence; although he could write a convincing account of a miracle, he could always add the saving clause that the ways of the Godhead were inscrutable.

Psellus's description of the miracle of the Virgin's cloak at the church of the Blachernae affords some explanation of why he so successfully avoided any condemnation for heresy.[3] There was an icon of the Virgin in the church and the miracle was the lifting of her cloak which was raised into the air. This took place on Fridays[4] and symbolized the Mother of God's longing to engulf the whole world anew 'as in a sanctuary and an inviolable refuge'.[5] The special event which occasioned Psellus's account was the settlement of a lawsuit which was referred to the Virgin's judgement. The dispute was between the spatharius and stratêgus Leo Mandalus and the monks of the monastery τοῦ Καλλίου;[6] it concerned the water rights of a certain mill, and if the Virgin's cloak rose the general was to win the case, if nothing happened the claim of the monks would be established.

---

[1] Sathas, p. 447.
[3] *Catalogue*, ed. Bidez, pp. 192–210.
[5] Ibid., p. 195.

[2] Ibid., p. 450.
[4] Ibid., pp. 194 ff.
[6] Ibid., p. 196.

The difficulty was that the Virgin's cloak at first showed no sign, but just as the general was admitting his loss it rose. Both sides claimed the victory, but Psellus's statement, written at the command of Michael VII, vindicated the general.

The interest of the account is the light which it throws on the attitude of both Psellus and his contemporaries. Then, as now, miracles were possible, these not being in themselves irrational, but rather something of which the human mind had not yet learnt the explanation. Psellus's point was that although reason should be used, yet it would be foolish to reject the manifestation of a supernatural power simply because no scientific explanation could be given. ποιητικοὶ μὲν γὰρ μῦθοι τὴν δίκην ἀπὸ γῆς εἰς οὐρανοὺς ἀναφέρουσι καὶ οὐρανίοις θώκοις ἐγκαθιδρύουσιν ἵνα μὴ παντάπασιν ἡμῖν ὁ βίος ἄδικος ᾖ καὶ πλήρης παρανομίας.[1] When Psellus writes about the miracle of the Virgin's cloak his account is full of instances of the working of the unseen powers,[2] nor does he question this particular μυστικὴ διαίρεσις. It is true that criticism would have been injudicious, but on the other hand, the *Accusation* shows that he could be outspoken. And to realize the limitations of the human mind is not incompatible with the desire to use it to its fullest extent. Nor did Psellus's enthusiasm for knowledge, and especially philosophy, 'the other half of learning', ever waver. The impetus which he gave to Platonic studies was undeniable, and, in spite of the intermittent attacks of the Church, this interest continued throughout the Middle Ages. It was, therefore, justly by reason of his scholarship rather than his statesmanship that Psellus stood high in the estimate of his contemporaries. The *Timarion*, probably written in the first half of the twelfth century, describes his very favourable reception into the underworld in contrast to that of his successor and pupil, John Italus; Anna Comnena, writing in the days of Manuel, says of him that he had reached 'the summit of all knowledge',[3] praise which, if somewhat exaggerated, is at least a fitting tribute to his love of learning.

[1] *Catalogue*, ed. Bidez, p. 192.
[2] Cf. ibid., pp. 200 ff. Bidez, ibid., p. 190, says: 'Nous ne cessons pas de le constater, chaque fois que Psellus parle de l'art hiératique, de la théurgie, de la magie et de la sorcellerie, c'est chez Proclus qu'il va chercher son érudition théosophique.'
[3] *Alexias*, v. 8 (i, p. 178).

CHAPTER V

JOHN ITALUS AND THE OTHER COMNENIAN HERETICS

My father had studied the Scriptures more than anybody else, so that his tongue might be sharpened for argument with the heretics.

Anna Comnena, *Alexias*, xiv. 8 (ii, p. 259).

THE battle of εὐσέβεια versus ἀσέβεια was fought more fiercely in the period of the Comneni than in that of the Macedonians. This was not because orthodoxy was any the less dear to the Macedonians, who were deeply concerned at the errors held by Paulicians and Manichaeans, Moslems, Armenians, or Latins: Basil I transported whole colonies of Paulicians from Asia Minor to the Balkans, where unfortunately they spread unorthodox teaching among the Bulgarians; Leo VI composed a letter on Saracen heresies to Omarus, King of the Saracens;[1] Photius wrote books against the Manichaeans.[2] Sects, churches in schism, different religions—these were the concern of the orthodox, whether lay or ecclesiastic, in both Macedonian and Comnenian centuries, and the Byzantine Church had always been faced with some such trouble, in addition to the possibility of the intellectual opposition of philosophers to the teaching of the Church. These difficulties were brought into prominence by the pugnacious orthodoxy of both Alexius and Manuel Comnenus, whose conflicts show very clearly that the Emperor, as well as the Patriarch, was the protector of orthodoxy, and emphasize the extent to which the spheres of Church and State were tactfully complementary in the Byzantine polity at its best.[3] On the other hand, when a strong Emperor chose to take too active an interest in any ecclesiastical problem he could be the dominating factor, and part of the interest of the twelfth-century disputes is the increasing importance of the Emperor in decisions which belonged rather to the Patriarch than to the secular authority.

Many Byzantine Emperors may have been as zealous for orthodoxy as Alexius Comnenus, but he alone had the fortune

---

[1] PG, cvii, cols. 315 ff.   [2] See Chapter I, p. 30.
[3] See Chapter VII.

to possess a daughter who carefully portrayed any detail that could add to the imperial reputation for εὐσέβεια. Anna Comnena considered this the crowning virtue of the Emperor and father whom she idealized, and a virtue equally shared by her mother the Empress. There is no doubt that the Comneni introduced into their court an austerity unknown in the Macedonian times. Anna Dalassena's dominating piety was perfectly reflected in the attitude of her son Alexius Comnenus and her daughter-in-law Irene Ducas. 'Any scholar who has visited the court will have seen the holy pair, my royal parents, completely absorbed both by day and night in their study of the interpretations of the Scriptures,' wrote Anna Comnena.[1] Such an Emperor was naturally anxious to suppress all signs of unorthodoxy, and his contests, if somewhat ruthless, were genuinely inspired by his care for the Church, in contrast to his grandson Manuel, who was often dominated by a desire to display his own skill in theological argument.

It was unfortunate that the zeal of the Comneni should have coincided with the renewed enthusiasm for philosophical studies. Michael Psellus, who had done much to stimulate this revival, had been able to clear himself from the charge of heresy.[2] His followers were not so fortunate. One of the problems of the medieval Church was the difficulty of reconciling freedom of philosophical thought with the maintenance of orthodox doctrine. It was easy enough to lay down the rules for the pursuit of learning, and to say with John of Damascus, or Michael Psellus, that pagan writings were to be explored for the sake of sifting the good in them from the evil; but this was a perilous task, for a man might be accused of heresy while in the act of sifting, or he might genuinely be converted to some philosophical theory alien to the doctrine of the Church. On the whole the years 867–1185 produced amazingly little evidence of controversy of this kind. Perhaps this is due to imperial tolerance or occupation elsewhere. Certainly there are hints of difference of opinion, as, for instance, in the case of Psellus and Xiphilinus quarrelling over their respective attachments to Plato and Aristotle. But the difficulty was brought into the open at the end of the eleventh century by the trial of John

[1] Anna Comnena, v. 9 (i, p. 181).   [2] See Chapter IV, pp. 86 ff.

Italus, Psellus's pupil. He had already been cautioned by Michael VII, but where the Ducas Emperor was easily satisfied with a profession of orthodoxy, Alexius Comnenus acted very differently.

Anna Comnena, as we have seen, emphasizes her father's marked interest in theology, and says, moreover, that the Emperor encouraged scholars to study the divine writings rather than Greek literature.[1] But Anna as an authority is clearly partial and even prejudiced. She praises her father and she praises Michael Psellus; yet she would not, or could not, see that John Italus was a worthy successor to Psellus and that her father's attitude to philosophy would have been no less unfavourable to her favourite Psellus than to John Italus. Both the nature of John Italus's teaching and the course taken by his trial remain uncertain, but as far as his own writings have been published they reveal the incompleteness and inadequacy of the existing evidence concerning his condemnation as a heretic.[2]

Something of John Italus has long been known from Anna Comnena's description of him. An uncouth Latin, quick tempered, swift to hit his opponents, unpolished in speech, at times even ungrammatical, he seemed to Anna a barbarian in no way suited to succeed Psellus as the chief professor of philosophy in Constantinople.[3] Nevertheless, Anna has to admit that he was an able philosopher and dialectician, who exerted a great influence and was eagerly listened to. She says that he lectured to his students on 'the doctrines of Proclus and Plato, and the two philosophers Porphyry and Iamblichus, but especially the rules of Aristotle'.[4] His influence, she continues, was bad, and it is clear that he and his pupils were suspected of reaching conclusions contrary to orthodox dogma. Anna only mentions by name metempsychosis, insults to the icons of the saints, and unorthodox teaching about 'ideas'. Italus, by order of Alexius, was questioned by Isaac the Sebastocrator, the Emperor's brother, and then subjected to an ecclesiastical inquiry. The Patriarch, Eustratius Garidas, was apparently infected by

---

[1] Anna Comnena, v. 9 (i, p. 182).

[2] Ed. Gr. Cereteli, *Johannis Itali opuscula selecta*. See also E. Stéphanou's discussion of and quotation from John Italus's Διάφορα ζητήματα, in EO, xxxii (1933), 'Jean Italos: L'immortalité de l'âme et la résurrection.'

[3] Anna Comnena, v. 8 (i, pp. 177 ff.).   [4] Ibid., v. 9 (i, p. 181).

the 'evil doctrines', and it was due to imperial authority that the heretical part of Italus's teaching was condemned and set out in eleven sections, while he himself was forced to renounce these publicly from the pulpit in S. Sophia. But again he was found teaching false doctrine and was this time excommunicated, although Anna ends her chapter by telling of Italus's genuine repentance late in life and his final submission to the Church.

Thus Anna's evidence gives little but a bare account of events, and provides no detail concerning the points on which Italus was accused. Fortunately there exists an account of the trial as well as the *Synodicon* containing the heretical beliefs attributed to Italus which were publicly anathematized on the first Sunday in Lent.[1] The account of the trial shows that Italus's orthodoxy had been questioned in Michael VII's reign, but that he had successfully appealed to the Patriarch Cosmas and had been acquitted of heresy,[2] perhaps because the Ducas court took an interest in philosophical problems. This interest is apparent from certain of Italus's Διάφορα ζητήματα, which are addressed to the Emperor Michael or to his brother Andronicus.[3] In Alexius's reign Italus was again accused, but this time his appeal to the Patriarch Eustratius was unsuccessful, not because of patriarchal opposition, but because the Emperor, suspecting the Patriarch of partiality,[4] insisted on a trial, while, as Anna tells, the people had already shown their disapproval of Italus by rushing into S. Sophia to interrupt the Patriarch's examination of him.[5] It is the report of the trial which followed that exists, and contains the six theological points upon which Italus was found unorthodox. The first four points were concerned with the doctrine of the Trinity and the Incarnation, the last two with the Theotokos and icons. There was a further list of Italus's philosophical errors, drawn up in ten headings, κεφάλαιά τινα δέκα τῆς ἑλληνικῆς ἀθεότητος γέμοντα.[6] These may well correspond to the errors given in the *Synodicon*, which are mainly concerned with the acceptance of some philosophical tenet at variance with the teaching of the Church. If so, then

---

[1] Both edited by Th. Uspensky. [2] *Trial*, pp. 38 ff.
[3] Stéphanou, op. cit., pp. 416–17; Cereteli, fasc. i, pp. 1 and 29, fasc. ii, p. 59. [4] *Trial*, p. 32.
[5] Anna Comnena, v. 9 (i, p. 183). [6] *Trial*, p. 59, note 1.

the existing evidence shows a trial, followed by condemnation
on both theological and philosophical grounds. Anna's story
of a second outburst, this time resulting in excommunication,
may imply a second trial, but there do not appear to be any
details of it.

John Italus's theological mistakes had evidently had their
roots in his dialectical activity and interest in philosophy, and
there was nothing strange, therefore, in compiling a list of his
philosophical errors to form the basis of the public recantation.[1]
But the headings in the *Synodicon* are so inconsistent as to
suggest a random collection of points at variance with orthodox
doctrine which it would be difficult to impute to the same person.
This may indicate inadequacy of philosophical knowledge on
the part of Italus's accusers, or, more probably, a desire to
anathematize the different heretical points arising at various
times among Italus and his followers. Anna tells how young
men flocked to his lectures, and in the discussions which would
inevitably follow in any living course of philosophical instruction it must have been easy for the errors anathematized in the
Synodicon to have appeared either in passing argument or as
deliberate conviction. Italus was willing to repudiate any error,
but how difficult it must have been to continue philosophical
studies and avoid heresy is shown by his second fall from grace,
even though he was deprived of his official position of professor
of philosophy and entered a monastery after his first trial.[2]

The interest of the *Synodicon* is, then, not in the light thrown
on Italus's philosophical convictions, for he could hardly be
credited, for instance, with believing in a resurrection with a
different body[3] as well as in the impossibility of any resurrection.[4] But behind inconsistencies and generalities the point of
the *Synodicon* is clearly this: to deny the study of philosophy
any but a subordinate place. Anna says that Italus taught philosophy to provide his pupils with 'a tool',[5] and the *Synodicon*

---

[1] G. Buckler in *Anna Comnena*, p. 323, takes the opposite view and suggests
that the *Trial* on the one hand, the *Synodicon* and the account of the *Alexias*
on the other, refer to two separate trials, on the ground that their respective
accusations do not agree.

[2] *Trial*, p. 63; Anna Comnena, v. 9 (i, pp. 183–4) says that he was excommunicated after his second reproof.   [3] *Synodicon*, 9th heading (pp. 423–4).

[4] Ibid., 3rd heading (pp. 421–2).   [5] Anna Comnena, v. 9 (i, p. 181).

deprecates the use of this weapon, except in so far as it accorded with ecclesiastical doctrine. 'The impious dogmas of the Greeks',[1] 'the stupid and so-called wisdom of the pagans',[2] and similar phrases frequently recur; and in the seventh heading the wrong use of philosophy is forbidden, 'Anathema to those who devote themselves to Greek studies, and, instead of merely making this a part of their education, adopt the foolish doctrines of the ancients and accept them for the truth; anathema to those who so firmly believe such doctrines that they unhesitatingly teach them and commend them to others, both secretly and openly.'[3]

To judge how far Italus's own philosophical teaching was more than a compilation is impossible until all his writings have been published. The one thing that can be affirmed with certainty is his interest in philosophy, and it has been usual in the past to speak of him as a Neoplatonist. So he may have been, but not exclusively; even Anna says that he 'taught especially the rules of Aristotle', and already those of his writings which have been edited show his use of Aristotle.[4] They show, too, the *Synodicon's* inaccuracy in accusing him of denying the immortality of the soul and the resurrection, while affirming the eternity of the world.[5] From the *Trial* and the *Synodicon*, then, little knowledge of the real Italus is to be found, and his denial of the charges brought against him is substantiated by such of his own writings which have been published.[6]

John Italus's was the most interesting instance in the Comnenian period of an open and prolonged controversy between philosophy and theology, but it was by no means the only disturbance of Alexius's reign. Leo, Bishop of Chalcedon, for example, was accused of paying too great a reverence to icons when he protested against the melting down of these for purposes of filling the imperial treasury. This protest may have originated in ecclesiastical opposition to the secular financial policy, but

---

[1] *Synodicon*, 2nd heading (p. 421).
[2] Ibid., 3rd heading (p. 421).   [3] Ibid., 7th heading (pp. 422–3).
[4] See Stéphanou, op. cit., and Cereteli.
[5] Ibid., where there is an analysis of Italus's treatment of these points.
[6] It is, however, true that he was at variance with the Church concerning the *manner* of the resurrection. See Stéphanou, op. cit., pp. 423–4, and pp. 427–8.

it is characteristic that the controversy at once assumed the nature of a theological dispute. Leo was accused by a synod of worshipping icons λατρευτικῶς, whereas they could only be reverenced σχετικῶς, the material of which they were made therefore ceasing to have any special value once it was melted down and no longer represented any special figure. As usual, the accused lost his case, and, according to the report of the synod, he repented whole-heartedly,[1] but Anna Comnena says that he was so difficult and obdurate that he was finally deprived of his see and exiled.[2]

Anna Comnena writes of a further controversy within the Church, but also involving the Armenian Church. This arose from the activities of Nilus, an uneducated and clever monk, who had evidently studied ecclesiastical literature closely, but without the necessary background or teaching. Even Anna had to admit that he was an austere and upright man, with a large following.[3] Nilus's error came from his inability to grasp the hypostatical union of the two natures in Christ, 'he had not learnt from the saints the manner in which the assumption of human nature was made divine, and was thus diverted from the true doctrine and foolishly thought that nature had made it divine'.[4] Alexius, having failed in his own attempt to convince Nilus of his mistake, called a synod of the clergy to censure him. Nilus evidently had many followers, particularly among the Armenians in Constantinople who had long been censured, especially for their unorthodox Christology, and against whom polemic was from time to time directed.[5] The synod condemned to perpetual anathema both Nilus and the Armenians.

Anna then immediately goes on to speak of a condemnation of a priest who was infected by the Enthusiasts and whom the Emperor could not convert by his personal efforts, being forced to hand him over to ecclesiastical judgement. These Enthusiasts were a sect who had adopted a form of Manichaean teaching. The Byzantine Church had continually waged war against developments of the Manichaean heresy, and had found it far

---

[1] PG, cxxvii, col. 984.   [2] Anna Comnena, v. 2 (i, p. 159).
[3] Ibid., x. 1 (ii, p. 56).   [4] Ibid., x. 1 (ii, p. 56).
[5] e.g. Archbishop Theophylactus, PG, cxxvi, Letters, *passim*; and Euthymius Zigabenus, PG, CXXX, *Panoplia dogmatica*.

more difficult to fight than the unorthodoxy of such as John
Italus or Nilus. Widely spread throughout the Empire, it could
not be eliminated by summoning a synod at Constantinople and
forcing a leader to recant. It was a way of life that had the power
of popular appeal to the Byzantine, as it had also in western
Europe, especially in the twelfth and thirteenth centuries.
Superficially akin to Christianity in some respects, it was funda-
mentally antagonistic, and was based on a belief in the antithesis
of matter and spirit, matter being irretrievably evil, and the
visible world being therefore created not by God but by Satan.[1]

During the years 867–1185 varying forms of Manichaeism
appeared under different names, the Paulicians, the Enthusiasts
or Massalians, and the Bogomiles. It is not possible here to
analyse their distinguishing features, but they were obviously
becoming a force in the life of the Byzantine people. Anna
speaks with great bitterness against them, and Alexius made
strenuous efforts to root out all such sects. Supported by ecclesiastics and his own son-in-law, Nicephorus Bryennius, the
Emperor led a special expedition to Philippopolis in order to
convert by argument and force those still incorrigible Manichaeans who had been transported to Thrace by John Tzimisces,
and who were perverting the whole district.[2] Of the reality of
his success it is difficult to judge, and although Anna writes of
many conversions, accompanied by lavish imperial gifts, she
has to admit that his arguments had no effect on the three
leaders, 'and since he was unable to convince them at all, he at
last grew tired of their stupidity'.[3] In the end one of the three
repented, the others were imprisoned and left 'to die in solitude,
with nothing but their sins around them'.[4]

The prevalence of such heretical activities is evident, nor is
Anna's reference to 'the great cloud of heretics' an exaggeration.
In Constantinople as well as in the provinces there was evidence
of the danger of Manichaean influence. 'A new kind of heresy
arose, which had not been known before in the Church. It was
compounded of two of the worst and most wicked doctrines of

---

[1] For a short account of the origin and early development of Manichaeism
see F. C. Burkitt, *The Religion of the Manichees*, Cambridge, 1925.
[2] Anna Comnena, xiv. 8 (ii, p. 256).   [3] Ibid., 9 (ii, p. 262).
[4] Ibid. (ii, p. 263).

former times, namely, the impiety, as it were, of the Manichaeans (which we call the Paulician heresy), and the shamelessness of the Massalians. This was the Bogomile teaching.'[1] The leader, Basil, a monk and an ascetic man, was trapped into giving an account of his teaching by the deceit of the Emperor, who pretended that he was anxious to join the sect. Once he had obtained proof of the man's unorthodoxy, Alexius dramatically drew back a curtain and revealed in the next room the senate and soldiers and ecclesiastics waiting with the Patriarch to condemn the unfortunate Bogomile. Nothing would move Basil, and he was burnt to death, while Alexius instituted a vigorous campaign against any suspected of the Bogomile heresy, which was anathematized under five headings in the *Synodicon*[2]. It was at this time that Alexius commissioned Euthymius Zigabenus, a learned monk and 'the best authority on ecclesiastical dogma',[3] to set forth all the heresies with the orthodox refutation of them. This appeared under the title of the *Panoplia dogmatica*, a work wherein everything may be found.[4] In spite of all Anna's pride in the personal activity of Alexius and his theological acumen, she is honest enough to admit that he did not always convert his opponents, even with the added weight which the imperial dignity must have lent to his arguments. But Alexius could always fall back on the help of ecclesiastical authority; on the whole there was little division of opinion concerning the religious policy, in contrast to the imperial overruling of ecclesiastical opinion in Manuel's reign.

Alexius's son, John Comnenus, was not much disturbed by heretical activities, but the one episode that comes to light concerns the suppression of 'doctrines more foolish than the Enthusiasts and Bogomiles'. These errors were detected in a manuscript setting forth the writings of a certain Constantine Chrysolamus, which was being used by the monks of S. Nicholas's monastery; two other similarly contaminated manuscripts were found, one belonging to an abbot, the other having recently been in possession of a monk. The offenders and the doctrines were condemned by a synod.[5] This may seem a small

---

[1] Anna Comnena, xv. 8 (ii, p. 294).   [2] *Synodicon*, pp. 425–6.
[3] Anna Comnena, xv. 9 (ii, p. 299).   [4] PG, cxxx.
[5] Allatius, pp. 644–9; Balsamon, *In Can. LX Apostolorum*, PG, cxxxvii, cols. 156 ff.

matter, but it does show the ease with which heresy could creep into any monastery, and perhaps remain undetected until it had grown to large dimensions. The Bogomile Basil had been a monk, and possibly the experience of Alexius's reign had increased the vigilançe of ecclesiastical authorities.

If the twenty-one years of John's reign have left little evidence of official action against heresy, this is more than counterbalanced by Manuel's activity. In his attitude to heresy and his relation to the ecclesiastical world he was singularly unfortunate, and that spirit of co-operation which was essential to the well-being of the Byzantine polity disappeared. The change is indicated by the comment of the chronicler Nicetas Choniates on Manuel's attitude.

'Although it is the duty of the theological experts to punish and refute those who, through ignorance or audacity, bring new and unfamiliar doctrines into the Church, yet even in these matters the Emperors cannot bear to take a second place, and they themselves introduce doctrines and make judgements and definitions in doctrinal matters and often go as far as to punish those who disagree with them.'[1]

This implied criticism is a contrast to Anna's adulation, and the reason is not far to seek. Manuel overstepped the bounds of his undefined prerogative in his eagerness to display his own theological ability. The disputes of his reign must seem trivial in comparison with the complexity and interest, for instance, of the accusation against the Patriarch Cerularius, or the trial of the philosopher John Italus. But there is no doubt that the Emperor made theological discussions fashionable, though in an artificial atmosphere, since his habit of inviting discussion of difficult doctrinal points was not always due to a genuine desire for help, but in order to provide an opportunity for a new imperial interpretation. 'Just as though', says Nicetas, 'he completely comprehended Christ Himself, and therefore taught things about Him more clearly and divinely.'[2]

The evidence for Manuel's reign points rather to minute theological disputes than widespread heresy. But there are some indications of the persistence of Bogomile teaching, which

[1] vii. 5 (p. 274).   [2] vii. 5 (p. 275).

only come to the front because of their connexion with the Patriarch Cosmas. There was a certain monk, Niphon, who had in 1143 been censured for preaching Bogomile doctrine,[1] while a few months before this two bishops had been similarly condemned,[2] thus showing the difficulty which even the higher ecclesiastics found in keeping within the bounds of orthodoxy. Again, in 1144 Niphon was punished by the synod,[3] and soon after this no less a person than the Patriarch became involved in the charge. The Patriarch in question was Cosmas Atticus, 'a man distinguished in both deed and word',[4] very learned and devout and living in great simplicity.[5] This Cosmas evidently considered that Niphon had been harshly judged, or that he had repented, for he not only allowed him complete freedom, but openly treated him as an intimate friend. Behind this lay the Patriarch's friendship with the Emperor's brother Isaac, which gave his enemies their opportunity of accusing him of conspiracy against Manuel in favour of Isaac.[6] The result was the reimprisonment of Niphon and the Patriarch's trial and deposition for partiality towards a monk accused of the Bogomile heresy. In spite of his indignant protests, Cosmas was deposed in 1147,[7] but it is impossible to say how far this was a cloak for political jealousy, or how far it was justified by an unwise patriarchal leniency towards an insidious form of heresy.

The more obviously religious activity of Manuel's reign was centred in two controversies concerning the orthodox interpretations of certain words. The first dispute[8] was about the meaning of a sentence in the liturgy, σὺ εἶ ὁ προσφέρων καὶ προσφερόμενος καὶ προσδεχόμενος (Thou art He who offers, and is offered, and receives).[9] The origin of this dispute had nothing to do with the Emperor, but it was a point discussed among men interested in theology, of whom there were a considerable number; Nicetas Choniates[10] and the *Synodicon*[11] speak of Soterichus Panteugenes, Bishop-elect of Antioch, Eustathius, Bishop of Durazzo, and Michael of Thessalonica and Nicephorus

---

[1] Allatius, p. 678.   [2] Ibid., p. 674.   [3] Ibid., p. 681.
[4] Cinnamus, ii. 10 (p. 63).   [5] Nicetas, ii. 3 (p. 106).
[6] Ibid.   [7] Cinnamus, ii. 10 (pp. 65–6); Allatius, pp. 683 ff.
[8] See Chalandon, *Jean II Comnène et Manuel I Comnène*, pp. 641 ff. for bibliography.   [9] PG, cxl, col. 137.
[10] vii. 5 (pp. 275–6); cf. Cinnamus, iv. 16 (p. 176).   [11] *Synodicon*, p. 428.

Basilaces, both theological teachers at S. Sophia. The point
was whether the words σὺ εἶ ὁ προσφέρων καὶ προσφερόμενος
καὶ προσδεχόμενος meant that Christ's sacrifice on the Cross
was offered to God the Father or to all three Persons of the
Trinity. To maintain, as some did, that it was offered only to
God the Father and to God the Holy Spirit was to attack the
orthodox doctrines of the Trinity and Incarnation, and as such
was condemned by a synod in January 1156,[1] and those who did
not retract were declared heretics. The discussion persisted and
was presented to the public by Soterichus Panteugenes in the
form of a dialogue.[2] However, in the following year (1157)
another synod was called, meeting this time in the imperial
palace under the direction of the Emperor himself. The
conclusion was foregone; Soterichus Panteugenes and also
Nicephorus Basilaces were condemned. Four sections of the
Synodicon[3] are devoted to this controversy, showing that not
only the Trinity but the Eucharist was involved, and the
Synodicon anathematizes those who claimed that this service was
a memorial and not a daily renewal of the actual sacrifice on the
Cross. And still more interesting is Nicholas of Methone's
answer[4] to Soterichus's *Dialogue*. He begins by remarking that
the subject is not one on which he would choose to write, and
then in reply to Soterichus's taunt of Nestorianism (the belief
that Two Persons co-exist in Christ in perfect harmony, thus
denying the Unity of the Person) he attempts to prove that
Soterichus himself is open to the charge of Monophysitism
(the belief in the one nature of the Divine Word Incarnate,
thus affirming the divine nature and denying the human) and
Arianism (the denial of the consubstantiality and co-equality
of the three Persons of the Trinity). From the references farther
on to Plato it is probable that Soterichus had drawn some of
his arguments from this source, though unjustifiably, as Nicholas
tries to show.[5]

In the next controversy it was the Emperor who took upon
himself the duty of the Patriarch in order to check an unorthodoxy rapidly being accepted by the higher ecclesiastics. The
discussion was started by Demetrius of Lampe, who often went

---

[1] PG, cxl, cols. 147 ff.   [2] Ibid., cols. 137 ff.   [3] *Synodicon*, pp. 428–30.
[4] Ed. Demetracopoulos, pp. 321 ff.   [5] Ibid., pp. 324–5.

as ambassador to countries in western Europe. About 1160 he returned full of scorn for the Germans who maintained the Son to be both less than, and equal to, the Father. Soon there were two schools of thought, those who agreed with Demetrius, and his opponents who accepted the orthodox interpretation of the text 'my Father is greater than I' (John xiv. 28), and maintained that the human and redemptive Christ was there referred to, and that He was distinct from the divine Christ yet co-equal with God the Father and God the Holy Spirit.[1] The Patriarch seemed to have been a nonentity, and it was the Emperor who interviewed Demetrius, and without success, since Demetrius then wrote a defence of his case and circulated it privately. When the unorthodox view gained ground Manuel summoned the suspect bishops individually to discuss the question with him, and was progressing excellently when he learnt that certain bishops, who had not yet been favoured with personal interviews, had united to refuse to consider any argument which the Emperor might bring forward. A synod was called (1166); the official, or rather the imperial, interpretation prevailed, and was summarized in five clauses of the *Synodicon*.[2] So brief an account can give no idea of the ramifications of this controversy, the widespread interest among the clergy, the extensive imperial quotation from patristic sources, the lingering traces of dissatisfaction with the verdict.[3]

To make any variation in the orthodox interpretations and custom was as difficult for the Emperor as for his subjects. When, in the interests of Moslem converts, Manuel tried to omit a certain anathema against their holosphyros, or eternal, God, he was fiercely opposed by both clergy and the Patriarch Theodosius Boradiotes.[4] He had a long and obstinate fight, during which he used every kind of method from public persuasion to coercion, even threatening to invite the help of the Pope. Finally he extracted consent to the replacement of the debated anathema by another against Mahomet, his teaching, and his followers.

[1] The controversy is mentioned by Nicetas, vii. 5 (pp. 276 ff.), and a full account given in his *Treasury of Orthodoxy*, PG, cxl; Cinnamus, vi. 2 (pp. 251 ff.).
[2] *Synodicon*, pp. 431 ff.   [3] See L. Petit, VV., vol. xi, pp. 465 ff.
[4] Nicetas, vii. 6 (pp. 278 ff.).

In his religious, no less than his political, activity, the scope of Manuel's activities was wide. Not only did he appear at Constantinople as the foremost theologian, but he was as anxious to convert both non-Christians and Christian churches in schism as to preserve orthodoxy at home. He negotiated with both the Roman and the Armenian Churches[1], but since he was animated largely by political motives, and neither attempt was successful, they will not be discussed here. The real interest of the zeal of the Comneni for orthodoxy is the gauge which this provides for measuring the vitality of theological and philosophical life at that time.

[1] There was, of course, individual polemic against the theological errors of Latins and Armenians, e.g. the writings of Theophylactus of Achrida, Eustratius of Nicaea, Nicholas of Methone.

CHAPTER VI

THE SCHOLARS OF THE COMNENIAN PERIOD

'I was not ignorant of letters, for I carried my study of Greek to the highest pitch, and was also not unpractised in rhetoric; I perused the works of Aristotle and the dialogues of Plato carefully, and enriched my mind by the 'quarternion' of learning.'

Anna Comnena, *Alexias*, Preface (i, p. 3)

As far as learning was concerned, the Macedonian tradition slipped quietly into the Comnenian, though certain differences of outlook and reflections of the increasing pressure of political difficulties became apparent during the course of the twelfth century. The sophistication and irony of the outstanding literary productions of this period came fitly, indeed, from an age that was living under the shadow of imminent disaster; although such qualities were to be found in Byzantine literature throughout its history, and were, moreover, inherent in its particular genius, yet the absence of the lives of the saints or of the devotional poetry so characteristic of earlier centuries can only be regarded as in keeping with the historical setting of the twelfth century. The best writings of the Comnenian period were the histories of well-educated authors, the satire of those who knew and admired Lucian, and the competent literary exercises of men trained in appreciation of classical learning and versed in the traditional rhetoric. Not without touches both of brilliance and interest, notably in satire and in the use of the vernacular, the work of the Comnenian scholars continued that of its predecessors, especially, as has already been shown,[1] in maintaining a lively interest in theological and philosophical problems.

In discussing the Comnenian period it is clear that 1185 cannot be taken as a rigid boundary, for many Comnenians naturally lived to see the disaster of 1204 and the Lascarids of Nicaea; such, for instance, were Michael and Nicetas Choniates. Nor can the many activities be more than barely indicated, while, even so, no claim is made to include all the men of letters of the period.

The continuity of the Macedonian and Comnenian learning

[1] See Chapter V.

has already been mentioned, and it is a commonplace too often forgotten, that the one inevitably had its roots in the soil of its predecessors. Any such activity as that of Psellus and his friends must have left its mark on many and fired with enthusiasm those who went to make up the numbers of the educated Byzantine public, even if these left no evidence of first-class ability. Concerning the problem of education under the Comnenians it is difficult to do more than suggest the implications of certain evidence. From the numbers of scholars it is clear that there can have been no dearth of teachers, but it is more difficult to determine how far instruction was obtained privately, or was given in a public institution such as the University or the Patriarch's school: and, further, how far Constantinople was the centre of learning. The concern here is not with the foundations of education, but with the higher courses of study. Anna Dalassena and the Empress Irene were educated women, and Anna Comnena must have penetrated far beyond the normal pre-university standard. And so must many of the men whose writings have survived, and who were the acknowledged leaders of their generation, such as Alexius Aristenus, Theodore of Smyrna, or Eustathius of Thessalonica. But whereas the imperial Anna as a princess would presumably have had the help of private teachers, supplemented, of course, by her own natural powers, as well as her opportunities for mixing with scholars,[1] it would probably be the custom for ordinary people to get higher instruction from the University or the Patriarch's school.

After the reopening in 1045, little is heard of the University, although John Italus seems to have succeeded to Psellus's title of ὕπατος τῶν φιλοσόφων,[2] and Theodore of Smyrna, who figures in the underworld of the *Timarion*, had a similar title.[3] Though little appears to be known of the University, in all probability it continued as a centre of learning. There is definite mention, on the other hand, of the Patriarch's school, and it is possible that the apparent growth in the importance of this, and the extension of the range of its studies, was due to the well-known Comnenian interest in theology and in the preservation of orthodoxy. Fuchs shows that the school was distinct

[1] Zonaras, 18, 26 (iii, p. 754).   [2] Anna Comnena, v. 8 (i, p. 179).
[3] See Fuchs, p. 35, n. 1.

from the secular University,[1] and he attempts to show who its
teachers were, and what was the extent of its curriculum.[2]
There were five professors: the διδάσκαλος οἰκουμενικός expounded the Gospels, and of the four others it is known that
one specialized in the Epistles, and another in the Psalter.
The fame of the school depended upon its teachers, and in the
twelfth century it counted among these such men as Michael
Italicus, or Eustathius of Thessalonica, whose interests were
by no means solely ecclesiastical in character. Michael, the
professor of exegesis of the Gospels, taught the secular sciences,
including medicine,[3] and Eustathius, a deacon of the Great
Church and Master of the orators there, was the centre of secular
learning in Constantinople, and famed for his lectures on Homer.

Constantinople, 'the heart of the universe',[4] was, then, the
acknowledged mistress of the Byzantine world of learning, and
those whose duties of office scattered them throughout the Empire could only bewail their enforced absence from so congenial
an environment. Like John of Euchaita in an earlier century,
Theophylact of Achrida or Michael Choniates found little in
the provinces to compensate them for the loss of the humanist
circles of Constantinople. Yet such men to some extent must
have stimulated interest in their dioceses; certainly Michael
Choniates, both in Athens and in exile, was not without friends
who appreciated his enthusiasm for learning, and who sent their
sons to be taught by him, or who helped to collect again his
treasured library which had been scattered during the Latin
conquest of the city.[5] And Michael's letters show a circle of
friends in Constantinople and elsewhere, mostly high officials in
departments of Church or State, who appear to have shared his
own humanist outlook.[6] Beyond fragments of evidence such as
these, it is difficult to say anything of the condition of learning
in the provinces. In the twelfth, as in other centuries, it was
considered expedient to send a boy to Constantinople to complete his education; but, as in the case of Symeon the Young,
or the two Choniatae, this was due not only to the desire to

---

[1] Fuchs, pp. 47 ff.   [2] Ibid., pp. 35 ff.
[3] Ibid., pp. 38 ff. See Michael's letters for the wide range of his knowledge.
[4] Theodore Prodromus, PG, cxxxiii, col. 1246.
[5] See Stadtmüller, *Michael Choniates*, pp. 200 ff.   [6] Ibid., pp. 165 ff.

utilize the best educational opportunities, but also to the very
natural realization that it was in Constantinople that all the
more coveted posts, both lay and ecclesiastical, were to be
obtained. The two motives were, indeed, often inextricably
interwoven, and scholarship was by no means the disadvantage
which the 'prodromic' poems would pretend.

The attempt to preserve the Empire was not without its
reaction on the world of learning. As its difficulties increased,
the emphasis on its classical heritage became, if anything, more
pronounced, almost as though the Byzantines felt that their
world was crumbling about their ears, and therefore treasured
all the more what they had. It might be wild honey that was to
be found in pagan learning,[1] but it was none the less sweet, and
a classical education was the foundation of Byzantine teaching.
But this is not to imply any disparagement of the Bible or
Patristic literature. The University might have no theological
chair, but theology was too important a subject ever to be
neglected in Byzantium, as the works of most Byzantine writers
show; nor were theology and classical learning in any way considered mutually exclusive. There were, of course, always certain
ascetic writers who decried secular learning. Such was Symeon
the Young in the eleventh century. But nothing was more usual
than to find a panegyric or letter full of references to pagan
writers and to the great ecclesiastical authorities. Michael
Choniates, in his *Funeral Oration* for Eustathius of Thessalonica, writes that the great archbishop has united the thrones
of learning and religion, having knowledge both of the paths
of rhetoric and of the spiritual life,[2] and he imagines that the
first to welcome him in heaven will be Clement and Dionysius,
who will come to rejoice in a kindred spirit, in one, who, like
them, had made Greek philosophy the servant of the divine
Christian wisdom.[3] Whatever may have been the outlook of the
hermit or mystic who banned all worldly learning, though without showing how he reconciled this with his use of the Church
Fathers who owed so much to the non-Christian tradition, it
cannot be sufficiently emphasized that the accepted canon of
Byzantine scholarship was the judicious use of all sources of

---

[1] Eustathius of Thessalonica, PG, cxxxv, col. 645 (Lent sermon, iii, ch. 15).
[2] Ed. Lampros, i, p. 290 (21 ff.).   [3] Ibid., p. 304 (3 ff.).

knowledge. The Greeks of New Rome prized above all the polished style and rhetorical power of a Thucydides or a Demosthenes; the very qualities which they so much admired in the Church Fathers were those of style as well as subject-matter. They praised Basil, and Gregory the Theologian, and John Chrysostom, not only for their devotional outlook, or for the intellectual capacity which enabled them to discourse on the mysteries of the Trinity, but especially for the forceful ease with which they expressed themselves. When, in the reign of Alexius Comnenus, there arose a controversy concerning the respective merits of these three Fathers, the point at issue appears to have been the value, not of the contents of their teaching, but of their eloquence. Chrysostom's 'polished phrases, . . . stream of sweetly flowing words, subtility of thought' are compared with Gregory's 'elegance and vividness of style, wide range of vocabulary, and ornateness of phrase'.[1] The Byzantines might recognize that the virtue of a saint transcended earthly knowledge, but for those who had to live in the world it was necessary to acquire the rhetorical polish and literary background from which there was no escape.

Eustathius of Thessalonica is in the twelfth century the personification of the Byzantine ideal. Unquestionably orthodox, and in his later years a wise ecclesiastical administrator, he was also a great classical scholar. Unlike eleventh century men such as Michael Psellus, John Mauropous, or John Xiphilinus, who in the early stages of their lives appear to owe little to the Church, Eustathius was brought up in a monastery, and was later associated with the Patriarch's school, where he was μαΐστωρ τῶν ῥητόρων. Here he gathered round him much the same circle as Psellus had collected when he was lecturer in philosophy in the imperial University. Michael Choniates and Euthymius Malaces[2] bear eloquent witness to Eustathius's influence and scholarship, and to the ready response which it found. If the swarms of students of whom Michael Choniates speaks were

[1] From the *Sunaxarion* for the festival of the Three Fathers, SS. Basil the Great, Gregory the Theologian, and John Chrysostom, in the *Menaion*, Office of Orthros, January 31.
[2] Euthymius Malaces, the Metropolitan of Neae Patrae, was the friend and contemporary of Michael Choniates. For his life and writings see G. Stadtmüller, pp. 306 ff.

as keen as he would have us believe,[1] and there is no reason to suppose otherwise, then there must have been in the second half of the twelfth century the enthusiastic and well-educated public which existing evidence has rarely failed to indicate. Eustathius arranged his curriculum in a manner similar to that of Psellus in the previous century: grammar is the foundation for the study of classical literature, and this is followed by rhetoric and philosophy.[2] It was especially as a lecturer on Homer that Eustathius was famed, and the most monumental portion of his works consists of commentaries on the *Iliad* and the *Odyssey*, obviously a favourite subject for lectures.[3]

The fruit of Eustathius's teaching and of his own personal love of classical writers is seen in his friend and pupil Michael Choniates, who became Archbishop of Athens. To Michael Athens had been the centre of all that he prized in the Greek tradition; and in the contrast between the economic poverty and destitution of the medieval city and the intellectual vigour and political pride of ancient Athens is to be found the underlying current of his writings during his residence in his metropolis. There is no doubt that the financial distress, for which Michael constantly sought imperial relief, inevitably had its effect on learning; but there must have been some exaggeration in his stream of lamentation that all the fame of Athens had perished,[4] for his own writings show that this city was not without men who could appreciate their archbishop's humanist outlook; and, it may be added, while Michael constantly bewailed the depressing condition of Athens, yet once he was exiled from it he wished himself back again.[5]

In the histories of the twelfth century its learning found a characteristic expression. Although its historians attempted to maintain the continuity of the classical tradition, yet nothing could have been more distinctly Byzantine than the *Alexias* of Anna Comnena or the *Epitome* of Cinnamus; however far the

---

[1] Ed. Lampros, i, p. 289 (21 ff.).   [2] See Fuchs, pp. 45–7.

[3] See the article in Pauly-Wissowa, vi (1), cols. 1452 ff. for an account of all Eustathius's commentaries (he worked on other authors besides Homer), and a discussion of their value, with special reference to his use of earlier commentators. For Eustathius's interest in folk-lore and local customs see Ph. Koukoules.

[4] Ed. Lampros, ii, p. 398 (26).   [5] Ibid., ii, p. 259 (19 ff.).

style or mode of presentation was supposed to approximate to
the ancient models, it was impossible to escape contemporary
influence and environment, and in the Byzantine histories there
is reflected a world very different from that of Herodotus or
Thucydides or Polybius. It is, on the other hand, equally different from that of medieval western Europe. The Byzantine
histories of the Comnenian period, together with Michael
Psellus in the eleventh century,[1] are more mature than their
western counterparts; they offer their readers something, both
in presentation and in psychological insight, that was the fruit
of a long and continuous tradition, not only of erudition, but of
culture. It is in the histories more than anywhere else that the
outlook and standard of Constantinople are revealed.

Byzantine historians had a definite conception of the aim of
'history'.[2] It was to be an objective account, related without
emotion, analysing the causes of events, and written in an Attic
style. It was, then, something different from the chronological
world histories, with their indiscriminating wealth of detail and
reliance on earlier traditions and compilations. But, in spite
of the exclusion of pathos or feelings, it was by no means a
colourless or purely impersonal piece of writing; the characters
of Anna or Cinnamus or Nicetas Choniates stand out on every
page of their story, while the individual likes and dislikes of the
author are in each case largely responsible for the selection and
mode of presentation. Anna's personality is as dominating in
the *Alexias* as Psellus's is in the *Chronographia*, Cinnamus's
idealization of the Roman Empire and the imperial Manuel is
as clearly revealed as Nicetas's ecclesiastical prejudices and
criticism of this same Manuel.

Of the three twelfth-century historians Anna is the greatest,
and the *Alexias* an excellent reflection of the Empire at that time.
The daughter of Alexius Comnenus, Anna was brought up in
the midst of continuous political and financial difficulty, and
she describes her world with a detail that is as welcome as it
is unusual: her book is no bare narrative of facts, but the living
drama of a life and death struggle for existence, an epic whose
hero is the Emperor Alexius Comnenus. Her unusual gifts as

---

[1] See J. M. Hussey, Michael Psellus the Byzantine Historian, *Speculum*,
x (1935), pp. 81–90.   [2] Eustathius of Thessalonica, PG, cxxxvi, col. 9.

a writer are well shown by her masterly story of the rise of the Comnenian house to power: the young Alexius and his brother emerge from a maze of politics, with subtlety and decision they make their way, propitiating both the Emperor Michael VII and the Empress Maria, gauging the danger of palace opposition to a nicety, striking at the identically right moment, working always under the shadow of their mother Anna Dalassena's able guidance and relying on her co-operation and judgement. Anna not only presents the larger issues, but she adds little details which make the picture alive and human; she stresses the dignity and majesty of 'my Father the Emperor', but she is not afraid to say that 'over the letter "r" his tongue lisped slightly and stammered a little'.[1] And not only events and people but the *Weltanschauung* of the 'Romans', is strikingly revealed in casual and sometimes seemingly unimportant sentences. Nicephorus Bryennius, Anna's husband, though an experienced soldier, 'had not neglected letters, but had read every book and applied himself to every branch of learning, and drawn therefrom all the wisdom of our own and of other times',[2] and even when on campaign he gave what time he could to his literary work.[3] Leo, Bishop of Chalcedon, who was accused of wrong views concerning the use of holy images, was described as 'virtuous but not particularly wise or intellectual', and after telling of his heated quarrel with Alexius Anna implies that nothing else could really be expected of him, for 'he was incapable of making a precise statement with conviction as he was absolutely untrained in the science of reasoning'.[4] In her opinion this was an unpardonable gap in a good education. And so in countless ways Anna's *Alexias* corroborates all that we know about the outlook of the Byzantines.[5]

The authors of the twelfth century not only knew how to portray the diplomacy of Emperors and the difficulties of a constant struggle against invaders, with all the lights and shades involved in the intricacies of personal relationships, but they had the insight and penetration to satirize as well as to describe. In this branch of literature, as in others, Byzantium lived under

---

[1] Anna Comnena, i. 8 (i, p. 30).   [2] Ibid. vii. 2 (i, p. 231).
[3] Ibid. Preface (i, p. 5).   [4] Ibid. v. 2 (i, p. 159).
[5] See G. G. Buckler, *Anna Comnena*, for a full account.

the shadow of a tradition, and in this case it was Lucian whose wit made so great an appeal to Byzantine sophistication. One of the most interesting writings of the twelfth century is the anonymous dialogue called *Timarion*, written in the style of Lucian. The interest of the *Timarion* lies not only in its satire, but in its account of contemporary life. The hero of the piece, when he returns from his visit to the underworld, his mouth full of poetic phrases, relates to his friend the circumstances in which this adventure befell him, and is thus afforded an opportunity of describing his visit to the great fair of Thessalonica, held each year at the time of the festival of the city's patron, S. Demetrius. Then follows a remarkable passage of description. The cosmopolitan crowds, the merchants and animals, the celebrations of the festival with the processions and all-night vigils, the wonderful singing of the double choir strengthened by the voices of nuns in one of the aisles, all this is so vividly presented to the reader that he himself might well be sitting on the heights behind the city, looking down upon the twelfth-century crowd as the author had, and as John Cameniates had done in more terrible circumstances when the same city was sacked by the Moslems in the tenth century.[1]

But the real point of the *Timarion* is the fun of its satire. This is directed, not only against general foibles, but also against particular individuals. The main speaker, Timarion, has a definite animus against the medical profession, who would rather a man died than recovered in defiance of some accepted medical maxim. Theodore Prodromus has the same bias in some of his writings, as, for instance, in *The Public Executioner or the Doctor*, where he satirizes the physician whose remedy for a cold in the head is to send the victim to a dentist to have a tooth extracted.[2] The author of the *Timarion* attacks not only the vagaries and inadequacies of doctors, but the prevalent gluttony of contemporaries, always a favourite point for satirists. Even his old teacher, Theodore of Smyrna, whom Timarion meets in the underworld, is made to confess how well he lived on earth, contrasting his plenty there and its inevitable ills, such as gout, with the frugal philosophical diet of the lower regions,

[1] Cameniates, pp. 99 ff.
[2] See *Notices et extraits*. . ., vol. 8, pt. 2, p. 104.

where he feeds from a sparse and meagre table, but yet admits
that he enjoys a peaceful and care-free life.[1]

The most pleasing part of the satire in the *Timarion* is the
account of the almost contemporary philosophers, Michael
Psellus and John Italus, and the way in which they were supposed
to be regarded by the company of established immortals.[2]
Italus is looked upon with suspicion and ordered to cast aside
his monk's clothes and the irrational beliefs implied by such,
or else to depart. He refuses to give up his 'Galilaean dress', and
so is forced to turn away from those who have devoted their
lives to wisdom and learning. Finally, after getting the worst of
a fight with Diogenes, from whom he is scornfully rescued by
Cato, he rushes off, sobbing, 'O Aristotle, Aristotle . . . where
are you?'—a characteristic remark, to judge from the extent to
which his recently published works show his frequent use of
Aristotle.[3] In the *Timarion* Michael Psellus, in contrast to
Italus, is greeted aimably by the quietly chatting philosophers;
they do not, however, ask him to seat himself, nor does he presume so to do, but he finds his appropriate place among the
sophists, where he is well received because of his style and
powers as an orator, and is, indeed, greeted with one of his own
phrases, "ὦ βασιλεῦ ἥλιε". Throughout these scenes the author
shows a shrewd sense of proportion as well as a delightful malice in apportioning to the great scholars of his age their
rightful places. Even his own friend and teacher, Theodore of
Smyrna, is characterized as not venturing to say much, except
among the rhetoricians, his own countrymen.

The anonymous author of the *Timarion* was not the only
satirist of the twelfth century. Theodore Prodromus, with his
wealth of output, was well known as a man whose pen spared
nothing, and whose complaints are far more biting than those
of the *Timarion*; his gifts of satire and irony had been only too
plainly sharpened by the disappointments and uncertainties of
poverty. The *Timarion* is a more complete work of art than
most of Theodore's writings because it is free from the element
of begging that too often creeps into the latter. The penury of
scholars was a favourite theme of Theodore Prodromus, and he
treats this subject with dignity, if with acidity, as, for instance,

[1] Ed. Ellissen, p. 67.   [2] Ibid., pp. 87 ff.   [3] See Chapter V, p. 94.

in his 'Invecta in illud: pauperies sophiam nacta est',[1] or 'In eos qui ob paupertatem providentiae conviciantur'.[2] In these, and other of Prodromus's poems, it is impossible not to feel that the author's complaints were born of a deep love of learning, though he is probably exaggerating the depressed condition of letters for his own purposes of satire.

It is considered probable that some of the writings under the name of Theodore Prodromus are wrongly ascribed to him.[3] In these so-called 'prodromic' poems there are certain affinities with the other poems of Theodorus, for the author's object is to expose abuses and difficulties and to appeal for relief, but the satire is of a different order and the verse is written in vernacular Greek. These poems are not without interest, and, apart from their philological value, they provide detail of domestic life, and are a contrast to the rather empty rhetoric which sometimes characterizes Byzantine prose and poetry, including some of Theodore Prodromus's writings. Many of his letters and poems appealing to the Comnenian family are full of heavy flattery and conventional phrases, somewhat reminiscent of Claudian, in distinction to the concrete vitality of the 'prodromic' petitions. In one of the 'prodromic' poems, probably addressed to one of the Emperor John Comnenus's sons, the author details his domestic needs:

'And surely I must have at home linen and cotton, . . . honey, vinegar, sweet-smelling oil, salt, mushrooms, celery, leeks, lettuce, cress, endive, spinach, mountain spinach, turnips, egg-fruit, Phrygian cabbage, beets, cauliflowers? And don't I want almonds and pomegranates and nut-kernels and hemp-seed and lentils and dried raisins and chick-peas for the festival of the remembrance of the dead? And doesn't my wife need a new skirt for Easter, and my mother a cloak and shoes?'[4]

Whatever the solution of the authorship of the 'prodromic' poems, there is in them far less poise and dignity than in the

[1] PG, cxxxiii, cols. 1313 ff.
[2] Ibid., cols. 1291 ff.; see also *Notices et extraits*. . ., vol. 8, pt. 2, pp. 78 ff.
[3] See Hesseling for a discussion of the disputed authorship of certain works attributed to Theodore Prodromus; I have accepted his distinction between the 'prodromiques' poems and the other writings.
[4] Ed. E. Miller and E. Legrand, p. 20 (35 ff.); and D-C. Hesseling and H. Pernot, pp. 42 ff. and see also p. 92.

other works ascribed to Theodore Prodromus. Their author is, for example, fond of railing at the hard lot of scholars, but in a different way from Theodore Prodromus. Take the opening passage of the 'prodromic' poem to John Comnenus, which deplores the fate of those who devote themselves to learning:

'From the time I was small my old father used to say to me: "My son, you learn your letters as well as you can. Look at that man over there, my child; he used to go on foot, but now he has a horse with a double breastplate, and goes about on a fat mule. While he was studying he had no shoes, and now you see him wearing fashionable pointed boots. While he was studying he never combed his hair, and now he is a well-groomed cavalier. While he was studying he did not know the entrance to the baths, and now he has three baths a week. He used to be full of fleas as big as almonds, and now he is filled with gold pieces with Manuel's effigy on them. So take the advice of your old father, and learn your letters as well as you can".'[1]

The poem continues in this colloquial strain, and contrasts the promising paternal vision with the actual lot of the author. It is, of course, conceivable that the difference in style between this poem and a more serious treatment of the same subject, as in Theodore Prodromus's 'In eos qui ob paupertatem providentiae conviciantur', is deliberate, in which case it would have been of set purpose that the one was colloquial and popular, the other dignified and rhetorical.

It is easy to imply that, apart from satire and histories, Byzantine literature of the twelfth century is not of outstanding interest. It is true that its letters and orations and theological works are often rhetorical and dull, full of empty phrases that have been overworked for generations, or merely compilations of facts taken from earlier authors. This was recognized by the Byzantines themselves. Michael Italicus, when he was asked to criticize a certain theological work, said frankly that it had no claim to originality and was not even well compiled.[2] There is, moreover, little real poetry. The epigram, the favoured mode of expression in Byzantium, has lost much of its flavour by the twelfth century; the freshness and spontaneity of such poets

[1] Ed. E. Miller and E. Legrand, p. 6; and D-C. Hesseling and H. Pernot, pp. 72–4.
[2] Ed. Cramer, pp. 196–7 (*Ep.* 25).

as the tenth-century John Geometres or the eleventh-century
John Mauropous have died away. But an adverse verdict
would only ignore much that justly claims attention. The letters
and panegyrics and homilies of the twelfth-century scholars are
in themselves the refutation of the usual charges of monotony
and lack of vitality. Without pressing any claims of outstanding
merit it may be suggested that the letters of Michael Italicus
or Theodore Prodromus, the orations of Michael Choniates or
Eustathius of Thessalonica, to mention only a few, are in themselves individual and interesting pieces of work, full of information for those who take the trouble to study them.

Such writings, quite apart from their historical value, show
the way in which Byzantine scholars thought, and how they
chose to express their thoughts. The most obvious influence
in them is that of rhetoric.[1] This had always been a highly
valued study in Byzantium, widespread in its effect; whether it
was a history or a letter or a sermon, in all literary forms it was
the mode of expression that counted as much as the contents,
for it was this that marked the well-educated man. 'The beauty
of rhetoric is unquestionably of the greatest service to men,'
wrote Michael Italicus,[2] who, like Michael Psellus,[3] emphasized
the importance of this art. There were, of course, numerous
treaties on rhetoric,[4] but, apart from these, the form and expression of other prose works shows the important place taken by
rhetorical studies in the normal curriculum. Eustathius of
Thessalonica's sermons were finished works of art, carefully
balanced and carefully expressed, and a contrast to the
orations of Michael Choniates; the letters of Theodore Prodromus or Michael Italicus differ in many ways—Theodore's are,
for instance, not so simple and direct as Michael's[5]—and yet
they both bear the same stamp of finish and care. And, like John
Mauropous, Theodore can use the conventional metaphor of
the spring and swallows with a charm that not all the smoothness
of a polished presentation can dim, and which is the antithesis
of the pompous rhetoric of much of his poetry.[6]

[1] See above, pp. 107 ff.   [2] Ed. Cramer, p. 161 (*Ep.* 2).
[3] See Chapter III, pp. 62 ff.   [4] See GBL, pp. 451 ff.
[5] Cf. Theodore Prodromus, PG, cxxxiii, cols. 1241 ff. (*Ep.* 2), with Michael
Italicus, ed. Cramer, pp. 196 ff. (*Ep.* 25).
[6] Cf. Theodore Prodromus, PG, cxxxiii, col. 1239 (*Ep.* 1) with any of his

There is need for careful distinction between the twelfth-century writers, especially in summarizing for purposes of general outlines. To dismiss the style and form of Michael Choniates's two famous Funeral Orations, the one written for his brother Nicetas, the other for his friend Eustathius of Thessalonica, with nothing but the same word 'émouvante'[1] is not only to do injustice to Michael, but to fail to convey to the inexperienced reader the real character of these orations, or to give any clue to the literary tradition from which they sprang.

For the general English reader the literary history of the Comnenian period has yet to be written. Krumbacher's *Geschichte der byzantinischen Litteratur*, invaluable as it is, has by now many gaps. Information remains, for the most part, in learned periodicals, often not easy to obtain in England; such articles are, moreover, usually on the more technical points. If it is too much to expect most readers to brave the difficulties of twelfth-century Greek, often with the added obstacle of poor editions, it remains to be hoped that they may at least soon be given an adequate account of the writings of the scholars who lived in this period. They would thus be able not only to appreciate the first-class work of these men, but would realize that much which is intrinsically second class is nevertheless full of interest and individuality.

poems to the Comneni, ibid., cols. 1339 ff. and again with John Mauropous, *Ep.* 1, ed. Lagarde, pp. 51–2.

[1] A. A. Vasiliev, *Histoire*, ii, pp. 153, 156 (this is the French translation; it is still worse in the English version where it is given as 'emotional').

CHAPTER VII

ECCLESIASTICAL ORGANIZATION

'It was the wise judgement of God which appointed these our rulers, and
they must receive due honour in our writings, the one as the Sovereign of
our human bodies, the other as the Shepherd of our souls.'
   John of Euchaita, *On the Icon of the Emperor and the Patriarch*, Lagarde,
   p. 42 (Poem 87).

THE Byzantine Church neither possessed, nor indeed desired,
the freedom of its western neighbour, as comparison with
the Latin Church will show. It had its traditions, its doctrine,
its Patriarch, its Emperor, and felt little impulse to enter upon
fierce dialectic concerning the relative powers of spiritual and
secular authorities. In the West the Pope and the Emperor were
separated by the Alps, and the imperial position was more
fittingly described by the scornful designation of the Byzantine
Chancery as that of "ῥήξ", rather than "βασιλεύς". The relations between secular and ecclesiastic were widely discussed in
western Europe of the tenth and eleventh centuries, and the
growth of the papal power showed itself in the reforms of Leo
IX and Gregory VII and the quarrel over investiture. Nobody
would have denied the superiority of the spiritual powers. In
the tenth century Sylvester II wrote that the crowns of kings
were but lead in comparison with the flashing gold of an episcopal mitre, 'wherefore you shall see kings and princes on
bended knee bowing before the priesthood';[1] in the eleventh
century Peter Damian, while recognizing, like Dante, that the
temporal and spiritual powers had each their own sphere, did
not hesitate to assert the ultimate superiority of the spiritual
authority and maintained that when the King disregarded divine
commands, he himself might justly be deposed by his subjects.[2]
   He would have been a brave man who had spoken in Constantinople of the leaden hue of the imperial crown, or the
deposition of the Emperor for his ecclesiastical policy.[3] The

---

[1] Sylvester II, *De Informatione Episcoporum*, quoted by A. J. Carlyle,
Medieval Political Theory in the West, vol. iv (1922), p. 41, n. 4.
[2] See A. J. Carlyle, op. cit., pp. 44 ff.
[3] The context of Peter Damian's remark was no question of doctrinal

fate of Michael Cerularius showed the strength of the imperial position,[1] and therein lies the difference between the Eastern and Western Churches. In the existence of Constantinople, New Rome, lay the guarantee for imperial stability, and it was said that he who possessed Constantinople possessed the Empire.[2] However fictitious the hereditary claim of an Emperor, once he had won Constantinople, the centre of both secular and ecclesiastical life, he was βασιλεύς and the ruler of the Empire. The Western Emperor had no such advantage, he took his stand in his own lands, and was little more than a *primus inter pares*, especially as the election was not necessarily limited to the rulers of any particular duchy or kingdom from among the heterogeneous collection which composed the Western Empire. The only parallel to Constantinople for the West was Rome, but that was some distance outside the effective sovereignty of the Holy Roman Empire. The Eastern Emperor had therefore the added advantage of a continuous tradition, and, though political revolutions were not infrequent and the new Emperor might be from any of the Asiatic or European provinces, Constantinople nevertheless remained the centre of government, and behind it was the tradition of a humanist education and of an Orthodox Church. Thus there were none of the difficulties which dogged the western Emperors, and no Alps to be crossed before the imperial coronation could be performed. So the Byzantine Emperor retained the bone, while his Western counterpart spent time and substance in pursuit of something that always ended by assuming the qualities of a shadow. The ultimate authority of the Eastern Emperor in ecclesiastical life was unquestioned. It is neither the absence of chronicles written with all the bias of a great monastic house, nor the layman's fear of the court resentment of criticism that can account for the prominence which was always given to the Emperor's verdict. This was a fact, and no boastful misrepresentation of writers whose aim was flattery, and, had monastic

heresy, but a matter of supporting Pope Alexander II against the anti-Pope Cadalous of Parma.

[1] See *infra* on Cerularius (Chapter VIII).

[2] Cecaumenus, p. 74 (c. 186): 'the victory always remains with the Emperor at Constantinople', quoted by Neumann, *Die Weltstellung des byzantinischen Reiches* . . ., p. 75.

houses produced chroniclers, they would have been the first to acclaim the glory of the imperial power.[1]

The clue to the understanding of Byzantine Church history is the realization that, in matters of individual spiritual development, Emperor and secular clergy could only stand aside and share, or envy, the reverence which rich and poor alike gave to those monks whom they could recognize as holy men; on the other hand, there was the everyday life of the Church, which meant the performance of the duties of a hierarchy of priests, with the daily liturgies in the cathedrals and churches, the spiritual supervision of those people who had not monastic confessors, the settlement of legal difficulties and the collection of church dues. The Eastern Empire never had the struggle between temporal and spiritual claims which dominated the history of western Europe, because, although the Orthodox Church had its inevitable organization, yet it never made the mistake of forgetting that organization of necessity implied a temporal element, and that therefore the highest authority in such matters was imperial. Had the Emperor supported doctrine contrary to orthodox teaching, he would undoubtedly have met with opposition, as indeed happened in the case of Manuel Comnenus; but he was unquestioned as long as he was concerned only to provide justice or regulation in cases which baffled the Patriarch or bishops, or which came to him by reason of some privilege of foundation. The Emperor had the right of access to synods, and was in practice a person of equal, if not greater, importance than the Patriarch. He may have honoured the Patriarch as a first-born son should honour his father, but this was only as long as the Patriarch acted in willing co-operation with him. There is no doubt that the office of Patriarch was important, and an obstructionist policy from its holder could seriously inconvenience the Emperor; it was therefore to the mutual advantage of both secular and spiritual authorities that they should be in agreement. In the event of opposition the Emperor usually proved the stronger, nor did the Patriarch often venture to dissent, unless he were sure of secular support, perhaps from the party of political malcontents.

[1] See Chapter IX.

If the Patriarch of Constantinople[1] had neither the opportunity nor the necessity to acquire the temporal powers which
the Pope was forced to claim, he remained, nevertheless, the head
of the Orthodox Church. Though he was inevitably over-
shadowed by the Emperor, the Byzantines did not deny the importance of one who was 'the living image of Christ'.[2] 'As the body
politic, like the human body, is composed of parts and members,
so the most important and the most vital parts are the Emperor
and Patriarch.   In the same way that the peace and happiness
of the human body depends on the harmony of soul and body,
so in the polity there must be perfect agreement between the
Emperor and the priesthood (ἀρχιερωσύνη).'[3]   The Patriarch
was assigned the higher part as was fitting for one who was 'the
shepherd of our souls', this could not be denied him; it was the
Patriarch who had the right of giving doctrinal instruction, of
explaining the canons and the Church Fathers. The extent to
which the Patriarch was regarded as the guardian of orthodoxy
is shown by Psellus in the *Accusation*, when he charges Cerularius with ἀσέβεια and emphasizes his betrayal of his trust.[4]
The Patriarch of Constantinople was canonically only the first
of the other Eastern Patriarchs, but in practice the latter had
little influence; Alexandria had long been lost to the Mono-
physite heresy and the Arabs, Antioch and Jerusalem again fell
a prey to Moslem invaders during the eleventh century.

Under the Patriarch there was the usual hierarchy of ecclesiastics—metropolitans, archbishops, bishops, priests, and deacons.
The organization of the Church had been modelled on that of
the state. Each union of several provinces was controlled by an
exarch or superior metropolitan, and under him were separate
provinces ruled by their metropolitans, and individual cities by
their bishops. Some archbishops were directly dependent upon
the Patriarch, and these, as Nicaea or Chalcedon, were known
as autocephalous sees. The frequency of changes and the

---

[1] On the Patriarchs of the eleventh century see Chapter VIII.

[2] PG, cxix, col. 909 A. ('Officium et definitio patriarchae', quoted from
the *Basilica, De jure*, Tit. II, cap. 1.)

[3] Ibid., col. 909 C.

[4] Cf. *Accusation*, ed. Bréhier, p. 393: 'this [i.e. the destruction of Chaldaean
heresy] should have been the duty of the upholder of right dogma and the
shepherd of true belief.'

difficulty of geographical identification introduce an element of
uncertainty into any statements concerning the detail of organization under the Macedonians and Comneni. But it was the
Emperor, no doubt in consultation with the Patriarch, who was
responsible for the territorial organization of the Church;
Nicephorus Phocas made Otranto a metropolis and at the same
time, partly for political motives, forbade the Latin rite in Apulia
and Calabria,[1] Basil II reorganized the Bulgarian archbishopric
of Achrida.[2] Changes in the eleventh and twelfth centuries
were sometimes effected by means of raising a bishop to the
rank of metropolitan, but this is misleading since this was often
only for a lifetime, and was primarily due to financial motives.[3]
Constantine X raised the Archbishop of Basileion (Galatia) to the
rank of metropolitan for his lifetime,[4] and this was confirmed
by Michael VII.[5] Romanus IV raised the bishopric of Nazianzus
to the status of a metropolis,[6] Michael VII did likewise to
Neocaesarea.[7] There are similar instances in the Comneni
period, both of imperial promotion to a higher rank,[8] and of
reorganization of dioceses.[9] The advance of the Turks must
necessarily have created havoc in the dioceses of Asia Minor.
As early as 1059 the Archbishop of Euchaita could speak of
'the terrible troubles' of the Moslem advance,[10] and in the reign
of Manuel Comnenus special imperial provision is made for
those bishops whose seats are in the possession of the Turks.[11]
The conferring of the dignity of a metropolitan was an imperial matter, and the Emperor must have had considerable influence in ecclesiastical elections. Nicephorus Phocas even went
so far as to assert that no bishop was to be chosen without his
consent,[12] but this was because he wished to suppress opposition

[1] Liutprand, *Legatio*, p. 370 (CB, with Leo Diaconus).
[2] Jus, iii, pp. 319–20 (Dölger 806).
[3] Scabalanovitch, p. 362 and pp. 269–70.
[4] Freh. i. p. 278 = Jus, iii, c. 4, n. 4, p. 326 (Dölger 964).
[5] Jus, iii, c. 4, n. 8, p. 330 (Dölger 1014).
[6] Scylitzes, ii. 705 (Dölger 974).
[7] Jus, iii, c. 4, n. 9, p. 330 (Dölger 1015).
[8] Ibid., c. 4, n. 23, p. 358 (Dölger 1086); ibid., c. 4, n. 25, p. 364 (Dölger 1112).
[9] Ibid., c. 4, n. 29, pp. 368–70 = PG, cxxvii, cols. 929–32 (Dölger 1140).
[10] See Chapter VII, p. 130.
[11] Balsamon, PG, cxxxvii, cols. 1444 ff., *In Can. VI Conc. Sardic.* (Dölger 1485).
[12] Jus, iii, c. 3, note to n. 24, p. 301; Leo Diaconus, p. 99; Cedrenus, ii,
p. 368 (Dölger 703).

to his Church policy. To claim complete control of the epis-
copacy was a very different thing from a less definite, but none
the less real, use of ecclesiastical patronage in the interests of
the imperial policy; and one of the first acts of Nicephorus's
successor, Tzimisces, was to abrogate this,[1] and to recall the
opposition bishops who had evidently been dismissed from their
sees. Nevertheless, this in no way meant any renunciation of
imperial influence in a useful branch of patronage, and, as Basil
I was persuaded to reward Photius's friend, Theophanes, by the
appointment to the archbishopric of Caesarea,[2] so later Emperors used ecclesiastical promotion to suit their own purposes.
John Mauropous was obviously made Archbishop of Euchaita
at the instigation of Constantine IX; bishops and archbishops,
like monastic foundations, no doubt found the Emperor a more
effective patron and ally than the Patriarch. John himself wrote
that his position was strengthened not by appeal to the Patriarch
but by the chrysobull of the Emperor.[3] Similarly imperial
chrysobulls of Nicephorus III confirmed the rights of the metropolis of Patrai,[4] and determined that, on the death of the
Metropolitan of Madytus, the metropolitan powers should revert
to the Bishop of Heracleia.[5]

The routine of ecclesiastical administration was based on an
organization very similar to that of secular life. Under the
Patriarch were important officials, each controlling some special
department. The six chief officials, who were also members of
the synod, were the great oeconomus (ὁ μέγας οἰκονόμος), the
great sacellarius (ὁ μέγας σακελλάριος), the great sceuophylax (ὁ
μέγας σκευοφύλαξ), the great chartophylax (ὁ μέγας χαρτο-
φύλαξ), the prefect of the sacellus (ὁ σακελλίου), and the
protecdicus (ὁ πρωτέκδικος).[6] The most important of these
officials was the chartophylax, who was the Patriarch's chan-
cellor, and who dealt with difficulties of ecclesiastical jurisdiction, for instance, disputes arising out of the marriage

---

[1] Leo Diaconus, pp. 98–9; Cedrenus, ii, p. 381.
[2] *Vita S. Ignatii*, PG, cv, col. 568.
[3] Lagarde, p. 34 (Poem 57).
[4] Jus, iii, c. 4, n. 16, p. 341 (Dölger 1055).
[5] Ibid., c. 4, n. 15, p. 341 (Dölger 1056).
[6] PG, cxix, col. 924; cf. Scabalanovitch, p. 363, who says that the protecdicus was added later; and Mortreuil, iii, pp. 69 ff.

laws. He was the Patriarch's official secretary, and assisted
with his correspondence and *sententiae*, and is sometimes
mentioned in the inscription of patriarchal edicts, as a certain
Nicetas, who appears in the letters of Cerularius and Xiphilinus.[1]
The great oeconomus had general charge of financial administration, and supervised the collection of money owing to the Great
Church and the Patriarchate of Constantinople, such as dues
from property, or from monasteries under the direct control
of the Patriarch. It was an important and profitable office, and
up to the end of the first half of the eleventh century the appointment rested with the Emperor. Not infrequently lay appointments were made; the office had been held by Romanus Argyrus,
afterwards to become the husband of Zoe.[2] Similarly the office
of sceuophylax was an imperial appointment;[3] the duty of the
department was to supervise the sacristy containing the sacred
vessels, the books and other possessions of the Great Church.
Under Cerularius both oeconomus and sceuophylax became
ecclesiastical appointments, when Isaac Comnenus granted
S. Sophia control of its exchequer and placed it once more under
the Patriarch's supervision.[4] The great sacellarius exerted control over such monasteries as came within the Patriarch's jurisdiction,[5] the prefect of the sacellus performed the same duties
with regard to nunneries or parish churches. The protecdicus
was a judicial officer, representing the interests of the Church in
the lay courts and assisting ecclesiastical plaintiffs or defendants.

The great officials of the legal, financial, and administrative
departments immediately under the Patriarch of Constantinople
were duplicated throughout the ecclesiastical hierarchy. Autocephalous archbishops, metropolitans, bishops, all had their
own officers and courts, their own financial problems and legal
difficulties. It was only in the last resort that they would appeal
to the Patriarch of Constantinople. In practice any degree of
independence was obtained not by gaining the support of the

[1] PG, cxix, cols. 748 B, 856 D.
[2] Cedrenus, ii, p. 485; Zonaras, xvii. 11. 2 (iii, p. 574).
[3] Zonaras, xviii. 4. 5 (iii, p. 666).
[4] Attaleiates, p. 60; Scylitzes, ii, pp. 641–2; Zonaras, xviii. 4, 5 (iii,
p. 666).
[5] Cf. Zhishman, *Die Synoden* . . . , on the duties of the prefect of the
sacellarius, pp. 103 ff.

Patriarchs, but by appealing to the Emperor, and it was not without point that the Emperor's name nearly always came first when the Emperor and Patriarch were mentioned side by side.[1] As with monastic foundations, so in the secular Church the normal routine continued; it was only the exceptional cases which were recorded, and hence the difficulty of depicting the ordinary business of the Church courts or the ecclesiastical exchequers.

The administrative departments of the Church functioned in the same way as their lay counterparts. The Church was not a body corporate within the polity, it was part of it, and this was but rarely disputed. Consequently, the Byzantine Empire had no development of canon law comparable to that of western Europe, nor, apart from the iconoclastic controversy in the ninth century, was there any serious conflict between lay and spiritual authorities.

Byzantine canon law never lost the imprint of the imperial stamp, and this indicates, not any quality of debasement or secularization, but rather that the Emperor was the source of Christian law, and its guarantor. The Church councils originally met to discuss points of dogma and discipline, they met under the imperial protection, if not at the imperial command, and their conclusions were ratified by the imperial consent. The difficult problems of doctrine were settled by the early councils, and, after the outburst of the iconoclastic controversy, there was in the Orthodox Church little either of protest or development, and, in comparison with Berengar or Abelard, the disputes of Psellus and John Italus and Demetrius of Lampe assume their true insignificance, while the Eastern Church has nothing which can compare with the Lateran Councils of western Europe. Almost the only points which were raised in the East were those of discipline, or problems in connexion with the marriage laws. The *synodales sententiae* of the years 867–1185[2] are few and relatively unimportant in comparison with the earlier councils.

[1] Lagarde, p. 28 (Poem 53) and p. 42 (Poem 87). There are probably exceptions, no doubt from motives of diplomacy; for instance, in Leo the Deacon's account of Tzimisces' speech before the election of a Patriarch to fill Polyeuctus's place, the Emperor speaks of the one divine principle and the two earthly powers, 'the priesthood and the empire' (*Historia*, vi. 7, p. 101).

[2] PG, cxix, cxxvii, and cxl.

The most important exceptions are the ninth-century councils which met to settle the controversy between Ignatius and Photius, and possibly the twelfth-century councils which tried to suppress various heresies.[1]

It was through the synod that the Patriarch acted. Since the rift with Rome, the loss of Alexandria, and the dwindling in importance of Antioch and Jerusalem, general councils or synods had ceased to serve any practical purpose, and the Patriarch in the synod of Constantinople formed the most effective organ in any important crisis.[2] This body was composed of all who held episcopal or higher rank, chosen normally by the Patriarch, in addition to the higher grades of the patriarchal secretariat, and imperial representatives, if not the Emperor himself.[3] The synod was the descendant of the earlier Church councils, and its business was to discuss matters of ecclesiastical importance. It was not often concerned with difficulties of heresy, but usually met to decide questions of administration or appointment. It was the synod which was summoned to discuss the cult of Symeon the Studite which Symeon the Young had instituted;[4] it was in the synod that the Patriarch proposed certain amendments of the marriage laws which he thought desirable.[5] The synod could be summoned by the Emperor, and the more important decrees were confirmed by him; Constantine X[6] and Nicephorus III ratified Xiphilinus's marriage decrees.[7] When the synod could come to no decision regarding Symeon the Young, the Patriarch was terrified lest the Emperor would interfere.[8] The very presence of the imperial officers showed how close was the relation between Church and State, an intimacy

[1] See Chapter V.
[2] Synods held at Constantinople by Manuel Comnenus for the discussion of heresy were sometimes attended by the Patriarchs of Antioch and Jerusalem who were invited perhaps because they happened to be in Constantinople, rather than by reason of an attempt at an oecumenical verdict (1156 synod, Patriarch of Jerusalem present, PG, cxl, col. 148; 1166 synod, Patriarchs of Antioch and Jerusalem present, PG, cxl, col. 237).
[3] Scabalanovitch, p. 363; Gasquet, *De l'autorité impériale en matière religieuse à Byzance*, pp. 135 ff.   [4] *Vita Symeonis*, p. 102 (ch. 75).
[5] PG, cxix, cols. 748 ff. (*Sententiae synodales*).
[6] Jus, iii, c. 4, n. 10, p. 331 (Dölger 966 says that Fischer, *Studien*, p. 36, note 5, doubts the authenticity of this).
[7] Jus, iii, c. 4, n. 13, pp. 338–40; PG, cxxvii, cols. 1481–4 (Dölger 1048).
[8] *Vita Symeonis*, p. 142 (ch. 102).

born of the days when councils and Church owed their existence
to the imperial protection, a tradition which in the East had been
continuous from the time of Constantine.

Local ecclesiastical jurisdiction, no less than central, showed
the limits beyond which it could not, and did not, expect to go.[1]
The supremacy of the State was naturally accepted to a far
greater extent than in western Europe, and ecclesiastical authorities had even to prevent their people from preferring the temporal to the spiritual courts, although it is difficult to say whether
this was legislation against monastic preference for secular
courts, or whether there was a general preference of both clerics
and monks for temporal justice. The Patriarch Alexius expressly
forbade κοσμικοὶ δικασταί to interfere in ecclesiastical cases
under pain of imperial displeasure: 'We will not suffer this
ecclesiastical and sacred and divine privilege to be snatched
from us, whether by the judges of the themes or the towns.'[2]
In the usual civil and criminal cases ecclesiastics were bound
by the common law, unlike western clerics with their pernicious
'benefit of clergy'. The ordinary ecclesiastical court was that
of the bishop, and civil disputes of clerk v. clerk[3] were decided
by him. A case of clerk or bishop v. bishop went to the pro-
vincial synod, of clerk or bishop v. metropolitan to the exarch
of the diocese or the imperial tribunal.[4] If the case were a
criminal one, it was investigated by the appropriate ecclesiastical
authority, and then sent, if it were proved, to the secular
authority for condemnation and punishment. In the case of
clerk v. civilian it was tried in the court to which the defendant
belonged, while, if a civilian defendant agreed, it could be
examined before the bishop,[5] and, if both sides then agreed
to the bishop's decision, this was executed by a magistrate,
otherwise, if the bishop's decision were disputed, the case was
referred to a secular court. It was possible for two civilians to
go to the bishop, or other ecclesiastical authority, for arbitration
on moral questions, such as marriage or divorce or difficulties
of doctrinal interpretation. Appeals against the bishop went to

[1] Cf. Gasquet, op. cit., pp. 170 ff.
[2] PG, cxix, col. 833 A.
[3] Or a monk, but cf. Chapter IX, pp. 177 ff.
[4] Cf. PG, cxix, col. 832.
[5] Cf. Scabalanovitch, p. 356; Jus, iii, c. 4, n. 18, pp. 341–2.

the metropolitan, against the metropolitan to the patriarchal synod. There was no appeal against the Patriarch's decision, and the only way of altering it was by obtaining a revision (ἀναψηλάφησις).[1] The safeguard against any abuse of the patriarchal authority lay in the imperial power. Balsamon wrote in the twelfth century 'Because it is a legal principle that no one shall suffer injury from another, if the Patriarch himself commits sacrilege or is unorthodox or errs in any other way he shall be subject to the judgement of the Emperor, the disciplinarian of the Church.'[2] And so, although it was naturally assumed that the Emperor and the Patriarch would work together in harmony 'like the ropes and sails of an ocean-bound ship, preserving the world unharmed by means of imperial counsel and spiritual exhortation',[3] yet it was clear that, if need arose, the Patriarch could be held responsible before the Emperor for his acts.

Revenue provided a problem as difficult for clerics as for secular authorities. The ordinary income of a bishop would be derived from Church property, from fees for ordination and marriages, and from the canonicon or hearth tax. Constantine IX determined that for a marriage in his diocese the bishop should receive one gold piece from the bridegroom and twelve ells of cloth from the bride;[4] Isaac Comnenus decreed that a bishop should receive for ordination or consecration not more than seven gold pieces, while the fee for the ordination of a priest or reader was one gold piece, and for a deacon or presbyter three.[5] And he fixed the episcopal canonicon from a community of thirty families at one gold piece, two silver pieces, one buck, six bushels of wheat, six measures of wine, six bushels of barley, thirty fowls, and proportionately for a community of twenty or ten families.[6] Alexius Comnenus made similar regulations for the various sources of a country bishop's income.[7] The town and village clergy received tithes and produce from glebe land, but the principal source of their income was derived from the fees and offerings in return for their spiritual services in the performance of the sacraments.

[1] Scabalanovitch, p. 357. [2] PG, cxxxvii, col. 1312 A.
[3] Ibid., cxxxviii, col. 1020 B. [4] Jus, iii, c. 4, n. 27 γ′, p. 366 (Dölger 923).
[5] Jus, iii, c. 4, n. 1, pp. 322–3 (Dölger 943).
[6] Ibid., c. 4, n. 1, p. 323 (Dölger 944).
[7] Ibid., c. 4, n. 27, pp. 365–7; PG, cxxvii, cols. 925–8 (Dölger 1127).

It is evident that both higher and lower clergy suffered from encroachments upon their financial sources, and this is partly due to the difficulty of monastic competition,[1] partly to the preference for imperial rather than ecclesiastical justice. The Patriarch Alexius in the synod of 1025 tried to protect the parish clergy by limiting the use of private chapels (τὰ τῶν οἴκων εὐκτήρια), and priests who used them at any but the appointed times were to be degraded.[2] These chapels were built with the permission of the bishop, and the sacraments could be administered in them, so that any widespread use of them meant a neglect of the parish churches, which became still more serious if the liturgy were performed by a monk and not a secular priest. Alexius's further insistence on the use of spiritual courts may have been partly caused by concern for episcopal finance, which must have been still further depleted by the monastic readiness to obtain the privileges of imperial justice, and the right of choosing whomsoever they pleased to perform their ordinations. Alexius's decrees were definitely on points of discipline which affected ecclesiastical finance. But it was by imperial decree that the amount of the canonicon and marriage dues was fixed; it was an imperial chrysobull that levied a tax to help build the cathedral at Ani;[3] and the secular church, like the monastic house, was grateful for the imperial protection and help. The Emperor, in finance, as in all other spheres, was the final authority. Important churches or cathedrals would have their patrons, and in Constantinople S. Sophia, with its official position, naturally hoped for imperial bounty. Basil I made special provision of oil for the lamps in S. Sophia;[4] Romanus III increased its yearly income by 80 lb. of gold,[5] Constantine IX gave special subsidies in order to enable the liturgy, which had previously been sung only on festivals, Saturdays, and Sundays, to be performed daily in the Great Church.[6] But such gifts were not entirely altruistic, they were part of an imperial policy, which was inextricably bound up with the relations between Emperor and Patriarch.

---

[1] Cf. Chapter IX, pp. 172 ff.   [2] PG, cxix, col. 837.

[3] Inscription on the west side of the Cathedral; Brosset, *Les Ruines d'Ani*, p. 28 (Dölger 852).

[4] Theoph. Cont., Basil, c. 79, p. 322; Cedrenus, ii, p. 238.

[5] Cedrenus, ii, p. 486; Zonaras, xvii. 11. 1 (iii, p. 574) (Dölger 831).

[6] Lagarde, p. 24 (Poems 44, 45); Cedrenus, ii, p. 609.

Moreover, in spite of benevolent grants of immunity and presentation of endowments, Emperors from time to time exercised
a close surveillance over ecclesiastical wealth, and drew upon
it in times of need. With regard to monastic property this
happened under Nicephorus Phocas, Isaac Comnenus, and
Alexius and Manuel.[1] As far as concerns non-monastic revenues
there is evidence that these, at least in the Bulgarian archbishopric, were very carefully watched. The problem revolved
round the difficulty of obtaining the payment due from those
paroikoi on an ecclesiastical estate who paid their tax to the
State and not the Church. There were a certain number who
were exempt from the state tax but who paid the canonicon to
the Church; frequently imperial officials would find that the
estate had more than its allotted number of exempt paroikoi,
the secular treasury thus being defrauded of its due revenue
from these. Alexius Comnenus, who had very grave financial
difficulties, made strict inquiries into this, and Theophylactus,
then Archbishop of Achrida, complained bitterly of the severity
and persistence of the secular tax collectors.[2] Both the power
and the greed of the Emperor in ecclesiastical matters are further
revealed in an analysis of the patriarchal activities in this period.[3]

The Patriarchs were important men, in spite of imperial
limitations of their power, and their doings are recorded in
the Byzantine histories. But unfortunately it is nearly always the
event of political significance that is noted, and, apart from
the Patriarchs, there is but fragmentary evidence concerning the
characters and work of the secular clergy. Occasionally metropolitans or bishops appear in the pages of a chronicle, but only
by reason of their entanglement in some difficulty of secular
life; thus Attaleiates writes that the metropolitans accused the
Archbishop and Metropolitan of Neocaesarea of uncanonical
behaviour in holding secular office.[4] But rarely is it recorded
whether a metropolitan was a just and faithful spiritual super-
visor, or whether he found the lower clergy in his diocese careful
in performance of their pastoral duties. Symeon the Young
speaks at the beginning of the eleventh century of the scarcity

---

[1] See Chapter IX, p. 174.
[2] PG, cxxvi, *Ep.* 24, cols. 405 ff.; and his other letters *passim*.
[3] See Chapter VIII.   [4] Attaleiates, pp. 278–9.

of spiritual rulers fit to guide their flocks,[1] and he emphasizes the unworthiness of the secular priesthood;[2] in the twelfth century Eustathius of Thessalonica complains that monks pretend they are weak from the asceticism of monastic life, while in reality they are bloated from overeating, as a glance at their hands and faces is sufficient to show.[3] Manuel Comnenus issued a novel to prevent bishops from lingering too long in Constantinople when they should be in their own dioceses.[4] The attempts of the Comneni to raise the standard of the clergy of S. Sophia[5] and to prevent ecclesiastical participation in worldly affairs[6] indicate that the standard of the secular clergy left much to be desired. These condemnations, perhaps in Symeon's case the result of a natural monastic bias, must have been true of some. But there were such as John of Euchaita, who, though forced into a position of virtual exile, fulfilled his duties with courage and perseverance. It might well have been John whom the two Georgian monks met when they visited Euchaita in 1059, and described its metropolitan as one who received them in the spirit of charity with all hospitality, 'for he was a holy man and full of the knowledge of God, and our arrival was a great comfort to him amid these terrible troubles [i.e. the advance of the Moslems], and we talked to him for a long while concerning the spiritual life.'[7]

The sources for the organization of the secular church in this period consist, therefore, of fragments, gathered chiefly from chronicles or imperial bulls or hagiographical writings. The framework of the Church remains that of earlier centuries and its condition is deduced as often from negative as from positive evidence. To speak of the spirit which animated the secular church at this time is almost impossible. It can only be said that in one place there was a metropolitan of saintly character, in another, one renowned for his greed. There is little record of everyday activities, of cases which came before the bishop's

---

[1] PG, cxx, col. 433 A (Or. 23).
[2] Epistola de confessione, c. 11, ed. Holl, p. 120.
[3] De simulatione, ed. Tafel, pp. 94–5 (ch. 27).
[4] Jus, iii, c. 4, n. 75, pp. 500–1; PG, cxxxiii, col. 788 (Dölger 1333ᵃ).
[5] Jus, iii, c. 4, n. 41, pp. 413–24; PG, cxxvii, cols. 945–68 (Dölger 1236).
[6] Jus, iii, c. 4, n. 71, pp. 492–3 (Dölger 1384).
[7] Vita S. Georgii Hagioritae, pp. 121–2.

court, of the exact sources of an episcopal income, or of the teaching of the parish priests. Apart from the sermons of a few men it only remains to read the liturgy which was in essence the same then as in earlier and later times, and which is a permanent witness to the beauty of the Byzantine Church service.

CHAPTER VIII

THE PATRIARCHS 867–1185

'He said that there was no difference between the priesthood and the empire, or very little, but that it was in the more important points that the difference was perhaps greater and really significant. But when the Emperor heard these words he was full of zeal to take action against such snarlings rather than to suffer them.'   Scylitzes, ii, p. 643.

'Did I not say to begin with, did I not protest, that I would never willingly have left true peace (ἡσυχία) to descend to such affairs?' 'But this is no down-fall,' I immediately replied, 'think how great a promotion it is to ascend to the office of Patriarch.' 'It is a descent and nothing else! for what could be higher than God, whose mysteries I have been performing?'

Psellus, *Funeral oration on John Xiphilinus*, Sathas, iv, p. 448.

T HE Byzantine Patriarch was chosen as an official of a Church that professed to contain all whether saints or sinners; he could not, and was not indeed expected to live in the devotional isolation that would win him the name of saint. To claim by reason of a right of suzerainty any powers of criticism, whether in the sphere of appointments, finance, or policy, was not within his prerogative. This is not to deny his importance, for in the routine of both political and ecclesiastical machinery his participation was as essential as that of the Emperor, while in any crisis of internal government his attitude was a vital factor. Patriarch and Emperor were integral parts of a single polity in which were united both ecclesiastical and political elements. Each had to play his part in the maintenance of an empire which was constantly menaced by external foes: disputes concerning their respective spheres of action were perilous and mutual support imperative. The history of the Macedonian and Comnenian Patriarchs admirably illustrates this finely adjusted balance, almost compromise, between Emperor and Patriarch, and it emphasizes the futility of any attempt at readjustment in favour of the Church; Nicholas in the tenth, and Cerularius in the eleventh century failed to achieve this, and justly so, since the only hope for the Byzantine Empire was in the continuation of its imperial traditions, unhampered by any suggestions of a dual control. Nor was there anything derogatory to the Church in such a tradition, for the Emperor was the protector not only of the secular well-being of his citizens, but of their orthodoxy.

Of the long line of Patriarchs holding office during the years 867–1185—thirty-five of them—nearly all were monks, but at least three were not fully ordained at the time of their election;[1] nearly all, at least before 1081, were of good family and were outstanding men. Of the three tenth-century Patriarchs who appear to be nonentities[2] two were deliberately appointed as such, and in the eleventh century the fact that nothing was known of Cosmas save that he was a pious monk with psychic powers was recorded by Scylitzes as though to suggest that this was an unusual occurrence.[3] The twelfth-century Patriarchs are of less interest than their Macedonian predecessors; they were almost completely under the control of the Comnenian Emperors, and less is known about them. There is, moreover, little that can compare with the vitality of the controversies between Ignatius and Photius in the ninth, Nicholas and Euthymius in the tenth, or the activities of Cerularius and Xiphilinus in the eleventh centuries. When the twelfth-century Patriarchs do appear from time to time, it is nearly always in the suppression of heresy, but even here it is plainly evident that the mainspring of the activity is imperial rather than patriarchal.[4] Theodosius (1178–83), who did show some signs of opposition to both Manuel and Andronicus Comnenus, could not affect a political situation already beyond recovery; in patriarchal as in secular politics, the impending disasters had already cast their shadows, and that contrast between the twelfth and the immediately preceding centuries is as strongly felt in ecclesiastical as in political spheres.

The duties of the Patriarch were such that they demanded qualities of statesmanship and capacity for administration, rather than those gifts usually associated with the monastic vocation; indeed, the monastic vows of Cerularius and Xiphilinus had been forced upon them by political reverses. It is therefore a mistake to suppose that the Patriarch was chosen because of his sense of religious vocation or his theological

[1] Photius, Cerularius, and Leichudes.
[2] Stephen II, Tryphon, and Nicholas II Chrysoberges.
[3] Scylitzes, ii, p. 731.   [4] See Chapter V.

ability. On the contrary, a Patriarch could not pursue the former, nor did the latter enter into consideration, save in so far as he was required to possess a knowledge of the canons and of the Church Fathers. It was too late for an Athanasius, and there had never been any place for an Innocent III; Byzantine theology had long since been stated in its classical form by John of Damascus, and Emperors normally chose for their Patriarchs men who lived reasonably good lives, who would co-operate with the secular departments, and administer their own special province with due regard to the wishes of the State.

The Emperor Basil I succeeded to a bitter ecclesiastical quarrel that had swept over Constantinople like 'a terrible storm'.[1] In 858 the Patriarch Ignatius, an austere and independent monk, had been deposed because he denounced the evil life of Michael III's minister, Caesar Bardas, and Photius, a layman and a man of great learning, had accepted the Patriarchate,[2] though Ignatius refused to abdicate. Consequently there was great antagonism between the Ignatians and monastic party, tending to look to Rome for support, and the Photians and upholders of a more independent policy, not that they hesitated to appeal to Rome if it suited their purposes. Basil I removed Photius 'and restored the saintly Ignatius, thus giving peace to the Church'.[3] To give peace to the Church was no doubt Basil's aim, but it was not so easy of accomplishment, especially as there was always the difficulty of the validity of the ordination of bishops consecrated by a Patriarch wrongly occupying a throne whose rightful owner was still alive. Each party in turn seems to have suffered, even to the length of exile and loss of office;[4] for instance, Nicholas, the abbot of the Studite monastery[5], refused to recognize Photius and was exiled.[6] Photius himself was twice exiled, the second time never to return. Even after the death of Ignatius, difficulties and hatreds must have lingered, for the writer of the

---

[1] *Vita S. Ignatii*, PG, cv, col. 497 D.

[2] Theoph. Cont., p. 195; Georg. Mon., p. 826.

[3] Theoph. Cont., p. 262; Georg. Mon., p. 841; Sym. Mag., pp. 688–9; Cedrenus, ii, p. 205.   [4] *Vita S. Ignatii*, PG, cv, col. 545 AB.

[5] i.e. the monastery of Studios in SW. Constantinople; cf. H. Delehaye, Stoudion-Stoudios, AB, 52 (1934), pp. 64–5, on the correct form of the wrongly called 'Studion'.   [6] *Vita S. Nicolai*, PG, cv, col. 909 B.

life of Ignatius's follower Nicholas, perhaps with natural exaggeration, implores his master to mediate for the peace of the
Church, 'you who guide the ship of your soul far from the
wild noise of tumults, . . . you who look down from the sky to
see churches being burnt and the land of the Christians stained
with blood. . . .'[1]

Photius, ὁ τολμητίας οὗτος,[2] if not 'the mainspring of the hypo-
crites and enemies of the cross' as the *Vita S. Ignatii* would like
to insist,[3] certainly had no desire to waste his time in exile, and
he endeavoured to return to Constantinople, perhaps not so
much 'corrupted by love of power and ambition', as it seemed to
his monastic enemies,[4] as longing to be once more in the centre
of all activity, the natural impulse of an enthusiastic scholar and
a vigorous statesman. He was restored to favour by Basil I, and
finally, when Ignatius brought his life to a close 'in a devoutness well pleasing to God', he again became Patriarch,[5] only
to be a second time deposed by the next Emperor, Leo VI,
who suspected him of poisoning his father's mind against him.
Famous as a scholar, and no less outstanding as a Patriarch,
he ended his days in exile. For this time he was not recalled,
and he lived only a few years after his final deposition.[6]

It is understandable that the Patriarch succeeding Photius on
his final deposition in 886 should be Stephen, the brother of the
Emperor. No doubt Leo VI hoped for a less partisan and more
amenable partner; nor was the choice unsuitable, for Stephen
was a cleric holding the important ecclesiastical office of syncellus.[7] This satisfactory arrangement did not last long, for
Stephen died in 893, and the monk Antony Cauleas became
Patriarch.[8] His *Life* speaks of a healing of the scars of the Church,
referring to the quarrel of Photius and Ignatius, and of the
understanding with the Pope of 900 when he, Antony, 'united

---

[1] *Vita S. Nicolai*, PG, cv, col. 925 A.
[2] *Vita S. Ignatii*, ibid., col. 573 B.
[3] Ibid., col. 573 C.   [4] Ibid., col. 548 A.
[5] Theoph. Cont., p. 276; Sym. Mag., p. 692; Cedrenus, ii, p. 213.
[6] See Hergenröther for a detailed account of Photius's activities and
writings.
[7] Georg. Mon., p. 849; Theoph. Cont., p. 354; Sym. Mag., p. 700;
Cedrenus, ii, p. 249.
[8] Georg. Mon., p. 852; Theoph. Cont., p. 357; Sym. Mag., p. 702; Cedrenus,
ii, pp. 253–4; *Vita S. Antonii*, PG, cvi, col. 190 AB.

the east and the west', which is somewhat of an exaggeration.[1]
Antony not only lived a holy life, which is described at length
in his biography, but, having the courage of his convictions, he
denounced that which seemed evil to him; in his protests against
the Emperor Leo's third marriage[2] he foreshadowed the out-
break of a fresh controversy under the Patriarchs Nicholas and
Euthymius.

When Antony Cauleas died, the Emperor's private secretary,
'a wise and prudent man', Nicholas Mysticus,[3] was elected
Patriarch,[4] and the Emperor no doubt imagined that he had
gained a willing ally. Leo VI's difficulty was that he needed an
heir, and had already married three times without success. When
he finally had a child in 905 he desired to have it both baptized
and crowned, and to legalize its future position by marrying its
mother. To baptism and coronation Nicholas agreed, but
nothing would persuade him to sanction the marriage, not even
a favourable opinion from the other patriarchates, including the
see of Rome. Therefore Nicholas was forced to abdicate, and
Euthymius, the syncellus, became Patriarch.[5] Although Euthymius appears in the chronicles as 'the syncellus',[6] his *Life* shows
that he was really a retiring and holy monk, who was pressed
against his will to accept this office, the duties of which he never
adequately fulfilled.[7] Euthymius acquiesced in Leo's fourth
marriage, and when, after this Emperor's death, he was deposed,
and even maltreated during the proceedings of the synod, he
quietly bore all insults and retired uncomplaining to monastic
life.[8] So in 912 Nicholas was once more Patriarch, and on the
death of the regent Alexander, Leo VI's brother, he gained an
increasingly large share in the government of Constantine VII,

---

[1] *Vita S. Antonii*, PG, cvi, col. 191 B.

[2] Georg. Mon., p. 858; Theoph. Cont., p. 361; Sym. Mag., pp. 702–3;
Cedrenus, ii, p. 258.

[3] The word *mysticus* here means private secretary.

[4] Georg. Mon., p. 860; Theoph. Cont., p. 364; Sym. Mag., p. 703;
Cedrenus, ii, p. 259.

[5] Georg. Mon., p. 865; Theoph. Cont., pp. 370–1; Sym. Mag., p. 709;
Cedrenus, ii, pp. 264–5.

[6] The syncellus appears to have been next in importance to the Patriarch.
See Du Cange, *Gloss. ad script. med. et infim. graec.* under σύγκελλος, and
Vogt, *Basil I*er, pp. 262–4.   [7] *Vita S. Euthymii*, ch. 4, pp. 11 ff.

[8] Georg. Mon., p. 871; Theoph. Cont., p. 378; Sym. Mag., p. 716;
Cedrenus, ii, pp. 274–5.

who was still a child.[1] Finally, after many palace intrigues, he was turned out by the queen-mother, Zoe, who told him to confine himself to the affairs of the Church.[2] But all the various parties in the regency fell to pieces before Romanus Lecapenus, who controlled the government from 919 onwards. Nicholas remained Patriarch, and the Church was united and peace made between all the metropolitans and clergy who had been divided by the rift between Euthymius and Nicholas.[3]

This great struggle had centred not so much round the Patriarchs as men, as round the principle of fourth marriages and the problem of imperial privilege. Nicholas wrote an uncompromising letter to the Pope, claiming that emperors least of all could demand uncanonical concessions;[4] but as usually happened in Constantinople, the Patriarch was forced to capitulate, in practice, if not in theory. The rift was healed by the Tomus Unionis, with which Nicholas had to content himself. This, a condemnation of fourth marriages in general, was accepted in 920 by a synod in Constantinople, which was attended by legates from Rome.

Nicholas arrests attention by reason of his development from an imperial official into a Patriarch with a definite conception of the duties of his high office. His conduct shows in him a readiness to concern himself with temporal affairs, even to the length of being implicated in treason: on the other hand, he consistently refused to legalize the Emperor's fourth marriage, and justly so, if the validity of the Church canons was to be maintained. The *Vita S. Euthymii* paints Nicholas as a worldly minded scholar in contrast to the virtuous and saintly Euthymius, but that was natural. Euthymius, who was so unwilling a syncellus that he grudged one day a month to his new duties, and who rightly refused to become Patriarch again when the queen-mother Zoe quarrelled with Nicholas, was clearly suited to the monastic life. Nicholas, in spite of his shortcomings, was an efficient Patriarch, and one who could ably take his stand by the Emperor on public occasions as demanded by Byzantine etiquette and custom; and

---

[1] Georg. Mon., p. 874; Theoph. Cont., p. 381; Sym. Mag., p. 718; Cedrenus, ii, p. 278. [2] Theoph. Cont., p. 386.
[3] Georg. Mon., pp. 890–1; Theoph. Cont., p. 398.
[4] PG, cxi, cols. 196 ff., *Ep.* 32.

when Romanus I met the Bulgarian Emperor Symeon, the
chronicles note that he was accompanied by the Patriarch[1]
who could fittingly symbolize that dignity of the Orthodox
Church which so impressed its neighbours. Nicholas's letters
reveal the wide range of his activity and the ability with which
he had grasped the meaning of his ecclesiastical duties in their
spiritual as well as their temporal sense. He writes to Popes,
Emperors, metropolitans, bishops, monks, and all kinds of laymen, and always with the appropriate feeling of balance, dignity,
decision. To monks he can speak of the excellence of monastic
life, even though realizing that this is somewhat outside his own
experience; to the Pope of the canonical authority for his opposition to the Emperor's marriage; to each of his many correspon-
dents in accordance with their needs, though perhaps sometimes
with a lack of enthusiasm.

As in the case of the eleventh-century Michael Cerularius,
to attempt to find in Nicholas any formulation of a theory of
the supremacy of the Church, is to misread Byzantine history;
there was, indeed, little practical assertion of this in Nicholas's
actions. Byzantine Patriarchs played with politics according to
their inclination and the needs of the moment, and, remember-
ing Nicholas's past experience as the adviser of Leo VI, there is
nothing surprising in his domination of the troubled regency of
Constantine VII. Once a strong secular ruler took command,
Nicholas sank into his proper place as adviser in spiritual, and
sometimes secular,[2] affairs; though he could write a somewhat
stiff letter to Romanus I, exhorting him to lead a life of integrity
and to give thanks to God for all His benefits to His creatures of
whom Romanus, the Emperor, was one,[3] yet he did not claim
any *right* of control in spheres other than his own, nor could he
successfully establish his claim to supremacy in matters which
fell within the ecclesiastical domain. There is no doubt that he
wished to maintain the dignity of the see of Constantinople:
witness his anxiety to retain control over the infant Church of
Bulgaria, and to gain Rome's acknowledgement that, at least in

[1] Georg. Mon., p. 899; Sym. Mag., p. 736; Cedrenus, ii, p. 304.

[2] Especially in the case of Symeon of Bulgaria, where there was a marked
interpenetration of secular and spiritual interests by reason of the position of
the Bulgarian Church in relation to the Patriarchate of Constantinople.

[3] PG, cxi, cols. 384–5, *Ep.* 156.

theory, he had right on his side in the question of fourth marriages. But such was a proper pride that in no way affected the practical subordination of the Patriarch to the Emperor.

Romanus I may have found working with Nicholas a strain, and he evidently considered that he would find a safer alliance in the appointment of a member of his own family as Patriarch. He selected his son, Theophylactus, and since he was still a boy on Nicholas's death, he meanwhile obtained the appointment first of Stephen,[1] and then, on his premature death, of Tryphon.[2] Stephen was Metropolitan of Amasea and a eunuch, and the chronicles note Romanus's intention and say that Theophylactus, although not yet old enough to become Patriarch, was already a subdeacon and the syncellus. Tryphon, a monk and a holy man from the Opsician theme, abdicated, but it is not clear why, and Romanus still waited for some months after this before he had Theophylactus elected Patriarch.[3]

The story of Theophylactus is often quoted to show the ease with which the imperial control over the Patriarchate could be abused. He was only sixteen years old at the time of his appointment, while all his life he showed an unbecomingly active enthusiasm for horses. Cedrenus gives the well-known story of how the report that his favourite mare had foaled was brought to him while he was celebrating the Eucharist; when he heard the glad news, he finished the liturgy 'in any old way' and rushed off to see what was happening.[4] This is all no doubt true, but even Theophylactus seems to have shown the reverence for a saint which is so marked a Byzantine characteristic; in the *Life* of S. Luke the Stylite it is told how Theophylactus was healed of an illness by the saint,[5] and mounting to the top of the pillar by means of the usual ladder, 'he visited the Stylite, not once or twice but often'.[6]

Theophylactus's twenty-three years of office covered a large part of Romanus I's reign, and nearly the whole of the period

---

[1] Georg. Mon., p. 902; Theoph. Cont., pp. 409–10; Sym. Mag., p. 739; Cedrenus, ii, pp. 306–7.

[2] Georg. Mon., p. 908; Theoph. Cont., p. 417; Sym. Mag., p. 742; Cedrenus, ii, p. 311.

[3] Georg. Mon., pp. 911–12; Theoph. Cont., p. 421; Sym. Mag., pp. 742–3, 744–5; Cedrenus, ii, pp. 313–15.

[4] Cedrenus, ii, pp. 332–3; Theoph. Cont., p. 444.

[5] *Vita S. Lucae Stylitae*, ed. Vogt, p. 34.   [6] Ibid., p. 35.

when Constantine VII was reigning alone. When he died in 956, Polyeuctus, described with the usual provoking monotony as 'a most devout monk', became Patriarch.[1] Polyeuctus was not only a man 'learned in human and divine philosophy',[2] but one who ably maintained the traditions of his office during difficult times. It was to Polyeuctus that Nicephorus Phocas appealed for protection when he feared for his command and even his life;[3] it was to Polyeuctus that Nicephorus, as Co-Emperor, sent to ask for recognition and coronation;[4] it was by Polyeuctus that he was reproved for his marriage with Romanus II's widow Theophano.[5] Polyeuctus, who dared to deny Nicephorus access to the sanctuary in S. Sophia, proved even more exacting to Nicephorus's murderer and successor, John Tzimisces. The Patriarch's expectations from the monastically inclined Nicephorus had certainly been shaken, first by the Emperor's marriage, then by his attack on ecclesiastical property; from John Tzimisces he abruptly and successfully demanded his terms at the outset, even to the sacrifice of a private fortune and a wife elect. Tzimisces's obedience was prudent: he made a better marriage with the daughter of Constantine VII, and part at least of his own wealth would inevitably have gone in the customary largess. As it was he gained the benefit of the Patriarch's support, with the necessary coronation, as well as creating on the public mind the effect of a devout and penitent Emperor.

When Polyeuctus died, Tzimisces produced the monk Basil Scamandrenus, a perfect mirror of virtue,[6] but after a short time he was deposed in circumstances which suggest treasonable activities.[7] Antony, 'an angelic man', was a Studite and syncellus.[8] Between his death and the election of the monk Nicholas Chrysoberges was an interval of four years according to Cedrenus,[9] but Schlumberger[10] puts this between Nicholas's death and the election of Sisinnius, during which time the Emperor Basil II was in Bulgaria. Basil's Patriarchs did not

---

[1] Theoph. Cont., p. 444; Cedrenus, ii, p. 334.   [2] Leo Diaconus, p. 32.
[3] Leo Diaconus, p. 32.   [4] Ibid., pp. 44–5; Cedrenus, ii, p. 351.
[5] Leo Diaconus, pp. 49–50; Cedrenus, ii, p. 352.   [6] Cedrenus, ii, p. 382.
[7] Leo Diaconus, p. 163; Cedrenus, ii, pp. 414–15.
[8] Leo Diaconus, pp. 164–5.   [9] Cedrenus, ii, p. 434.
[10] L'épopée byzantine, ii, p. 117, note continued from p. 116.

have as much occasion for secular activity as their immediate
predecessors, and once Basil Scamandrenus had been disposed
of, they take no prominent place in the politics of the period.
Sisinnius (995–8?) was a layman and a well-known doctor, but
with the latent Byzantine interest in theological matters, he
considered it his duty to make a final statement on the invalidity
of fourth marriages.[1] Sergius, an abbot and a relative of Photius,
was Patriarch after Sisinnius for nearly twenty years of Basil's
reign, and Cedrenus records that he vainly protested against
Basil's reimposition of the allelengyon tax;[2] he had become well
known since it is supposed that during his reign the Pope's
name was omitted from the prayers of the liturgy. When he
died (1019), Eustathius, chief presbyter of the imperial Church,
was elected,[3] and he only died a few days before Basil's own
death (1025).[4]

The end of Basil II's reign is often said to coincide with the
end of the prosperity of the Macedonian house, and this is
indeed true, but it might be added that, although during the
years 1025–81 politics fell upon evil days, yet in some ways these
years mark a steady growth, as in the interest in learning, and
in others they at least show no falling away, as in the standard
maintained by their Patriarchs.

Alexius the Studite (1025–43) fulfilled the duties of his office
admirably, and his experience as abbot of the important Studite
monastery, as well as his own common sense, enabled him to
maintain good relations with the secular authorities during the
very difficult period which ended with the defeat of the Emperor
Michael V, while at the same time he parried with success the
intrigues and attacks of his enemies. Michael I Cerularius (1043–
58) was of other calibre, and his election was a mistake, except
that it was probably safer to have him as Patriarch than as a
rival for the imperial throne. Constantine III Leichudes (1059–
63) was more like Alexius, but cast in a finer mould; by nature
and vocation a statesman,[5] he was as successful in his short
tenure of ecclesiastical office as he had been in the service of

---

[1] Cedrenus, ii, pp. 448–9.   [2] Cedrenus, ii, p. 475.
[3] Ibid., p. 476.   [4] Ibid., p. 479.
[5] He was the only Patriarch during the eleventh century who was not a
monk.

the State. John VIII Xiphilinus (1063–75), the best, and certainly the most single-minded, of the eleventh-century Patriarchs, used his legal training and his monastic experience in order to improve the standard of his secular clergy, and as far as he could he avoided political controversy.

The period of the Comneni was fittingly inaugurated by Cosmas I of Jerusalem (1075–81), 'a certain monk',[1] who was a failure, for he could neither control his own bishops nor retain his office against imperial opposition. Nevertheless, before he could be persuaded to abdicate, he insisted on crowning Alexius Comnenus's wife, Irene Ducas, as Empress, to the anger of the Emperor's mother, Anna Dalassena, who bitterly hated the Ducas family and wanted the marriage dissolved.[2] By his very failure Cosmas marks the contrast between Church and State. Hitherto the assumption had generally been that the Patriarch was to be an active partner in a single polity: henceforth there is little evidence of any real partnership, and even such purely ecclesiastical matters as the morale of the clergy or the suppression of heresy appear to fall to the imperial decision. To insist on this is neither to over-emphasize the imperial control nor to suggest that the Emperor acted without due regard for the ecclesiastical machinery, but it became increasingly evident that the vital factor was the imperial power and that the Patriarchs took a subordinate place. Compare Photius's activity in his councils, Polyeuctus's successful refusal to allow the Emperor Nicephorus his customary right of access in S. Sophia, or Xiphilinus's care for justice and admonishment of Constantine X, with the twelfth-century acquiescence and stifled opposition, when the only real dissent of the Patriarch Theodosius is unavailing, and, in spite of popular support, he retires to his monastery in 1183, giving way to a successor who promised to obey the Emperor in all things.[3]

Cosmas, whose abdication had opened the period of the Comneni, was followed by Eustratius Garidas, a monk and nominee of Anna Dalassena, who was forced to resign his office after three years;[4] the reason of his offence was not stated by the

[1] Scylitzes, ii, p. 731.   [2] Anna Comnena, iii. 2 (i, pp. 97 ff.).
[3] Nicetas Choniates, p. 339.
[4] Anna Comnena, x. 2 (ii, p. 60); Zonaras, xviii. 21 (iii, p. 734).

chroniclers, but he was known to be in sympathy with John Italus's heretical doctrines.[1] After these two troubled patriarchates neither Alexius nor John Comnenus had any further difficulties; during the years 1084–1145 there were three Patriarchs, Nicholas the Grammarian,[2] John Agapetes,[3] and Leo Stypes.

Manuel Comnenus had nine Patriarchs. The first, Michael, a monk from the monastery on Oxeia, abdicated soon after his election because he longed to return to monastic life.[4] Cosmas, a deacon of S. Sophia, a learned and good man, was deposed against his will for suspected complicity in a political plot, the alleged excuse being his friendship with Niphon, a monk accused of heresy.[5] Then followed Nicholas III Muzalon (1147–51), an important ecclesiastic of Cyprus, who had to abdicate apparently because of an uncanonical election.[6] Theodotus (or Theodosius), a man 'well versed in the monastic life', succeeded him[7] for three years. After this the Patriarchs disappear more and more out of the chroniclers' eyes and a casual remark such as 'Luke, who was then ruling the Church' suffices.[8] But, on the other hand, they took their due part in the synods for the discussion of heresies and they figure in accounts of these, but never as leaders.[9] Nicetas Choniates does give some information concerning the most courageous of the twelfth-century Patriarchs, Theodosius Boradiotes (1178–83) but rather as throwing light on the imperial conduct than reflecting upon the Patriarch, and in any case by Andronicus Comnenus's time the situation was beyond the control of the wisest Patriarch. Perhaps if the twelfth century had anything corresponding to Psellus's eleventh-century history and funeral orations it would be easier to understand what manner of men its Patriarchs were, and if they were as lifeless and subservient as they nearly all appear to be in comparison with those of the Macedonian times.

The normal canonical mode of appointment had been the election of a cleric by the bishops and people, subject to the imperial confirmation. But it had long been clear that the

---

[1] Anna Comnena, v. 9 (i, p. 183).
[2] Zonaras, xviii. 21 (iii, p. 734) and xviii, 25 (iii, p. 750).   [3] Ibid., p. 751.
[4] Nicetas Choniates, p. 70 and pp. 105–6.   [5] Ibid., pp. 106 ff.
[6] Cinnamus, ii, 18 (pp. 83–4).   [7] Ibid., p. 84.
[8] Ibid., vi, 96 (p. 278).   [9] See Chapter V.

Emperor's pleasure could in the end outweigh any genuine elective element. Ignatius's fate in the ninth century well illustrates the importance of the imperial influence. And when Photius writes of his own election he speaks of the bishops and metropolitans, but justly stresses the part played by 'the Emperor, who, with them [i.e. the clergy] is the upholder of the true faith and of Christ . . .'[1] It was equally clear that the imposition of an imperial policy was not unquestioned in the ninth and early tenth centuries, as is shown by the open opposition of the partisans on either side. It is not without point that during these years members of the imperial family were twice deliberately selected some time in advance as Patriarch elect; obviously the Emperor must have been sure of his control over the election, but he must also have felt some need for ensuring peaceful co-operation. But according to the *Life of S. Anthony Cauleas*, at the beginning of the tenth century there was still some semblance of choice left with the elective bodies; it speaks of 'the votes of all the bishops and priests, and of those who were leading the monastic life, and also of the Senate', and of the imperial confirmation of the election.[2]

By the middle of the tenth century the legal fiction of an election had evidently become regularized. The canonical procedure described in the *De cerimoniis* was for the synod to select three candidates, present their names to the Emperor, and await his choice. But apart from the intangible pressure of imperial influence before the selection of the three names, should the Emperor still be unable to find among the three a name of which he approved, he would then set these aside and make his own nomination. In either case the synod then proceeded to ratify the imperial choice, though this was usually spoken of as an 'election'.[3]

The patriarchal elections most fully described within this period are those of the eleventh century, and a study of these provides proof of the imperial influence. Alexius was nominated by Basil II just before his death in 1025, and there is not even evidence of any ratification by the synod. Cedrenus writes: 'A

[1] PG, cii, *Ep.* 1, col. 588 C.   [2] PG, cvi, col. 190 A.
[3] Constantine VII Porphyrogenitus, *De cerimoniis aulae byz.*, ii. 14 (CB, i, pp. 564 ff.); cf. W. Fischer, *Studien*, p. 51, note 8.

few days before his death [i.e. Basil II] the Patriarch Eustathius
died; and the Emperor appointed as his successor the monk
Alexius who was abbot of the Studite monastery, and who had
come to visit him bearing the head of John the Baptist for him
to venerate. He was at once enthroned by the protonotarius
John, who assisted the Emperor in important public matters'.[1]
It is possible that the formality of election by the synod was
postponed owing to the death of the Emperor, and was not
considered necessary by his indolent brother, but it was the
charge of Alexius's political opponents in Michael IV's reign
that his appointment had been uncanonical.[2]

Cerularius at first appears to be likewise an imperial nomination. He was a man high in the favour of Constantine IX,[3] and
not inclined by nature towards any religious vocation or ecclesiastical office. He was, in fact, reported to be reluctant to accept
the appointment.[4] Cedrenus only says: 'After the death of the
Patriarch Alexius, on the Feast of the Annunciation, Michael
Cerularius, who had lived as a monk since he was exiled by
the Orphanotrophus for political intrigue, was raised to the
patriarchal throne[5].' There is nothing to suggest that Michael
Cerularius was elected by the synod, except the words of the
Accusation which was to have been brought against him by
Isaac Comnenus. Here Psellus, who had been chosen to voice
the imperial charges, speaks of corruption towards 'electors',[6]
which would suggest the synod, and it is unlikely that he would
have introduced into a public speech before that body facts
which it would be the first to recognize as false. Moreover,
there is further difficulty over Michael Cerularius's appointment, since circumstances point to some disreputable understanding with the Emperor. During the months that elapsed
between Alexius's death and Michael Cerularius's investiture
Constantine took a large sum of money from Alexius's private
monastic coffers[7] and there is no evidence of any protest from

[1] Cedrenus, ii, pp. 479–80.
[2] Cedrenus, ii, p. 517. The reproach was that he had not been chosen by
'the votes of the archbishops'.
[3] Psellus, *Funeral Oration*, ed. Sathas, iv, p. 324.
[4] Ibid., pp. 326–7.   [5] Cedrenus, ii, p. 550.
[6] Psellus, *Accusation*, ed. Bréhier, p. 63. Ἀφίημι . . . τὴν ἐπαγγελίαν, τὸν
δεκασμόν, τὴν ψῆφον.   [7] Cedrenus, ii, p. 550.

the Patriarch, while it is possible to connect this episode with
the discreditable 'promise' mentioned by Psellus in connexion
with Cerularius's election, but without any detail concerning
it.[1] At the time of his appointment Michael Cerularius was not
yet ordained, and this was one of the charges which Leo IX
later made against him;[2] but according to the *Anonymous
Chronicle* of the thirteenth century he had been 'a syncellus
at the time of his appointment',[3] that is, the deputy of the
Patriarch, who always had the rank of a bishop. Moreover, if
Psellus's panegyric is to be believed, Constantine IX had destined Cerularius to be Patriarch since their first meeting, when the
Emperor exclaimed, 'Here is the man who should be Patriarch
of Constantinople'.[4]

With the appointment of Leichudes, for the first time in the
eleventh century there is mention of an election. 'In his [i.e.
Michael Cerularius's] place Constantine Leichudes the proedrus
and protovestiarius was chosen Patriarch, after he had been
elected by the votes of the metropolitans and clerics and the
whole people.'[5] Psellus, though he does not mention an election,
speaks of other candidates who failed in competition with
so illustrious and virtuous a man who could bring to his
ecclesiastical office the seasoned wisdom of a πολιτικὸν
φρόνημα.[6] The interesting words in Scylitzes' evidence are
' the clerics and whole people', since the normal organ for election was the synod. Fischer argues that the inclusion of other
elements was a stroke of policy, in order to conciliate the people,
who venerated Cerularius for his opposition to Rome, and the
clergy, who upheld his attempt to assert the spiritual supremacy

---

[1] Psellus, *Accusation*, ed. Bréhier, p. 74. This supports Gfrörer's suggestion that there was an arrangement between Constantine and Cerularius;
but his surmise (iii, pp. 267–76) that the month's interval was used for purposes of a bargain whereby the Emperor was to be given the nomination of
the officials of the Great Church is probably unjustified, because as Scabalanovitch points out (p. 375) the interval could well have been filled with ceremonies, and further the Emperor already had control of such officials.

[2] 'Diceris neophytus.' Will, p. 90 (26), quoted by L. Bréhier, *Le schisme
oriental*, p. 63.

[3] Sathas, vii, p. 164, quoted by Bréhier, *Le schisme oriental*, p. 63, note 1.

[4] Psellus, *Funeral Oration*, ed. Sathas, iv, p. 324.

[5] Scylitzes, ii, p. 644. Cf. Attaleiates, p. 66, who only says that Leichudes
was 'chosen' Patriarch.

[6] Psellus, *Chron.* vii. 66 (ii, p. 124).

of the Church.[1] The arguments against this are that there
appears to be no evidence to support the statement that the
people attached any importance to the schism, which was largely
a question of politics, and, secondly, that to impute to the
Byzantine clerics a desire for a strong demarcation between the
spheres of State and Church would be to interpret the history of
the Eastern Empire in the light of the experience of western
Europe. If the statement of Scylitzes is accurate, and there
seems no reason for doubting it, then the most natural explanation is found in the difficulty, and perhaps unpopularity, which
Cerularius's untimely death brought to Isaac Comnenus. As he
had already been forced to enlist the aid of a synod in his plan
for the deposition of Cerularius, he no doubt felt it judicious to
employ the same authority to give a canonical seal to the
election of the new Patriarch. Not that this indicated any
real diminution of his power, as the incident of the πρόνοια[2]
of the Mangana shows. Leichudes had been given this by
Constantine IX, and on his election as Patriarch still retained it.
There arose, however, some hindrance in his ordination, and
hence in his enthronement, but once he resigned the πρόνοια
of the Mangana to the Emperor, his ordination proceeded
smoothly and he was invested as Patriarch.[3]

Leichudes' successor was chosen with equal formality, though
the precedent of the previous election was not followed so far
as concerns the participation of the clergy and the whole people.
Some months elapsed between Leichudes' death and Xiphilinus's appointment, because there was evidently difficulty in
finding a suitable candidate. Scylitzes says the Emperor chose
Xiphilinus and, after a brief discussion of his virtues, he adds
'since there was nobody else worthy of appointment to the
high honour of the patriarchal rank, and, though reluctant and
hesitant, he was forced to accept this honour'.[4] This is confirmed by Attaleiates.[5] Neither mentions the mode of appointment, and Gfrörer argues from the passage in Scylitzes that the
choice, though in accordance with the imperial wishes, was the

[1] W. Fischer, Studien, pp. 52–3.
[2] For a discussion on the πρόνοια see A. A. Vasiliev, On the question of
Byzantine feudalism, B, viii (1933), fasc. 2, pp. 590 ff.
[3] Scylitzes, ii, pp. 644–5.   [4] Ibid., p. 658.
[5] Attaleiates, p. 93; cf. Psellus, Sathas, iv, p. 448.

result of activity on the part of the court and senate.[1] Fischer
considers this improbable and quotes Psellus's words in
the *Funeral Oration*, when he says that everybody voted for
Xiphilinus, adding 'for it was the decision and preference
not of those from afar (πόρρωθεν), but of those within the
walls',[2] interpreting οἱ ἐντὸς τειχῶν as referring to the metropolitans.[3] In this oration Psellus describes the dearth of
good candidates, the anxiety of the Emperor, the suggestion of
Xiphilinus, who was then abbot of Mt. Olympus, that Mt.
Olympus might furnish the right man, and the realization that
the solution lay in Xiphilinus's own acceptance of the office.
There seems no ground for Gfrörer's suggestion that Xiphilinus
had always considered the possibility of this appointment, and
that, as with Michael Cerularius, his reluctance was feigned,[4]
or for the doubt which Fischer casts upon the influence which
Psellus claims to have exerted on Xiphilinus's behalf.[5] 'I have not
striven for this office of Patriarch', said Xiphilinus to Psellus, 'it
is your influence with the Emperor that has accomplished this.'[6]
Scabalanovitch accepts Psellus's statement,[7] and, although the
funeral orations are always open to suspicion, there appears to be
no reason for questioning this passage. Xiphilinus's subsequent
attack on Psellus is consistent with the logic and directness
of his character,[8] he would not have been moved from what he
considered his duty whether his friend had or had not rendered
him assistance in obtaining the patriarchal throne.[9]

[1] Gfrörer, iii, p. 674. Scylitzes, ii, p. 658, says Ξιφιλῖνος προχειρίζεται,
and then goes on to speak of the election to the Bulgarian Archbishopric
with the words "προχειρίζεται ὁ βασιλεὺς Ἰωάννην . . ." But προχειρίζεται
without any definite mention of the Emperor is the usual word for the patriarchal election, at least in the chronicles of the Macedonian period. Cf.
Theophanes Continuatus, p. 357, where he uses it of the elevation to the
Patriarchate of Antony Cauleas, who, according to the *Vita S. Antonii
Cauleae*, PG, cvi, col. 190 A, was chosen by the clergy and senate, the election being subsequently confirmed by the Emperor.
[2] Sathas, iv, p. 446. [3] Fischer, *Studien* p. 24, note 4.
[4] Gfrörer, iii, p. 673. [5] Fischer, *Studien*, p. 24, note 7.
[6] Sathas, iv, p. 448. [7] Scabalanovitch, p. 396.
[8] Cf. Xiphilinus's sermons, PG, cxx, cols. 1201–92.
[9] It is possible that the later enmity of Xiphilinus and Psellus has been
exaggerated,due to a tendency to over-emphasize what was really a difference
arising from the essential antagonism of their temperaments and interests.
In the *Chronographia* Psellus speaks of Xiphilinus in terms of admiration and
affection, nor is this inconsistent with their disputes.

When Xiphilinus died after sixteen years of office, he was succeeded by Cosmas, who was chosen by Michael VII, while practically nothing is known about the mode of his appointment; Scylitzes says: 'the Emperor chose another Patriarch, a man not of senatorial rank, or of the Church, nor indeed any Byzantine famous in word and deed, but Cosmas, a certain monk from the Holy City, who was held in great honour by the Emperor on account of his sanctity.'[1]

The imperial concern shown throughout the Macedonian period over the elections indicates the importance of the office, and the Comnenian appointments show no deviation from the principles of previous centuries. There is little doubt that in practice the will of the Emperor was responsible for what he considered to be a judicious choice. The delicacy of relationship between Emperor and Patriarch can be explained not only by the importance of the ecclesiastical well-being of the Empire, but by the inevitable necessity for the Patriarch's co-operation in matters of secular politics.

The outstanding example of this necessity for co-operation was the performance of certain ceremonies with which the Emperor could not dispense. Coronation, whatever may have been its origin, had by the time of the Macedonians acquired a spiritual as well as a secular significance, fittingly symbolizing the ultimate union of Church and State which characterized the Byzantine polity; and the accession of every Emperor was marked by the patriarchal sanction, not that this really increased the power of the Patriarch, because in most cases he did not dare refuse. Akin to coronation was imperial marriage, and again the Patriarch usually had to condone in practice what he could only condemn as an infringement of canon law. This has already been well illustrated by the imperial difficulties of Leo VI and Nicephorus Phocas. It is true that in case of patriarcha obstinacy, marriage might be performed by a priest, but coronation was the Patriarch's prerogative for which there was no substitute, and a ceremony of such importance that it is nearly always mentioned by the chroniclers. For instance, Constantine VII was crowned and married by Nicholas,[2] the same Patriarch crowned Romanus I,[3] Romanus II's infant son was crowned by

[1] Scylitzes, ii, p. 731.   [2] Theoph. Cont., p. 394.   [3] Ibid., p. 398.

Polyeuctus,[1] and both Nicephorus and Tzimisces, knowing it to
be vital to obtain an immediate coronation, hastened to gain the
support of him 'who held the key of things divine'.[2] As in the
case of patriarchal elections, the fullest information concerning
the imperial coronations comes from Psellus and the eleventh
century. When Romanus III died, or was poisoned, in 1034, the
first thought of John the Orphanotrophus, who was responsible
for the intrigue, was to arrange for the immediate recognition
of his brother Michael as Emperor, and at midnight the Patriarch
Alexius was hastily summoned to marry the ancient Empress
Zoe to Michael, as a preliminary to the coronation. Though
Romanus was scarcely dead, Alexius found Zoe and Michael
crowned and sitting on the imperial thrones, in the royal gar-
ments which were woven of the famous gold tissue.[3] The horrified Patriarch was hastily presented with fifty pounds of gold for
himself, another fifty for the clergy, and 'thus he was persuaded
to perform the marriage ceremony'.[4] Neither Cedrenus nor
Psellus mention a ceremony in S. Sophia, but it is in any case
evident from Cedrenus that the Patriarch's assistance was an
essential preliminary to the recognition of Michael as Emperor.

In the case of Michael V, who ascended the throne in 1041 as
the adopted son of the Empress Zoe, Psellus is more explicit,
and mentions 'the mystery of recognition as Emperor, the procession, the entry into the church, the blessing of the Patriarch, the
coronation and all else that customarily attends the ceremony',[5]
while Cedrenus only remarks that 'he was crowned by the
Patriarch'.[6] After the forced abdication of Michael the reluctant
Theodora was hurriedly crowned at midnight in S. Sophia,[7]
but this proved only a temporary solution, and Zoe insisted on
finding an Emperor and third husband in Constantine Monomachus. The Church forbade third marriages, but since he
could not prevent the marriage the Patriarch Alexius withdrew
until this ceremony had been performed by a protopresbyter of
S. Sophia. 'He himself would not lay his hands on them during
the coronation, but once they were married and crowned, he

---

[1] Theoph. Cont., p. 473.
[2] Leo Diaconus, pp. 44–5; p. 98; Cedrenus, ii, p. 351.
[3] Psellus, *Chron.* iv. 2 (i, p. 54); there is no mention here of the Patriarch
Alexius.   [4] Cedrenus, ii, p. 505.   [5] Psellus, *Chron.* v. 5 (i, p. 88).
[6] Cedrenus, ii, p. 535.   [7] Psellus, *Chron.* v. 37 (i, pp. 108–9).

saluted them.'[1] Cedrenus, however, says that, after they had been married, 'they were crowned on the following day by the Patriarch'.[2] There seems to be here some confusion between the marriage ceremony and the coronation, but the marriage service of the Orthodox Church contains the ritual of crowning which would naturally not take the place of the ceremonial of the coronation service.

There is no need to mention in detail the coronations of the second half of the eleventh and the twelfth centuries; it will suffice to say that this ceremony is never omitted, and it is always the Patriarch whose special function it is·to officiate. He might show his disapproval by refusing personal attendance at an imperial marriage, and Cosmas even went so far as to degrade the priest who married Nicephorus III Botaneiates to Maria, whose husband was still alive,[3] though he himself made no effort to prevent the marriage. But to refuse to assist at a coronation would have been a dangerous action. It is significant that although during the years 1025–81 no less than seven Emperors owed their accession to a revolution, basing their claims to the throne on political necessity rather than right of inheritance, yet no Patriarch refused coronation. Whatever may have been their influence in advancing or retarding a particular candidate to the throne, they dared not take the risk of opposing a *fait accompli*. They realized that Byzantium had sufficient troubles without complicating the issue by the assertion of any misplaced ecclesiastical prerogative.

It is, nevertheless, not to be denied that the Patriarch could, and did, exert influence in secular affairs, although his disapproval was on the whole that of an unpleasant rather than a dangerous enemy. Alexius's antagonism to the Paphlagonian régime and sympathy for the deluded Zoe forms one of the definite undercurrents of the reigns of Michael IV and Michael V. The realization of this probably accounts for John the Orphanotrophus's determination to depose Alexius on the ground that his election was uncanonical, and to obtain his own appointment to so important an office. Alexius cleverly defeated his opponent, who was supported by certain of the metropolitans,

[1] Psellus, *Chron.* vi. 20 (i, p. 127).   [2] Cedrenus, ii, p. 542.
[3] Scylitzes, ii, p. 738.

by stating that if his election were uncanonical, then all his appointments were equally invalid.[1]   Michael V, antagonistic as he was to the policy of his uncle John, realized the enmity of Alexius, and considered the possibility of his removal.[2]   The Patriarch was virtually imprisoned in his monastery at the Stenum, and only by bribing the guard did he contrive to escape to S. Sophia.[3]   He undoubtedly encouraged the opposition to Michael V; he did nothing to protect the unfortunate Emperor, but supported the revolution which produced first Theodora as Co-Empress, and then Constantine IX as Emperor.

Alexius's successor, Michael Cerularius, was still more predominant a figure in contemporary politics.   His story centres in his attempt to make the Church more powerful than the State, and as such deserves special treatment; but it may be noted here that he facilitated the accession of Isaac Comnenus, both by his personal support and by persuading Michael VI to abdicate and enter a monastery. He was, moreover, so difficult an enemy that Isaac Comnenus was preparing to depose him when the Patriarch died before the sentence could be pronounced.

Leichudes, Xiphilinus, and Cosmas all assisted at an abdication of some kind, though they were not primarily responsible for these political revolutions.   Leichudes used his influence to persuade Isaac Comnenus to become a monk;[4] Xiphilinus sanctioned the succession of Romanus IV in contradiction to Constantine X's express intentions;[5] Cosmas, obviously as the mouthpiece of the Comneni, urged Nicephorus III to abdicate.[6] The Patriarch thus stood in the position of moral tutor to the Emperor, and was often employed as the agent through whom political opponents might dictate their terms.

Cerularius's attempt to become the master of both Church and State was an exception which formed a strong contrast to the normal attitude of the Patriarch, and its attendant difficulties explain the wisdom of the Byzantine insistence, at least in practice, on the subordination of the Patriarchate to the Empire. In

---

[1] Cedrenus, ii, p. 517.

[2] Schlumberger, L'épopée byzantine, iii, pp. 343–4, quotes the evidence of the historian Ibn el-Athîr.   [3] Cedrenus, ii, p. 536; Schlumberger, loc. cit.

[4] Psellus, Chron. vii. 18 and 79 (ii, p. 93 and p. 132).

[5] Cedrenus, ii, p. 666; cf. Zonaras, xviii. 10 (iii, pp. 685 ff.).

[6] Anna Comnena, ii. 12 (i, p. 92)

the *Funeral Oration* Psellus gives a picture of Cerularius's character which, with obvious reservations, is not incompatible with that of the *Accusation* and *Letters*. The *Accusation* explains the reasons why Isaac Comnenus wished the synod to depose Cerularius, and is therefore hostile in tone, but, allowing for rhetorical exaggeration and some misinterpretation of facts, as, for instance, the events after Michael VI's abdication, its portrayal of Cerularius is consistent with his character. The *Funeral Oration* was written in the following reign, when Constantine X established a yearly festival in honour of the dead Patriarch, whose niece Eudoxia he had married, and as a panegyric it naturally gives a favourable interpretation of his life. Cerularius was a man ruled by reason rather than feeling, relentless and calculating, capable of private ascetic devotion, but proud and overbearing in public life, believing that his power was derived from God. He was destined by nature for imperial rule, and it was the misfortune of fate that he was constrained to take refuge in the office of Patriarch. But it would be a mistake to attribute to Cerularius theories which he did not formulate, and which are only deduced from actions which can just as easily be explained by his personal character. It was not so much that Cerularius thought the Church to be superior to the State, as that his pride gradually refused to submit to restraint, and his theory, if he had any, resulted from his action.

If regarded through the eyes of a Byzantine, Cerularius's conduct during Constantine IX's reign was only what might be expected from a Patriarch of his temperament; and to isolate the episode of the dispute with Rome to the neglect of other events, would be to give disproportionate emphasis to that which was, apart from its political roots, of little significance, and which owed its dramatic form to a singularly tempestuous and difficult Patriarch. During these years 1042–55 Cerularius was, in reality, less important than the 1054 outburst would suggest, and it is possible that he may have been absorbed by that interest in science and in precious stones and occult practices which he shared with Psellus, and which was unjustly turned to his reproach in the *Accusation*.[1] During the greater portion of

---

[1] Cf. the charges of ἀσέβεια and ἀδιαφορία, especially REG, xvi (1903), chs. v–xxiii, pp. 386–408, and xvii (1904), chs. lxv–lxvi, pp. 69–72.

Constantine's reign Cerularius, like Psellus and his friends, led a pleasant but not conspicuous life, and he figures in no public event except the rebellion of Leo Tornicius, when he gave moral support to the Emperor and led processions of suppliant clergy through the city.[1] Apart from this the only evidence for his activities appears in the *Funeral Oration*, and Psellus, anxious as he is to magnify the dead Patriarch, only describes such indefinable duties as befitted an ecclesiastic, such as exhorting Constantine to keep his promises or attempting to correct his vacillating habits.[2] In fact the Emperor was occupied with war, and Cerularius must have realized that this was no moment for him to interfere. Towards the end of the reign there is evidence for a change of policy,[3] and under the advice of new counsellors Constantine was not so favourably disposed towards either the Patriarch or the secular church. This showed itself in various ways. He evidently opposed the Patriarch's attempt to make the monks of the monastery of Studios conform to the general rule of the Church by renouncing their claim to wear special girdles.[4] More important still was the imperial infringement of the rights of ecclesiastical property, due probably to financial difficulty, which Cerularius either thought it injudicious to oppose, or was more probably powerless to prevent.[5]

Even in the quarrel with Rome, the clue to events is found in politics rather than in the attempt of an ecclesiastical autocrat to proclaim his superiority over the Papal See; the question to consider is not only how far did Cerularius win a victory over both Eastern Emperor and Papacy, but also how far did political necessity make it expedient for Constantine IX to capitulate to the Patriarch. This is not to deny that there were points of difference between the Greek and Latin Churches, but these were recognized and discussed; the trouble of 1054 arose from a combination of circumstances of which the most important were political in origin. The question at stake was the Byzantine position in South Italy, where the Normans were gradually conquering the country, while the Pope was uncertain of his attitude

[1] John of Euchaita, ed. Lagarde, pp. 184–5 (No. 186).
[2] Sathas, iv, pp. 341–2.
[3] Cedrenus, ii, p. 610; Attaleiates, pp. 50–1.
[4] Cerularius's Letter to Peter of Antioch, PG, cxx, cols. 808–9, quoted by Scabalanovitch, p. 382.　　　　　　　　　　　　　[5] Attaleiates, p. 51.

and open to an alliance with Constantinople against their common enemy. On the other hand, the Pope was then Leo IX, a strong upholder of the papal position, who would admit no compromise with the Greek Church on theological questions, hence the attitude of the legates who came to Constantinople prepared to propitiate Constantine IX, but unfavourably disposed towards the Patriarch. As long as political purposes demanded it the Emperor forced Cerularius to make a show of submission to the legates, when this was no longer expedient he suffered his outburst against the Pope when the papal bull was destroyed in S. Sophia.[1] As Michel says, the truth is that the rift between the Churches had long existed and religion (as distinct from any questioning of dogma) was at the service of politics, the two being inextricably interwoven and the actual control of both resting with the Emperor.

Those who describe Cerularius as a man bent on asserting the supremacy of the Church find the culmination of the attack of 1054 in his quarrel with Isaac Comnenus, and there is some evidence for attributing to him the desire to play the leading part in both secular and ecclesiastical politics. During the short reigns of Theodora and Michael VI Cerularius was not in favour. His original hope of controlling Theodora was frustrated by her ministers, nor apparently could Cerularius prevent the exile of his favourite prophetess, Dosithea, and her two monks, but he was eventually helped by the growth of opposition to Michael VI, whom he finally persuaded to abdicate in favour of Isaac Comnenus. At first Isaac and Cerularius preserved some degree of friendship, however feigned this may have been. But Cerularius made an error of judgement when he attacked Isaac for infringement of the rights of Church property, and threatened him with deposition when he proved obstinate.[2] Then he rapidly brought matters to a crisis by his assumption of the

[1] The history of the 1054 quarrel with Rome is given at length by L. Bréhier, *Le schisme oriental*, Paris, 1899, although he tends to overestimate the importance of Cerularius. A counterbalance to Bréhier and a more recent analysis of these events is found in A. Michel, *Humbert und Kerullarios*, Paderborn, pt. i, 1924, pt. ii, 1930.

[2] Scylitzes, ii, pp. 642–4; Attaleiates, pp. 62–3; Psellus, *Chron.* vii. 55 (ii, p. 123), a very guarded account, in marked contrast to the emphatic charges of the *Accusation*.

imperial insignia, and by his claim to a status equal to that of Isaac. There was no question of his fate; he was exiled and preparations made for his deposition. There seems no doubt that Cerularius did claim an authority at least equal to that of the Emperor. The independent evidence of Attaleiates and Scylitzes confirm Psellus in this respect. It may be suggested that in his letters and in the *Accusation* Psellus over-emphasizes both Cerularius's claim and his hope. It seems improbable that Cerularius aimed at the imperial throne, possibly in combination with the Patriarchate, which is one of the main charges of the *Accusation*.[1] It is difficult to say how far Psellus is right in attributing to Cerularius the theory that the priesthood was superior to the Empire, as his well-known letter implies[2] and as Scylitzes hints.[3] This was a thought antagonistic to the practical necessity of Byzantine life. It may be suggested that the primary factor in Cerularius's attack against the powers of the State was his own overbearing temperament, for he was quite capable of exploiting the divine character of his office in order to justify his own ambition. Nor is there any evidence that Cerularius found support, in marked contrast to the numbers of papal theorists of the West, and indeed his failure emphasizes the difference between the Latin and Greek Churches.

The history of Cerularius shows, then, how firmly the Church was under the control of the Emperor; and this is confirmed by such evidence as there is concerning the Patriarch and Church government. The sequestration of ecclesiastical property under Constantine IX was imitated to a far worse degree by Michael VII, and if Cerularius was unable to prevent this or obtain restitution, it can readily be understood that Cosmas was still more impotent, even though a strong and independent protest was voiced by his metropolitans.[4] The Patriarch's control over

[1] Ed. Bréhier, REG, 1904 (xvii), pp. 35–46 (chs. xxxi–xliv), while Psellus makes the charge of τυραννίς on the ground that Cerularius had intended to supplant both Michael VI and Isaac Comnenus.

[2] Sathas, v, pp. 505–13 (*Ep.* 207), note p. 511. 'You despise Emperors and oppose all authority.' Cf. *Accusation*, op. cit., p. 45 (ch. xlii). 'He sought to unite under one authority that which had been separated' [i.e. the Empire and priesthood].

[3] Scylitzes, ii, p. 643.

[4] Attaleiates, pp. 278–9; the protest was directed against the Metropolitan of Neocaesarea, who was the leader of Michael VII's Church policy.

his metropolitans and lower clergy varied with his own personal character. Alexius did not check the rapacity of his bishops,[1] Cosmas was obviously unable to control his ;[2] Xiphilinus, on the contrary, instructed his young clergy,[3] and checked such secularization as participation in lawsuits before the civil courts.[4] But the evidence is very fragmentary, and there is little to suggest the extent to which the Patriarch showed any pastoral interest.

The Patriarch's activities were not altogether political or administrative. By the ninth century theology was, it is true, interpretative rather than creative, but there was always the necessity of guarding against the intrusion of false teaching, and Xiphilinus had been careful to warn Psellus against the dangers of certain Platonic doctrines. It may, however, be emphasized that the Emperor was the protector of orthodoxy as well as the Patriarch. It was to Constantine IX that Psellus made his confession of faith.[5] Under happy circumstances both Emperor and Patriarch would co-operate in the synod, but were the Patriarch indifferent, or worse still, tainted by heresy, then the Emperor acted independently. Such was the case when Isaac Comnenus called a synod to hear his accusation against no less a person than the Patriarch himself.[6]

In the Byzantine Church there was, then, no possibility of pushing the problem of ecclesiastical supremacy to its logical conclusion. Moreover, it becomes clear that the Patriarch's duties were so inextricably interwoven with imperial politics, that this only served to strengthen the close connexion between the Church and State. The Patriarchs of this period were not famed for their reorganization of the dioceses or for their contribution to the growth of canon law, because there were no such developments in the Byzantine Church of this period. With the exception of Michael Cerularius, and possibly of Nicholas Mysticus, they were rightly concerned with the maintenance of the tradition which they had inherited.

[1] Cf. Cedrenus, ii, pp. 518–19.
[2] Attaleiates, pp. 278–9, where the Metropolitan of Neocaesarea not only held secular office but scandalously robbed the Church.
[3] Sathas, iv, p. 451.   [4] PG, cxix, cols. 760–1.
[5] See Chapter IV, p. 86.
[6] See Chapter V for the imperial attitude towards heresy in the Comnenian period.

CHAPTER IX

THE PLACE OF MONASTICISM IN THE BYZANTINE POLITY

'Monasteries are the harbours which shelter those voyaging over the sea of this world.'

John, Patriarch of Antioch, PG, cxxxii, cols. 1132-3.

MONASTICISM is an element in the life of a people which it is extraordinarily difficult to assess, because so often it is the unusual or the unworthy that comes to the surface.[1] It was in all good faith that Symeon the Young described a monastery as the only refuge of those who would escape the troubles of the world. But he was not the only man who thought thus, and many who frequented Byzantine monasteries did so from motives which he would indeed have judged unworthy of so high a calling. Because scandals or unfitting conduct did attract unfavourable comment, we may perhaps infer that they were the exception rather than the rule. Nevertheless, Byzantine monasticism presents outstanding defects due to conditions somewhat different from those of western monasticism, differences which will emerge from an analysis of the circumstances of eastern religious life.

The Byzantine had a definite reverence for the life of the monk and an equally definite desire to protect his own soul. To him the monastic life was the highest life, and it was certainly to the monastery that he looked for the solution of all his ills. After political defeat, before public discomfiture, in financial embarrassment, in search of the best confessor, as a place of interment, at every stage of his life and in every crisis it was to the monastery that he turned. If he felt that any endowment or gift to a monastery might ensure his earthly future, he was no less convinced that, behind this admittedly lesser motive, lay the desire to contribute towards the greater glory of God. The popular attitude towards monastic life was, then, composed of

---

[1] This difficulty is increased by the scarcity of records which makes it impossible to compare Byzantine monasteries in Europe with those in Asia Minor, or to discover if there was any difference in the life lived by monks in those parts of the Empire which were affected by heresy.

many and varying elements, all of which vitally affected the manner in which monasteries were founded, and the characters of the men who became monks, or who sojourned as birds of passage within their walls, while, further, they determined the relations which existed between monasteries and outside authorities, whether secular or ecclesiastical.

However critical an eye is cast on these monasteries it remains true that they did stand for a great deal in the life of the Byzantines. Whoever a man might be—Emperor, Patriarch, civil servant, peasant—when he wished to show his piety, it was in endowing or restoring a monastery, or in bearing some share of this task, that he found the expression of his religious faith. Particularly was the Emperor thus concerned, for εὐσέβεια was part of the imperial ideal, while he never knew when the uncertainty of his secular life would demand a refuge. Religious zeal was stimulated by the instability of politics and the need for securing some sure retreat. In addition there was the problem of finding a place of burial, and the monasteries with which Constantinople abounded were freely used for this purpose by the imperial families.[1] In the early Macedonian period the church of the Holy Apostles was the traditional imperial burial-place; Basil I, Leo VI, Constantine VII were buried there, and it was only at the last moment that Basil II changed his mind and rested elsewhere, with pilgrims and saints in the little church of S. John the Evangelist.[2]

But although an Emperor was, even in distress, free to enter any monastery, including the great house of Studios, it was more in accordance with the imperial dignity to establish a new foundation which would not only receive the founder in the hour of his death and give a resting-place to his bones, but would in itself perpetuate his magnanimity and his piety. Basil I not only restored churches and monasteries in Constantinople and built the magnificent New Church,[3] but he was a lover of holy men.[4] Romanus Lecapenus gave generously both to the poor

[1] Monasteries seem to have been used as cemeteries by the general public of Constantinople. Cf. *Vita Symeonis*, p. 46 (ch. 34) ... 'the monastery ... was used as a burial place for the dead'.

[2] Cedrenus, ii, p. 480.

[3] Theoph. Cont., pp. 321 ff.; Georg. Mon., p. 843; Cedrenus, ii, pp. 237 ff.; Sym. Mag., pp. 691–2.   [4] Theoph. Cont., pp. 314 ff.

and to monasteries,[1] and he himself founded a monastery where his wife was buried;[2] and it was in a monastery as a monk that he spent his last days, while after his death he was brought to Constantinople to lie with his wife.[3] Nicephorus Phocas, famous for his leaning towards the monastic life, was the patron of his friend Athanasius, the founder of the Laura, the first monastic house on Mt. Athos.[4] In the eleventh century Romanus III, being, as Psellus says,[5] jealous of Solomon and Justinian, built a most magnificent, even extravagant, church to the glory of the Mother of God, calling it the church of the Peribleptos.[6] Psellus speaks first of a church being built and then says that a monastery was added and that there was no end to the number of the monks who were encouraged to come to live in it. Within this foundation the unfortunate Romanus was buried, enjoying, writes Psellus, only just as much of the church as was occupied by his corpse.[7] Michael IV built a superb church in the monastery of SS. Cosmas and Damian,[8] and it was here that he became a monk during the last stages of his terrible illness, being finally buried in the same church outside the holy sanctuary.[9] Constantine IX with equal magnificence entirely rebuilt the church of S. George in the Mangana, and was buried in it.[10] The foundations of these eleventh-century emperors are described in all their splendid detail not only by Psellus and Cedrenus, but even by the curt Attaleiates. But it is evident that they were no exceptions, others acted likewise and, if in a quieter manner, with no less sincerity. Romanus IV after he had been blinded was taken to the monastery which he had founded on the island of Protê, and there he died[11] and was buried.[12] The Comneni, in spite of a certain severity towards ecclesiastical shortcomings, were no exception to the imperial patronage of monasteries.

---

[1] Theoph. Cont., p. 417; Sym. Mag., p. 744.
[2] Theoph. Cont., p. 402; Georg. Mon., p. 894.
[3] Theoph. Cont., pp. 440–1.   [4] Meyer, pp. 102 ff.
[5] Psellus, *Chron.* iii. 14 (i, p. 41).
[6] Ibid. iii. 14–16 (i, pp. 41–4). The Virgin was the special patron of Romanus III, cf. his coin which shows him being crowned by the Theotokos (Wroth, ii, Pl. LVII, 13, and Psellus, *Chron.* iii. 10–11 (i, p. 39).
[7] Ibid. iv. 5 (i, p. 55).
[8] Ibid. iv. 31–2 (i, p. 72).   [9] Ibid. iv. 52–5 (i, pp. 83–5).
[10] Ibid. vi. 185–7 (ii, pp. 61–3); Attaleiates, pp. 47–8; Cedrenus, ii, p. 608.
[11] Psellus, *Chron.* vii b, 43 (ii, p. 172).   [12] Attaleiates, p. 179.

Alexius I founded orphanages and hospitals,[1] as well as the monastery of SS. Peter and Paul, and of Christ Philanthropos where he was buried,[2] his wife Irene endowed a house for women where she herself retired,[3] John Comnenus founded near his monastery of the Pantocrator an almshouse for old men,[4] Manuel endowed with an annual grant from the treasury a monastery on the shores of the Black Sea, in his eyes a fittingly isolated spot for monks.[5]

Patriarchs no less than Emperors displayed their piety and their magnificence. Ignatius built a monastery where he was buried,[6] Nicholas Mysticus was buried in his monastery,[7] Alexius had a monastery in Stenum,[8] Cerularius built one outside the city, in which the festival of S. Michael and All Angels was usually celebrated,[9] while Leichudes founded a church and monastery in honour of the Mother of God.[10]

Only the rich, or those in command of public funds, could afford so splendid a testimony to their belief and gain so costly a burial-place, so certain a remembrance in the intercession of the monks. Constantine IX could grant the right of possession of Bessae to the monk Lazarus on condition that he would pray for his soul and for that of Sclerena:[11] such was within his power. Yet peasants as well as Emperors desired to found monasteries, but they did this in co-operation with neighbours of their own class, or with monks, as in the case of Dorotheus and his friends who sought to rebuild a foundation that had fallen into decay and become deserted.[12] Psellus tells of a nun, who had built a nunnery with the help of other peasants, and who became involved in difficulties because one of her neighbours refused to meet his obligations.[13] A peasant could build a chapel on his

---

[1] Anna Comnena, xv. 7 (ii, p. 292).   [2] *Anonymou synopsis chronice*, p. 186.
[3] See Chapter X, pp. 185 ff.   [4] See Chapter X, pp. 186 ff.
[5] Nicetas Choniates, vii. 3 (p. 270).   [6] Vogt, *Basile Ier* . . ., p. 237.
[7] Theoph. Cont., p. 410; Georg. Mon., p. 902.
[8] Cedrenus, ii, p. 536. The Stenum (στενόν) was really the strait between Byzantium and Pontus, but the term ἐν Στενῷ was used of the European shore, where there were numerous monasteries and buildings. (Du Cange, iv, p. 167).
[9] Attaleiates, p. 63; Zonaras, xviii, 5 (iii, p. 669); the monastery was dedicated to the 'Nine Orders' (τὰ ἐννέα τάγματα), cf. Du Cange, iv, p. 788.
[10] Sathas, iv, p. 415.
[11] *Vita S. Lazari Galesiotae*, 245 DE (ASS, Nov. iii, p. 584).
[12] PG, cxx, col. 1064 c.   [13] Sathas, v, p. 376 (*Ep.* 130).

own land, and, becoming a monk, could live in it until his death. To found a monastery was, then, an act well pleasing to God, in which both rich and poor could freely participate.

The monastery was therefore an integral part of Byzantine life and was the concern of all, both those who had a vocation for a holy life and those who had not. But the world was an uncertain place at the best of times and what could be more comforting than to know that there was somewhere a monastery which would welcome its patron when the world rejected him, and provide a burial-place and prayers for his soul after death?[1] Hence, it was the monasteries to which men turned in the moment of their distress, and to deny the presence of this thought in the mind of those who founded new houses, or supported old ones, would be to deny human nature.

The difficulty, certainly in Byzantium of the Macedonian and Comnenian periods, was the abuse of this privilege, and the consequent effect on the standard of monastic life. There is no lack of evidence to show the very general reliance which was placed on the monasteries. Psellus writes of a man who lost nearly all his money and who then went into a monastery, and lived on the income obtained from the remnant of the property.[2] There were doubtless many instances of this kind in private life had they been chronicled; the histories of the period are concerned with public life, and afford endless evidence of the unfailing regularity with which politicians and soldiers, Emperors and scholars entered monastic life, but only for as long as was convenient. Herein lay the great weakness of this popular reliance on monastic foundations. Faced with defeat and possibly with death, either of his own free will or compelled by the victorious party, one political figure after another appears in the records of his time only to be dismissed with the all too familiar words 'he became a monk'.[3] Before the days of imprisonment as a general penalty,[4] when blindness was often the secular punishment for over-bold offenders or for defeated

---

[1] Cf. the chantries of western Europe.
[2] Sathas, v, p. 342 (*Ep.* 99).   [3] Cf. Cedrenus, ii, p. 487, p. 514.
[4] There were some prisons; cf. Attaleiates, p. 15, who says that the prisons were opened when the mob rose against Michael V. From time to time certain important political offenders were confined in prisons. Cf. Buckler, *Anna Comnena*, Index, s.v. 'Punishment'.

Emperors, the usual imperial means of housing enemies was confinement within the walls of a monastery. In Romanus I's reign John the rector, fearing disgrace, left the palace feigning illness, like Michael Psellus, and went to his monastery near Galacrevae where he became a monk;[1] in the same reign Bardas Boilas accused of treason was by the imperial clemency condemned, not to death, but to the monastic life.[2] In the eleventh century John the Orphanotrophus had been a monk before he controlled the policy of Michael IV, and after he was disgraced by Michael V it was as a matter of course that he re-entered a monastery.[3] Michael V was led to a monastery after his eyes had been put out,[4] likewise his uncle; and so with Romanus IV and numberless other political refugees.

Virtual confinement for life was not the only political use of monastic houses, nor was this so difficult a problem, since the unfortunate man who was deprived of all hope of a secular life was the more likely to find that the vocation which had been forced on him was indeed the true solution of all his troubles. But it was otherwise with those birds of passage who unhesitatingly flitted from the secular to the monastic life as suited the occasion, and whose inability or refusal to realize the real purport of a monk's life could not fail to weaken monasticism. The supreme example of this is the philosopher Psellus who, with his friends, John Mauropous and Xiphilinus, sought monasticism as a temporary solution when they fell under the imperial displeasure. Psellus's behaviour is only characteristic of many others, some of whom may have acted in perfectly good faith, while others undoubtedly regarded the monasteries as fulfilling the functions of an alms-house, often of a luxurious kind. The Emperor Isaac, for instance, abdicated and spent his days writing in the monastery of Studios[5] and if it is debatable whether or not he made this decision under pressure, it is almost certain that he found there a rest which he had not known in political life.

[1] Theoph. Cont., p. 406; Georg. Mon., p. 898; Cedrenus, ii, p. 304.
[2] Sym. Mag., p. 734; Cedrenus, ii, p. 302.
[3] Cedrenus, ii, p. 543. John had fled to the monastery of Monobatae and was transported thence to the island of Lesbos.   [4] Ibid., p. 540.
[5] Psellus, *Chron.* vii *a*, 13 (ii, p. 145). The various stages by which the decision was reached and the choice of a successor are described by Psellus, ibid. vii. 74–vii *a*. 13 (ii, pp. 129–145).

Women, no less than men, availed themselves of the monastic life. On her husband's death the Empress Irene Ducas went to live in the nunnery which she had founded. The women of the imperial family could be political offenders, and often received banishment to a convent for this reason. Zoe, the mother of Constantine VII, was twice sent into a monastery by her opponents; Theophano the wife of Romanus II and of Nicephorus Phocas met the same punishment. Even women against whom there was no charge were, willingly or unwillingly, made to accept the tonsure. Basil I, when he came to the throne, sent his daughters into a convent;[1] Theophano insisted that her husband Romanus II should send his five sisters into a convent, and despite their innocence of any offence, and their open protestation, they were tonsured by the abbot of the Studite monastery;[2] in the eleventh century Michael V ordered the Empress Zoe to be forcibly shorn.[3]

Evidence shows, then, the frequency with which men and women founded monasteries, or took their vows as an escape from present evils, and it makes clear the prevalent thoughtlessness in taking advantage of monastic help. There is no doubt that monasteries did perform a great public service, nor was the chroniclers' emphasis on imperial bounty unjustified: the State money, which was lavished on monastic gifts, was repaid, in that those same establishments well fulfilled the manifold functions of prisons, hotels, alms-houses, places of retreat and refuge for those of every kind and degree from the young Comneni who were sent to the monastery of Studios and were there educated in letters and manners,[4] to the Latin bishop who came to live in Symeon's monastery.[5] But what is so often lacking is any positive evidence of the extent to which men who were forced into monastic life could, and did, develop a religious vocation. This did, in fact, sometimes happen. John Xiphilinus was a lawyer fearing political disgrace when he entered Mt. Olympus, but he became, first a monk, and then an abbot exercising a

---

[1] Vogt, *La jeunesse de Léon VI le sage*, p. 400.
[2] Theoph. Cont., p. 471; Cedrenus, ii, pp. 343–4.
[3] Psellus, *Chron.* v. 23 (i, p. 100).
[4] Bryennius, i. 1 (p. 18), who says that the monastery was conveniently situated for getting outside the City for hunting and military training.
[5] *Vita Symeonis*, pp. 68–76 (chs. 52–7).

salutary discipline over his house, before he was elected Patriarch of Constantinople. Nevertheless, monasteries must have found it difficult to maintain a high standard of spiritual life, and the institution wherein people found their one stability and security was itself often open to criticism. This was partly because of the close connexion of monasticism with secular life, by reason of the performance of public services, and partly because of other defects in the ecclesiastical organization and in the internal economy of the various houses.

Herein lies the contrast between monasticism in the Byzantine Empire and in western Europe, and the explanation of the unsatisfactory condition of the former. Byzantine monasteries were intimately interwoven with the secular world, which, though not a fault confined to the East, was present there in an acute form; there was in the East no central ecclesiastical authority comparable to the Papacy, for the Patriarch was, in matters of administration, subordinate to the Emperor who was a secular ruler and could not be exclusively, or even primarily, concerned with ecclesiastical organization or monastic reform; and, finally, it had none of the creativeness that could produce a Cluniac or a Cistercian order with its daughter houses and its very definite sense of a spiritual vocation, a vocation that in practice, if not in intent, combined, at its best, detachment from the world with real service to secular life. Byzantine monasticism seemed, on the contrary, to be used almost as though it were a part of secular existence, and it had none of the force and vigour which monks of the West derived from the consciousness of a definite place in a well ordered Church hierarchy; there was no lack of monasteries, but these were isolated and rarely outlived their founder, and they produced, generally speaking, neither statesmen nor ecclesiastics, neither scholars nor schools, but monks, whose concern was the orthodox performance of their monastic vows, and who lived usually according to the rule of St. Basil, or rather, in accordance with the very general principles which he had formulated.

It would be difficult to enumerate the various kinds and species of monasteries which were founded, or were already in existence, during the Macedonian and Comnenian periods, because of the paucity of records. An imperial chrysobull, or still more rarely a *Vita S. Dorothei*, may show perhaps a hermitage, or small monastery, in course of construction, but the duration of its existence remains unknown, though it might be surmised that it was often scarcely longer than the lifetime of its founder. There are certain differences of evidence during the centuries of this period. The ninth and tenth centuries are comparatively rich in the lives of saints, but without much concreteness of detail concerning the nature of the life lived or the rules of foundation of the house to which the saint belonged; such are, for instance, the lives of S. Ignatius, S. Nicholas the Studite, S. Luke the Younger, S. Antony Cauleas. In the eleventh century there are fewer lives, but more evidence from imperial bulls, usually of immunities granted to monks about whom little or nothing is known. To this century belongs Attaleiates' *Typicon*, or rule of life drawn up by himself, a layman, for the house which he founded, a custom followed in the Comnenian period, and providing valuable detail concerning the internal economy of such houses. There is in addition, by reason of frequent appeal to imperial protection, certain information about the foundations on Athos from the middle of the tenth century, and the monastery of Christodoulus on Patmos from the end of the eleventh century onwards. The only real insight into the spirit of the monastic life both at its best and worst, is provided by the sermons of Symeon the Young, abbot of S. Mamas at the end of the tenth and beginning of the eleventh century. However, despite the gaps, certain facts do emerge and serve to illustrate the variety of Byzantine monasteries.

There were the large and powerful foundations such as the monastery of Studios in Constantinople, the houses on Mt. Olympus in Bithynia, and the great monastic republic of Athos. They seemed to provide the only external stability which Byzantine monasticism knew, and even they were often unsatisfactory, as will be seen when the kind of life lived by their monks is examined. A glance at a map will show the splendid isolation of the site of the Holy Mountain, and indicate the inevitable difficulties of inter-monastic relations. The peninsula had been used in the tenth century by hermits, notably Euthymius and Athanasius, and it was the *typicon* which Athanasius drew up probably in 964 for his Laura that became the model for other foundations. Athanasius's foundation was a monastery or *coenobium*, based on the Studite rule, and was, therefore, a 'laura' only in name; the mode of life adopted by the Athos monks had hitherto been that of the laura, which consisted of a number of separate monastic cells. But Athanasius followed the Studite rule, which was the only definite supplement to Basil's which the East had produced, and which was generally used, though naturally in conjunction with necessary individual rules to meet particular circumstances. The tradition which lay behind the Studite rule was complete renunciation of the world, and those who made this sacrifice shared a status and a holiness which could not be known by men, even clergy, who were involved in secular relationships. Hence the inevitable and repeated difficulties of monastic government, and the opposition to any outside interference. The Laura, for instance, originally formed a self-governing and self-contained community, answerable only to its own abbot, who was elected by representatives from the community (fifteen brothers and the ἐπίτροπος). The important thing about Athanasius's *typicon* is that the community was a *coenobium*, not a collection of hermits. This form of ascetic life, i.e. the *coenobium* or monastery, prevailed in the later foundations of Mt. Athos, no inconsiderable number of which dated from the eleventh century.[1] The *typicon* of 1045 shows how extensively Mt. Athos was occupied by monasteries which, though nominally independent, were forced to admit co-operation among themselves if only for the purpose of combating the secularization that inevitably invades the best regulated communities. Though the Laura was founded by Nicephorus Phocas, both the Laura and the other houses claimed immunity from any secular interference, and owed obedience only to their abbot. In questions of difficulty they appealed to the most appropriate power, almost always the Emperor who, since their difficulties arose usually from some conflict over boundaries, or outside claims to jurisdiction, provided the quickest and most effective mode of

---

[1] Brockhaus, pp. 7–8, gives the following list: Xeropotamou (*c.* 1028–34), Esphigmenou (early 11th century), Docheiariou (before 1046), S. Paul's (*c.* 1050), Karakallou (*c.* 1070), Xenophontos (*c.* 1070), Kastamonitou (*c.* 1086), Koutloumousi (1081–1118).

settlement. The Holy Mountain, an important section of the monastic community, thus followed its own adaptation of the Studite rule, and set up as its ideal renunciation of the world and complete immunity from any outside control, whether secular or ecclesiastical.

Though it was a special case, Athos shows an attitude that was not peculiar to its own communities. Byzantine foundations show none of the difference of purpose, and consequently of organization, which characterized the Western orders. Cistercians, Carthusians, Dominicans, Franciscans, these were all dedicated to a religious way of life, but they were more militant, more assured of their definite place in the Church, they knew to whom they were responsible and to whom they could appeal, and points of doubt were settled, as they arose, in the legal and concise manner of the Roman See. It was otherwise in the Byzantine Empire. Seek for distinct orders of monks or for any fundamental differences in regulations of religious foundations, and they are almost non-existent. There are the big houses and the Holy Mountain, and, apart from these, the multiplication of foundations was due to individual effort. Attaleiates, a layman, drew up the rule of his Institute of Mercy,[1] Dorotheus took the rule of Arsenius as his model,[2] sometimes the diocesan bishops wrote rules for new foundations;[3] when the foundation consisted of an individual ascete he was no doubt a rule unto himself, such as S. Luke the Stylite in the tenth century, who enjoyed a great reputation. Some foundations are known only by reason of some appeal which was made to the Emperor, such as the monastery on the island of Strobelos[4] which was established by the sister of Constantine Cabalures, or the hermit cells of Nicodemus,[5] and Arsenius Scenures.[6] The variations for which there is evidence are not in the kind of religious life to be led, there was no doubt concerning that, but in other duties which were the result of the founder's wishes. Attaleiates desired to provide for service to the aged, Michael IV to found a home where prostitutes would be welcomed, or orphans cared for. Often the only duty was intercession for the soul of the founder,

---

[1] MM, v, pp. 293–327.   [2] PG, cxx, col. 1064 D (ch. 11).
[3] Sathas, v, p. 159.   [4] MM, vi, pp. 19–21 (Dölger 1045).
[5] *Corpus inscriptionum graecarum*, ed. Boeckh, iv, pp. 327–9, No. 8704 (Dölger 826).   [6] MM, vi, pp. 21–3 (Dölger 1046).

which would naturally have been performed in the daily liturgy, or in the private devotions of the monk. The conclusion is that in their organization Byzantine monasteries wished to be their own law and provided for no outside correction to check any signs of sloth or decadence.

But nobody can entirely ignore his neighbours or claim complete immunity from all civic responsibilities, and Byzantine monasteries were for ever discovering this. They had their economic and financial burdens, and were bound by legal rulings on these matters; and in the performance of their spiritual duties they inevitably came into contact, and even conflict, with the secular Church. The imperial decisions show the diversity of practice and the difficulty of adjustment which monastic houses experienced in this respect, and it becomes clear that there was no effective ecclesiastical control to check their instability.

Undoubtedly the Patriarch should always have held supreme control, but in monastic government, as in other ecclesiastical affairs, he was, in practice, subordinate to the imperial authority. Balsamon in the twelfth century considered that the Patriarch of Constantinople had immediate authority over the monks in any province of the East,[1] but that was, of course, saving the Emperor's authority over those houses which came directly under his jurisdiction, and of which there were no small number. In this latter case the Patriarch had right of visitation only if he were invited or if notified of some irregularity. It is true that the Patriarch was regarded as the natural authority to whom appeal should be made in certain cases of difficulty. When Symeon's monks in the eleventh century revolted against their abbot's sermons, it was to the Patriarch's house that they rushed in a body to protest, and the next day the Patriarch, having summoned Symeon, and finding that the revolt was unjustified, passed judgement on the rebels.[2] In such a case there were obviously no outside interests at stake, and the Patriarch's sentence passed unquestioned. But it was otherwise in the charge which was brought against this same Symeon the Young, when the Patriarch could neither control his synod, nor prevent the

---

[1] PG, cxxxviii, col. 296. Cf. PG, cxxvii, cols. 941–5; and Balsamon, *In 19 Can. Conc. VII. oecumen.*, PG, cxxxvii, cols. 980 ff. (Dölger 1076).

[2] *Vita Symeonis*, pp. 50–4 (chs. 38–41).

Emperor overruling his decision. The abbot had been brought to account for a matter that was nominally of a purely ecclesiastical nature, namely, his right to institute the cult of his spiritual father, Symeon the Studite, but the charge was actually prompted by jealously on the part of the secular clergy, and the Emperor interfered to close an unfortunate episode. The ineffectiveness of the Patriarch's control was often apparent. Constantine IX had to order the monastery of the Virgin of Stylus on Latros to obey the abbot appointed by the Patriarch.[1] Or, again, the same difficulty was shown by the trouble which arose at Mt. Athos at the end of the century. Nicetas tells the story of one of Symeon's followers who, when officiating at the Eucharist with Symeon, beheld the saint as though clothed in the patriarchal robes, immersed in divine mysteries.[2] There was nothing to which a monk could not aspire, and throughout there is this conviction that it is in monastic life that the highest spiritual development can be found. This lay at the basis of the monastic claim of complete autonomy, and often neither Patriarch nor ecclesiastics could hope to assert any right of visitation or control.

This difficulty of the patriarchal control of monastic houses was complicated by the antagonism between the secular and monastic clergy. It was this which underlay the quarrel between Stephen, Archbishop of Nicomedia, and Symeon, abbot of S. Mamas,[3] and there was always an over-readiness for monks to contrast the secular way of life, and its secular learning, with the contemplative life and its complete reliance on the knowledge which comes from the Holy Spirit, to the detriment of the former. Nicetas, the author of the *Vita Symeonis*, says that it was φθόνος against the saint which roused Stephen's hatred,[4] and he makes the very human omission of forgetting to state that Symeon, when asked by Stephen to write a dissertation on the relation between the Father and the Son, had been inspired to devote most of his verse to emphasizing the advantage of the knowledge which came from the Holy Spirit, in contrast to the

---

[1] MM, vi, p. 430 (Dölger 866). It may be asked whether this was a case of Cerularius's action, either in attempting to assert his rights or in overruling the privileges of the monastery. If the latter, then even as forceful a Patriarch as Cerularius had to appeal for imperial support.

[2] *Vita Symeonis*, p. 44 (ch. 33).

[3] Ibid., pp. 100 ff. (chs. 74 ff.).

[4] Ibid., p. 102 (ch. 74).

vanity of secular learning.[1] The whole controversy which
Symeon provoked serves to illustrate the independence of individual monastic houses, an independence that unfortunately
thrived on the possession of an abbot of saintly life. Both the
patience and the finances of secular clergy must have been often
sorely tried by the difficulty of competing with monastic prerogative and monastic superiority. The monk's claim to holiness
made him seem highly desirable as a confessor; Symeon the
Young was sought by the richest families in Constantinople.[2]
A monk was evidently equally in demand to take services in
private chapels, and the Patriarch Alexius made a protest in his
Sententiae Synodales, which forbade any private services save
on festivals and with the bishop's permission.[3] But the efforts to
eradicate the monastic preference for imperial justice to the
neglect of the bishops' court[4] must often have been frustrated
by obtaining a ruling from the Emperor.

In secular difficulties, no less than in spiritual, the monasteries
continually resented any interference or claims from the secular
clergy, usually the bishop of the diocese, nor was it the Patriarch
to whom they appealed. Monastic houses fought tenaciously
for privilege and immunity, whether in matters of finance or
possessions, and they inevitably found the safeguard for their
claim to special treatment in the imperial sanction. So valuable
was the imperial word that each successive Emperor was usually
called upon to confirm the more important concessions made by
his predecessor. In the eleventh century the privileges of Constantine IX's foundation of Νέα Μονή, on the island of Chios,
were confirmed by Michael VI,[5] by Constantine X,[6] by Romanus
IV,[7] and Nicephorus III Botaneiates,[8] the concessions which
Attaleiates had obtained from Michael VII were confirmed by
Nicephorus, when he gave his guarantee to the judge's new

---

[1] The poem is given by Hausherr in the introduction to the Vita Symeonis,
pp. lxiii–lxv.

[2] Vita Symeonis, pp. 142–4 (ch. 104). Cf. Epistola de confessione: 'he . . .
who has provoked the wrath of God, can find no other reconciliation save in
the mediation of some holy man, the friend and servant of Christ, and in
flight from all evil.' Ed. Holl, p. 115, ch. 5 (18–21).

[3] PG, cxix, col. 837 A.

[4] Ibid., cols. 832–3.   [5] K, pp. 558–9 (Dölger 937).

[6] Ibid., pp. 559–61 (Dölger 949).   [7] Ibid., pp. 562–4 (Dölger 971).

[8] MM, v, pp. 8–10; p. 448, and K, p. 566 (Dölger 1030, 1050).

foundation.[1]   There was nothing unusual in the case of *Néa Μονή*, which was an imperial foundation and dependent upon imperial bounty; but Attaleiates clearly judged a guarantee from the Emperor of far more value than the sanction of the Patriarch. And the eleventh-century evidence is abundantly confirmed by that of the Comnenian period. The monastery of Christodoulus on Patmos, founded under the auspices of the Emperor Alexius, appears with unfailing regularity in the imperial bulls of the years 1081–1185;[2] and the same is true of Athos which relied exclusively on imperial assistance, both for the confirmation of privileges and for the regulation of internal disorder.[3] Byzantine foundations persistently proclaim that their religious life is their own concern, and that, in mundane questions or organization, they prefer to obtain secular help, preferably through the Emperor.

This is indeed apparent in those difficulties of finance and jurisdiction, which even the most remote house found it impossible entirely to avoid. Monasteries undoubtedly desired to escape financial obligation, whether to the ecclesiastical authorities of the diocese, or to the secular departments of the administration. This could only be effected with imperial aid, and most monasteries must have been unable to obtain complete immunity from a certain amount of financial liability. The most fortunate monasteries appealed to the Emperor on such points, usually with success. The favoured *Néa Μονή*, which appears so often in the eleventh-century imperial chrysobulls, was freed from land taxes on its possessions both present and future,[4] the monastery Dochiariu on Mt. Athos was exempt from ground rent on its land in Perigardikon and Satublion,[5] and Iberon, the Georgian monastery on the Holy Mountain, was to be immune from any taxation by the epoptes of Thessalonica;[6] the monastery founded

[1] MM, v, pp. 138–45 (Dölger 1042). Michael VII's concessions are found in MM, v, pp. 135–8.
[2] Dölger 1141, 1142, 1147, 1148, 1150, 1151, 1153, 1170, 1214 (Alexius's reign); 1296 (John); 1339, 1411, 1423, 1439 (Manuel).
[3] Ibid., 1154, 1171, 1226, 1227, 1240, 1248, 1249, 1250, 1252, 1265, 1276, 1277, 1293, 1294 (Alexius); 1307 (John).
[4] K, pp. 545–9 (Dölger 862).
[5] Usp Vost, iii, p. 198 gives a Russian summary (Dölger 1000). But see Soloviev, pp. 234 ff. for a criticism of P. Uspensky.
[6] Usp Vost, iii, pp. 198–9 gives a Russian summary (Dölger 1040).

on the island of Strobelos by the sister of Constantine Cabalures
was freed from all taxes or tribute,[1] and likewise the cells which
Arsenius Scenures founded on the island of Cos.[2] These immunities sometimes involved the monastic property, or the
peasants who lived in the neighbourhood of the monastery, and
so the letters to Νέα Μονή make provision for the monastic funds
to be aided by the Jews of the island, who are in future to pay
their taxes to the monastery, and not to the secular authorities.[3]
Nor was the imperial graciousness confined either to remission,
or to diversion of taxes, it went farther, and the generosity of
its gifts must have done much to convince monasteries that it
was indeed in the Emperor that they found their protector and
their patron; the Patriarch could not compete. Νέα Μονή on
Chios had a yearly gift of 72 gold pieces, as well as a document
signed by the officials of the secretariat as token of the perpetuity
of this excellent arrangement;[4] moreover, upon occasion of their
visiting Constantinople, the monks were provided with quarters
in which to stay, as well as food and money.[5] Similarly, the
monasteries on Mt. Athos were from time to time granted sums
of gold from the State chests,[6] or from the private imperial
treasury;[7] sometimes the money was paid for a definite purpose
such as the prayers for some dead person.[8] Even in matters of
debt the Emperor did not fail those who appealed to him; thus
the abbot Joseph was freed from the obligations which he could
not fulfil,[9] while the monk Arsenius Scenures, finding that he
and his monks could not subsist, by reason of the barrenness of
the district, was granted an annual solemnium, to be paid from
the treasury of the theme of Cyclades, and was exempt from all
taxation.[10]

These instances of financial gifts or immunity all fall between

---

[1] MM, vi, pp. 19–21 (Dölger 1045).
[2] Ibid., pp. 21–3 (Dölger 1046).
[3] K, pp. 550–1 (Dölger 892); ibid., pp. 561–2 (Dölger 950); MM, v, pp.
8–10 (Dölger 1030). But for a discussion of the nature of this Jewish tax see
Andréadès, 'Les Juifs et le Fisc dans l'Empire byzantine' (*Mélanges Charles
Diehl*, i, pp. 7–29).   [4] MM, v, pp. 1–2 (Dölger 865).
[5] Ibid., pp. 5–6 (Dölger 878); ibid., pp. 6–7 (Dölger 887).
[6] Usp Vost, iii, p. 185, gives a Russian summary (Dölger 932).
[7] Ibid., pp. 198–9, gives a Russian summary (Dölger 1040).
[8] K, pp. 557–8 (Dölger 940).   [9] Ibid., pp. 562–4 (Dölger 971).
[10] MM, vi, pp. 21–3 (Dölger 1046).

the years 1025–81 and can be paralleled by imperial bounty at other times; the Macedonians before 1025 were not lacking in generosity,[1] while the Comneni gave freely to their own foundations and to such as the Holy Mountain, Christodoulus's monastery on Patmos, and the Theotokos Eleusa near Palaiocastro. But in proportion to the number of years there appear to be more imperial concessions to all kinds of foundations between 1025 and 1081 than before or after; it is possible that this was due to the brief space for which most emperors ruled during those years, and perhaps also to the fact that they were not such good generals. Isaac Comnenus, who did realize the gravity of the military position, was the one Emperor between 1025 and 1081 who made an effort to limit monastic wealth. Nicephorus Phocas and Basil II before 1025, Alexius and Manuel Comnenus after 1081, soldiers only too cognizant of the financial need, especially for military purposes, all these made some attempt to regulate both ecclesiastical and monastic property. It is difficult to assess how far the monasteries really were unjustifiably wealthy. Ideally the monastic life was one of poverty, but it was impossible in practice to maintain this, for even the most saintly house had to live. And monasteries must sometimes have been in financial difficulties; the Council of 869 forbade the sale of Church vessels or equipment,[2] S. Eustratius in the tenth century tells how his monastery on Mt. Olympus would have been in difficulties had not financial help arrived,[3] and Christodoulus would have been unable to live on the arid island of Patmos without generous imperial support.

But if monasticism was the practical manifestation of Byzantine faith in the world to come, it was also a source of weakness in the secular vicissitudes of this life. As the military and financial difficulties of the Empire steadily increased and at the same time monastic houses multiplied in number and possessions, it became apparent that imperial resources were being drained of both men and money. As early as 934 Romanus I attempted to prevent the increase of monastic property by ordering monks to bring not land but its value in money to their monasteries.[4] In 964 Nicephorus Phocas proposed to limit the foundation of

---

[1] See above pp. 159 ff.

[2] Mansi, xvi. 168. Canon XV.

[3] *Vita S. Eustratii*, p. 378.

[4] Jus, iii, c. 3, n. 5, pp. 242–52.

monastic houses. While explicitly stating that he was in no way inimical to the monastic life or to the endowment of monasteries and alms-houses, he insisted that the older houses must be repaired before new ones were founded.[1] The unpopularity of this novel is evident since both John Tzimisces and Basil II hastened to abrogate it. Nevertheless, Basil himself could not but stress the greed of ecclesiastical bodies, and when he tried to protect the poor from the depredations of the rich he pointedly included a clause against bishops or metropolitans who hastened to claim as monasteries peasant foundations in a village community. Sometimes a peasant would build a chapel on peasant land and himself become a monk. Basil insisted that such land was to remain peasant property, even in the case of not one but several peasants professing the monastic life; on the death of the founder it was to return to the village, not to the ecclesiastical jurisdiction of the diocese, and as peasant property it was to pay all the State taxes, obviously the important point for the imperial exchequer.[2]

An attack as direct as Nicephorus Phocas's had been proved unwise, and was not imitated until Manuel Comnenus in the twelfth century forbade the increase of monastic and secular Church property;[3] but he at the same time guaranteed all present possessions, even though the title to them were unproved by documentary evidence.[4]

The more indirect method, used specially against monastic property, was to grant it to the care of a layman. He, known as the *charisticarios*, was nominally responsible for its welfare, but in practice did not fail to reap considerable profit from its revenues. In the first half of the eleventh century the Patriarch Alexius protested in synod against episcopal abuse of this;[5] in the middle of the century Isaac Comnenus had roused opposition during his short reign by his appropriation of ecclesiastical and monastic property;[6] but it was most extensively used by Alexius Comnenus who had no other means of rewarding his followers. The evil affects of such a policy are described in the

---

[1] Jus, iii, c. 3, n. 19, pp. 292–6.   [2] Ibid., c. 3, n. 29, pp. 306–18.
[3] Nicetas Choniates, vii. 3 (p. 271).
[4] Dölger 1347, 1372, 1418–19, 1425.
[5] PG, cxix, cols. 828 ff.   [6] Attaleiates, pp. 60–1.

vigorous protest of John, the Patriarch of Antioch.[1] Writing in
Alexius's reign, he shows that the roots of this abuse were not of
recent growth. Patriarchs and Emperors had granted monastic
houses to laymen for the purposes of restoration, and in order to
help the monastery, not the lay patron.[2] John is not precise as
to date, but he evidently thought it was after the iconoclastic
controversy in the ninth century; by the middle of the tenth
century there is evidence that many monastic houses were
wealthy, and it must have been then that there began the abuse
of an originally well-intentioned policy. By the time of the
Patriarch Sisinnius (995–8?), whom John mentions, rich and
flourishing monasteries were everywhere granted to the care of
laity both men and women. Sisinnius attacked this prevalent
evil, but without success,[3] as is evident from the synodal decrees
of the Patriarch Alexius not long after, and there must have been
considerable truth in John's outcry, when he says, speaking
of Sisinnius's failure: 'And now it was a question not of a
monastery here and there, but all alike were granted to laymen,
small or large, poor or rich, whether for monks or nuns, the only
exceptions being a very few of the newly built houses.'[4] The
result of this secularization was, according to John, the trans-
formation of the monastery as the haven amid the waves of this
life into 'a general shipwreck'.[5] Monasteries became dis-
organized and their abbots were innkeepers; the celebration of
the liturgy within the monastery, the distribution of charity
without, the isolation from the world which was the aim of the
monastic life, all this was ruthlessly set aside by the intrusion of
the *charisticarios*, or worse still, the *charisticaria*, with the consequent submission of monks to laity.[6]

It is difficult to believe, as John would have it, that this was
the common fate of monasteries during the Macedonian period.
The place of monasteries in the Byzantine polity was such, that
an outcry would have been raised before Alexius Comnenus's
reign if the evil had been as acute as it was then. As described
by John it was an expedient that would have deprived the

---

[1] PG, cxxxii, *Oratio de disciplina monastica et de monasteriis laicis non
tradendis*, cols. 1117 ff.
[2] Ibid., col. 1129 C.   [3] Ibid., col. 1132 A.   [4] Ibid., col. 1132 B.
[5] Ibid., col. 1133 A.   [6] Ibid., cols. 1140 ff.

ecclesiastical authorities of the monastic revenue which evidence shows them to have been anxious to enjoy; it would have been bitterly resented by those monasteries which had been fortunate enough to obtain the imperial exemption from any ecclesiastical control. The one person who could employ this method of payment extensively was a strong Emperor, such as Alexius Comnenus, and even then John's evidence is corroborated by only one instance of an imperial grant, that of the peninsula of Cassandra to Alexius's brother Adrian, recorded because it contained property of the Laura on Athos whose rights as proprietors were carefully safeguarded by an imperial bull.[1] It is not possible to do more than state that such Macedonian evidence as exists does not indicate grants to *charisticarioi* as the cause of deterioration of monastic life; this is only too often due to the successful financial immunity which houses coveted in denial of the spirit of their way of life.

Instances of financial privileges were usually coupled with immunity from jurisdiction, whether that of the secular court or the bishop's court. The monk obviously preferred imperial justice. *Νέα Μονή* was exempt from all regular jurisdiction, and responsible only to the Emperor,[2] the hermit Nicodemus was completely withdrawn from the power of the bishop,[3] the monastery on the island of Strobelos was exempt from all jurisdiction,[4] Athos's complaint of outside jurisdiction was supported by the Emperor,[5] and disputes between individual monasteries on Mt. Athos went to be settled by the Emperor.[6] During the years 1025–81 Dölger finds only one instance of a monastic difficulty being referred to the Patriarch and synod, and then this was at the Emperor's command.[7]

Normally a monastery would be subject to the bishop's court, it would make financial contributions to the ecclesiastical funds of the diocese, in addition to being taxed by the secular authori-

---

[1] VV, 3 (1896), pp. 121–4 (Dölger 1118).
[2] MM, v, pp. 2–5 (Dölger 868).
[3] *Corpus inscript. graec.* iv, pp. 327–9, No. 8704 (Dölger 826).
[4] MM, vi, pp. 19–21 (Dölger 1045).
[5] Meyer, pp. 36–8 (Dölger 874).
[6] *Akty russkago na svjatom Afonê monastyrya ... Panteleimona*, Kiev, 1873, p. 20 (14) (Dölger 886).
[7] T. Uspensky, *Mnêniya i postanovleniya*, p. 16 (5 ff.) (Dölger 986).

ties, nor would the peasants on monastic land be excused their financial obligations towards the government. It would be difficult to escape ordination or consecration fees. All the advantages were with a monastery that obtained imperial privileges. The instances of imperial concessions are relatively few, in comparison with the number of monasteries in existence, and such evidence must therefore be read as the exception rather than the rule. Nevertheless, nobody would deny the *de facto* independence of Byzantine monasteries, whatever the nominal ties of jurisdiction or taxation by which they were bound. The superiority of the monk over the secular, and indeed the very nature of Byzantine religious life, made it inevitable that the monastery should be universally regarded as the home of the saint and the refuge of the sinner, and as such it enjoyed special treatment from both Emperor and people, and for the Patriarch to exercise any effective control was not in the nature of the Byzantine economy.

This, then, was the privileged position of the Byzantine monastery, and, like a spoilt child, it showed only too plainly its lack of discipline. Its refusal to submit to any consistent and impartial authority, and the very lack of any such authority, made possible the undesirable frequency of small foundations, which were not affiliated to a larger house and could often last only for a season, after which they lapsed into disrepute and disrepair, in signal contrast to the vitality and stability of Western houses. Again and again the lives of the saints tell how the site chosen for the new building was one on which stood the ruins of a church or oratory or monastery, and often the history of a particular monastery passes into obscurity with the death of its founder and the end of the life. Such was the case with the church which S. Dorotheus rebuilt in the eleventh century, and with S. Marine near Chrysopolis where Symeon the Young lived in voluntary exile. Since such foundations would seem to be without any inspiration save that of their abbot, and often without the stability of organization afforded by a written constitution, it is probable that the gradual disappearance of the monks, due to secular temptations, occurred even during the life of the founder. Such difficulty was certainly faced by S. Dorotheus, whose monks went away on business from time

to time, and lingered on the return journey;[1] while the ease with
which Symeon the Young was transferred by his spiritual father
from the monastery of Studios to the neighbouring S. Mamas,
shows how difficult it must have been for the abbot to maintain
discipline, when the outcasts from one monastery found so ready
a refuge in another;[2] had he not offered to receive them back into
his monastery,[3] Symeon's thirty howling rebels would have gone
to join that eternal floating population of unattached monks
which was not only a menace to the integrity of monastic life
but a drain on the economic resources of the Empire. Effective
control, either from within the monastery, or ultimately from the
Patriarch's supreme power, would have supplied that continuity
which Byzantine houses seem to lack. But in any case they did
not possess the vitality and creativeness which impelled Western
monasteries to throw off daughter houses, to bind them to the
original in a constructive unity, which yet possessed sufficient
elasticity to allow of development, the whole being, moreover,
subordinated to the authority of the Pope.

The defects of organization could not but react on the
standards of monastic life, especially when monasteries were so
freely and intimately used by all sorts and conditions of people.
Monks travelled, an activity which seems to have been expected,
and consequently provided for, by Constantine IX, who first of
all suggested that the monks of *Νέα Μονή* should share the Constantinople quarters of the monks of Mt. Olympus.[4] Two years
afterwards, perhaps when this arrangement had proved unsatisfactory, the abbot obtained the privilege of a separate house
in the district of Angeria (?), near the church of S. Nicholas.[5]
Thus monks evidently travelled on what may have been a
legitimate purpose; even the monks of the Athos Laura had a
secular trustee in Constantinople.[6] But they also seem to have
engaged in a great many worldly activities. It may have been

---

[1] PG, cxx, col. 1069 B (ch. 15).
[2] *Vita Symeonis*, p. 32 (ch. 22). Cf. Attaleiates who definitely states in his
Diataxis that he does not generally wish monks from other monasteries to be
received in his foundation, MM, v, p. 313 (30).
[3] *Vita Symeonis*, p. 54 (ch. 41). See also *infra*, p. 197.
[4] MM, v, pp. 5–6 (Dölger 878).
[5] Ibid., v, pp. 6–7 (Dölger, who gives Angeria (?) for MM's Ἀγγύριον, 887).
[6] Meyer, p. 27.

necessary to engage in a certain degree of trade, but the Athos
monks had employed themselves as though they were primarily
merchants, as the difficulties of 1045 showed;[1] Psellus wrote of
the monk Elias, who felt himself bound to travel and trade, in
order to support his mother, but who did realize the consequent
difficulty of fulfilling his vocation as a monk.[2] In the case of
Athos, it can only be concluded that monasteries sought to make
money, a desire completely at variance with the monastic traditions of self-renunciation and retreat from the world.

Equally inconsistent was the ease with which monks freely
mixed with the world, whether at social functions, or in court
life, or in legal activities.[3] If the ordinary man could fly to a
monastery when he so wished, the monk seemed at liberty to
re-enter the world; the attempt of the Council of 861 to prevent
monks from leaving their monasteries would seem to have been
unavailing. Monks surrounded Michael IV,[4] while Zoe, though
tonsured, had no scruple about emerging to share the imperial
throne, first with a sister who had likewise left a convent for the
purpose,[5] and then with a third husband. What reality could
there have been in monastic vows when such were the occur-
rences of everyday life? Even the spiteful canon of Psellus[6]
assumes an air of probability, when such monks as his Jacob
must have filled, not only the monasteries, but the very streets.
Xiphilinus was struck with the defects of life in the monasteries on
Mt. Olympus, Symeon the Young fled in desperation from the
monastery of Studios, and the Emperor had to intervene to stay
the secularization of Mt. Athos. Nor did the abbots escape condemnation. Almost as a Cistercian censuring the Cluniac lapses,
Symeon described the abbots who would ride abroad frequently
in rich trappings, preceded and followed by a cavalcade of atten-
dants.[7] Small wonder that he deplored the lack of true leaders,
and stressed the need of spiritually minded confessors, 'for there

---

[1] Meyer, pp. 36 ff.   [2] Sathas, v, pp. 402–4 (*Ep.* 153, 154).
[3] Cf. Xiphilinus's *De clericis causas agentibus*, PG, cxix, cols. 760–1.
[4] Psellus, *Chron.* iv. 37 (i, p. 75).
[5] Though it is true that both Zoe and Theodora had been tonsured under
compulsion, and that Theodora did not wish to leave the monastery on the
Petrion where she had lived so long in virtual confinement.
[6] Sathas, v, pp. 177–81.
[7] PG, cxx, col. 438 D.(*Or.* 24).

are indeed few, and especially in these days, who know the proper
care of souls or who can rightly cure spiritual diseases'.[1]

By the end of the twelfth century, Eustathius, who became
Archbishop of Thessalonica in 1175, could assert that monks
were more worldly than the layman. Ignorant, greedy, undis-
ciplined, they spent their lives in thought for their material
comfort, increasing their facilities for hot baths and procuring
the most luxurious clothes.[2] Eustathius probably wrote in exile
after the fall of the Comnenian house, having failed in his attempt
at monastic reform within his diocese. The truth in his treatise,
as with John of Antioch, is presented with emphasis and irony,
in order to make his case more forceful. Without denying the
validity of such criticism, it may be suggested that it is only one
side of the story. There is other evidence which points to the
continued maintenance of the best traditions of Byzantine
monastic life.

[1] Ibid., col. 433 A (*Or.* 23).
[2] *De emendanda vita monachica*, PG, cxxxv, col. 749 (ch. 26); ed. Tafel.
p. 220.

CHAPTER X

THE BYZANTINE MONASTERY

'And so monks ought to live in a monastery as though it were some solitary island in the midst of the sea and to regard themselves as being completely cut off from the world.'
Symeon the Young, *Divinorum Amorum Liber*, xxviii (PG, cxx, col. 570 D).

> Bound fast in the faith let us strain every nerve,
> We who have bidden farewell to the body,
> For those who hate us attack unceasingly,
> So let us be armed that they may take to flight.
>   What is the weapon of a monk?
> Even to submit in all meekness to his abbot,
> To love God and be charitable towards his brothers,
> To show all zeal at each appointed office, singing
>   Alleluia.

S. Romanus, *Canticum de Mortuis* (ed. Pitra, *Analecta Sacra*, i, pp. 48–9).

CRITICISM of the life lived by monks implied a clear conception of the monastic ideal, and the Macedonian and Comnenian periods were not without both exposition of this ideal and attempts to put it into practice. The *typica* of the late eleventh and the twelfth centuries supply minute details concerning the regulation of monastic devotions and charities in certain houses founded by laymen; the lives of the saints, though without any formal account of the internal economy of monasteries, give valuable information about the habits of various houses; the better known ecclesiastical foundations such as the houses on Athos or the house of Christodoulus on Patmos, by reason of their appeals for imperial sanction, frequently obtained chrysobulls concerning their government which supplement the hagiographical sources; and most important of all, there are the sermons of Symeon the Young, an abbot and mystic living at the end of the tenth and beginning of the eleventh century, containing unusually constructive criticism, in that emphasis on the faults of monastic life is balanced by suggestions for their remedy, and these suggestions touch not only the details of external conduct, but more important still, the devotional life of the monk.

Throughout this evidence certain monastic principles run, and there is little deviation from the well-accepted Studite

rule. Under the Macedonians there are three quite different
houses which well illustrate how far there was any variety in
Byzantine monastic foundations, and which were the result of
definite thought and determination to ensure that the monks
should lead a good life, according to the intent of the founder.
Each of these houses was somewhat different in purpose; Attaleiates' was an alms-house and hospital administered by monks,
Dorotheus's rule was based on a careful balance between practical duties and spiritual devotions, Symeon's was more like
Dorotheus's, but obviously something deeper and wider, owing
its inspiration to one who was a mystic and a saint. In the period
of the Comneni no new development is found, but the sources
of the previous centuries receive confirmation and expansion;
Christodoulus's house shows the collection of a valuable library
of ecclesiastical writers, the *typica* of the Comneni are full of
minute regulations for their hospitals, while the devotional life
of their monks is based on the Studite principles which it was
usual for Byzantine houses to follow. From such evidence, then,
it is possible to reconstruct a picture of Byzantine monasticism
at its best. Not that this is to claim for it any measure of perfection, but it would be untrue to leave unemphasized the good of
which it showed itself capable, both in the spiritual life of its
monks, and in the practical fruits of such an experience.

The eleventh-century Attaleiates was a wealthy lawyer, who
carefully explains in his *typicon* that he wishes to found his institutions, not for any lack of heirs, but solely because he desires
to devote some of his money to the glory of God:[1] and in Attaleiates' διάταξις[2] are to be observed all the characteristics of
the Byzantine's attitude to the religious life, as well as those
features which distinguish Byzantine monasticism. His intention was to use monasticism for purposes of social service,
and it would be interesting to know how often the 'alms-giving'
which is so familiar a part of the monk's life meant as definite
a work as that performed by Attaleiates' monks. Attaleiates
dedicated to Christ a property in Rhaedestos, which was to be

---

[1] MM, v, pp. 298 (26)–299 (2).
[2] The *Diataxis* is edited in Sathas, i, and in MM, v. My references are to
the latter edition. It has been fully commented on by W. Nissen, *Die
Diataxis des Michael Attaleiates von 1077* (Jena, 1894).

a poorhouse affording rest to beggars,[1] distributing daily food
and wine, as well as an annual present of gold and corn to twelve
old men;[2] and in Constantinople he founded another alms-house[3]
with much the same duties, except that its special charge consisted of providing daily food for six old men, and corn for
eighteen deserving poor.[4] The house in Constantinople had a
chapel dedicated to John the Baptist, and monks to look after
the poor.[5] There were seven monks and an abbot, in addition to
a porter.[6] Attaleiates makes very definite provision for every
contingency, from the disobedience of the monks to the failure
of external control in the event of the extinction of his heirs.[7]
He knew exactly what he meant his monks to do. Although
he insists on employing monks, not secular clerics or laity, yet
his foundation is not a monastery, it is to be known as the Poor-
hostel of the All-merciful.[8] Nevertheless, his monks are not
merely distributors of charity, they are to live the vocational
life in the best sense of the word, hence the regulations for the
right ordering of the services[9] and the library of religious works
which is provided for their guidance.[10] The principle is obviously
that of the Studite rule, only the alms-giving and good works
are to be in accordance with the specific demands of the founder's
typicon. There is an emphasis on the independence of the
foundation; it may not seek any outside jurisdiction, it is to
settle its own affairs, and Christ is its only Lord.[11] In any real
difficulty the heirs of Attaleiates would intervene, and failing that,
it was the abbot of the monastery of Studios who was the final
authority.[12] Week by week a liturgy was to be performed for Attaleiates and for his parents and others, especially for the Emperor
who had so graciously extended his protection to the foundation.[13]

[1] MM, v, p. 297 (4–24).   [2] Ibid., pp. 306 (17)–307 (15).
[3] Ibid., pp. 297 (24)–298 (18).   [4] Ibid., p. 306 (6–17).
[5] Ibid., p. 298 (12–26).   [6] Ibid., pp. 311 (6) ff.
[7] Ibid., pp. 307 (15)–321.
[8] Ibid., pp. 302 (25)–303 (15), Πτωχοτροφεῖον τοῦ Πανοικτίρμονος.
[9] Ibid., p. 314 (19–22).   [10] Ibid., pp. 324 (29) ff.
[11] Ibid., pp. 303 (26) ff. οὔτε γὰρ βασιλικοῖς δικαίοις, οὔτε πατριαρχικοῖς, ἢ
βασιλικῇ σακέλλῃ ἢ πατριαρχικῇ ἢ ἑτέρῳ τινὶ σεκρέτῳ κοσμικῷ τε ἢ ἐκκλησιαστικῷ
ἢ μητροπόλει ἢ ἐπισκοπῇ ἢ ἄλλῳ τινὶ τῶν ἁπάντων προσκυροῦσθαι τὸ τοιοῦτόν μου
πτωχοτροφεῖον καὶ τὸ μοναστήριον ἢ ὑποκεῖσθαι βούλομαι. . .
[12] Ibid., p. 317 (24–33). The abbot of the monastery of Studios could
claim an honorarium of 3 gold nomismata, ibid., 320 (4) ff
[13] Ibid., p. 314 (10–18).

The principles which inspired this eleventh-century foundation remain unaltered in the period of the Comneni, when
Gregory Parcourianus, the grand domestic for the West under
Alexius I, and Isaac, the brother of the Emperor John Comnenus, founded monastic houses on lines very similar to those
of Attaleiates.[1] The additional interest of the twelfth-century
typica is the detailed description of the hospitals attached to
the monasteries. Although this foundation of monasteries with
the practical addition of alms-houses and hospitals had long been
an expression not only of ordinary lay devotion but of the imperial virtues of εὐσέβεια and φιλανθρωπία, it is not until the
twelfth century that there is much illustration of the practical
thought with which lay founders endeavoured to secure the
permanent well-being of the material as well as the spiritual
needs of their foundations. The detailed *typicon* of the Emperor
John Comnenus shows the well-ordered domesticity of Byzantine institutions of charity.

John's foundation was on a far more lavish scale than Attaleiates'. He had at least eighty monks under his abbot, fifty for
the care of the church, thirty for social service,[2] and the endowments[3] of the monastery included whole villages, as well
as six different monasteries, so that the administrative offices,
especially that of the oeconomus, entailed great power and
responsibility. The *typicon* begins with a dedication to Christ
by whose aid alone John has overcome his enemies; this thank-
offering characteristically is extended to the Mother of God, to
whom a church is built beside that of the Pantocrator.[4] The
foundations are to provide for prayer and charity, to perpetuate
the memory of the family of the Comneni, and to give them a
place of burial in a chapel set apart for this purpose.

The hospital[5] had fifty beds, and was divided into ten wards
in each of which special diseases were treated, except that one
ward was devoted exclusively to women. These wards each had
their own two doctors, and day and night nurses, all men,
except in the women's ward, where in addition to the two men
doctors there was a woman doctor, while the nurses were women.

[1] See Bibliography, under the name of the founder, for editions of the
typica.
[2] p. 671.   [3] pp. 698 ff.   [4] p. 657.   [5] pp. 682 ff.

There was a consultation room with two dietetic specialists (διαιτητικοί) and two surgeons (τραυματικοί) as well as a herniary specialist (κηλοτόμος). Except for two doctors attached to the hospital, the rest were only visiting physicians, taking their turns in alternate months, and presumably having their own private practices. The welfare of the patients was in the hands of the πριμικήριοι, almost corresponding to the matron of a modern hospital; these visited the patients each day, hearing complaints and noting progress. Then there is a long list of various members of the hospital staff, including bakers, laundresses, cooks, a miller, and a groom. There were two chaplains and two readers to supervise the spiritual welfare of the sick, and a teacher of medicine to instruct the children of the hospital doctors, presumably that they might take their fathers' places. Each of these hospital officials and servants had a fixed salary.[1]

There was also an alms-house for twenty-six crippled old men,[1] having its own chapel and priest, servants and provisions; this was supervised by a monk who was responsible for its prosperity. John takes care to ensure that only the genuinely poor and crippled are to be admitted, and he excludes clergy, or monks, or slaves, or those in the service of officials (ἀπό τινων ἀρχόντων). Near to this alms-house was a home for epileptics.[2]

The outstanding feature of John's *typicon* is its detail. For example, the hospital bedding is described and its renewal and cleaning provided for;[3] in each ward there is to be a copper basin in which the doctor may wash his hands after attending to a patient;[4] each patient is to have two baths a week or more if necessary,[5] while the cripples in the alms-houses are allowed only two a month.[6] This very careful regulation emphasizes the thoughtfulness of the founder.

But it is an element of fear that is suggested by the *typicon* of the Empress Irene.[7] While the organization of John's hospital and alms-houses naturally invited a more detailed description, Irene's convent had nothing of this kind, and her multitude of rules were all for the benefit of the nuns. Although Irene's

---

[1] pp. 694 ff.   [2] p. 695.   [3] p. 682.
[4] p. 692.   [5] p. 686.   [6] p. 695.
[7] Ed. MM., vol. v, pp. 327–91, and PG, cxxxvii, cols. 985–1128. Reference here is to the chapters, which are the same in both editions.

typicon was for women, the life prescribed differs very little
from that of monks, and the intentions of the foundress present
a striking similarity to those of other founders. The aim is the
same: to make an act of thanksgiving to the Mother of God, and
in this case to provide a home and burial-place not only for nuns
but for the women of the imperial family; the government is
the same: for the convent is an independent house (αὐτο-
δέσποτος) under the supreme control of its abbess, subject only
to a final appeal to a princess of the royal family. There were
to be twenty-four nuns, but this number could be increased at
the discretion of the abbess to a maximum of forty;[1] besides
these there were six servants. The various offices of the convent
were to be held by nuns, appointed by the abbess in accordance
with the ceremony described in the *typicon*;[2] the outside business
of the convent was in the control of the oeconomus, who was
a eunuch.[3] At great length Irene makes provision for the worldly
welfare of her convent, forbidding any reclaiming of gifts, or the
sale of property except in unusual circumstances.[4]

She is equally careful to outline the kind of life which her
nuns are to lead, and to prevent temptations. All the men they
meet within the convent are if possible to be eunuchs; their
priests are to be eunuchs who have taken monastic vows, but if
such are not obtainable a eunuch rather than a monk is to be
chosen.[5] The convent is not to be overlooked by other buildings,[6] and the nuns are to go out only under strict supervision,
and only on some such errand as visiting a sick parent.[7] No
man, even a father or brother, is to be admitted,[8] nor may the
choir be augmented by male voices on festivals, but the nuns
must content themselves with their own voices and those of
their devout chaplains.[9] Thus safeguarded from the world, the
nuns are to spend their time between their duties and their
devotions. The services are described at length[10] with the
appropriate psalms and *troparia*, and the various festivals to be
specially observed. Then the food is prescribed for the different
days and seasons, and dignified behaviour at meals is essential;
the nuns process to their meal singing Psalm 145, and while they

[1] Ch. 5.   [2] Chs. 18 ff.   [3] Ch. 14.
[4] Chs. 8–10.   [5] Ch. 15; cf. chs. 16 and 57.   [6] Ch. 74.
[7] Ch. 17.   [8] Ibid.   [9] Ch. 75.   [10] Chs. 32 ff.

eat they listen in silence to a book read aloud.[1] Only the abbess
may speak at meals 'in a quiet voice', and she is to be answered
in 'a still quieter voice, with a minimum of words'. Unfitting
or untimely words, struggles for a better seat, lingering for conversation, private eating, or the removal of food from the table
are all alike condemned,[2] and if reproof fails to correct these
faults, the culprit is to be expelled from the convent. Such
correction appears to be in the hands of the abbess, and in the
event of her failure, there is no suggestion of any appeal to
another house, or a higher authority. Should the abbess herself
be at fault she can be removed by the patroness, and a new abbess
chosen in accordance with the form of election in the *typicon*.[3]

The second part of the *typicon*, written later and after the
death of Alexius, concerns the residence of the dowager Empress
herself. This was built on to the convent and provided the
ladies of the imperial family with more than ample comfort.[4]
It is interesting not so much as throwing light upon the monastic
life of this period, but as reflecting the character of the Empress,
and confirming the inconsistency of outlook suggested by the
rest of the *typicon*. Poverty and the ascetic life are praised, yet
exceptions are made should the Empress's daughters wish to
reside in the convent;[5] and a logically minded nun might wonder
why the Empress and her daughters did not avail themselves of
their opportunity to accept a life of complete poverty with the
rest of the sisters, why should they enjoy their luxurious suite
with its two sets of bathrooms, while the nuns had only their
common dormitory and one bath a month?[6]

Irene's *typicon* is that of a woman brought up in an atmosphere
of devotion, but with no innate capacity for the ascetic way of
life. The descriptions of the services show her carefulness for
the spiritual welfare of the nuns, but her true self comes out
in her economic and practical and almost fussy details. She
suggests buying when prices are cheap;[7] she insists that the
sisters genuflect as one, taking their time from the abbess;[8]
and there was clearly no place here for spiritual concentration
in such a stifling atmosphere. But although there are some

---

[1] Chs. 40 ff.   [2] Chs. 41, 42, 45, 49.
[3] Chs. 13 and 11.   [4] Ch. 79.   [5] Ch. 4.
[6] Chs. 58 and 79.   [7] Ch. 52.   [8] Ch. 32.

digressions in the nature of spiritual exhortations, she gives no convincing instruction. Perhaps that was not within her experience, and she betrays herself when she says that prayer is of less value than charity or love;[1] whereas Symeon the Young would have said that they were the complement of each other. Irene's *typicon* is not attractive to read and it has none of the spontaneity or simplicity of Attaleiates', perhaps because both her emphasis on her imperial majesty and her care for her own family are too prominent. But it does show the difficulties against which Byzantine monasticism had to struggle, and it can only be hoped that the abbess of Irene's convent was both strong minded and spiritually minded.

In these *typica*, then, are excellent examples of all that monasticism meant to the laity; it was a means of executing those good works which were the corollary of the Christian faith; it was essentially an individual matter, independent of any other ecclesiastical body, but appealing in ultimate necessity to a great monastic house such as the monastery of Studios; it found its firmest assurance of continuity in the imperial guarantee; and it naturally perpetuated the memory of its founder. In their use of this combination of devotion and good works, the founders show their realization of the strength of monasticism, and the details of their *typica* convey a reality which is missing when the only record is a brief sentence in a chronicle, 'He founded a monastery' or 'He endowed an institute for orphans'. It is so much easier to remember the disastrous independence, the falling off in the standard of life, the fight for financial privileges, than the substantial good which such houses as these must have performed.

It is refreshing to come upon evidence of monasteries founded by men who were themselves the spiritual leaders of their monks. It is perhaps natural that a layman in drafting his *typicon* should be specially concerned with domestic economy and external safeguards for the welfare of his foundation, and it is from ecclesiastical sources that the normal devotional life and the less elaborate structure of ordinary religious houses is disclosed.

Similar to Attaleiates' ideal was that formulated for his monks by S. Dorotheus. The differences are those naturally attendant

[1] Ch. 25.

upon environment; Attaleiates' houses had been in the crowded quarters of a great city, while Dorotheus chose for his site a ruined church in a scantily populated country district in Pontus.[1] His biography, which is the only source of information about him, was written by John, the Archbishop of Euchaita, whose conception of monastic life must have found its practical expression in this saint. John's admiration for S. Dorotheus is indeed consistent with his ideals. Is it possible, he asks, to describe the virtue of the saint's way of life? 'Who indeed could tell of his poverty, his frugality, his moderation towards all, his zeal in vigils, his insatiable fervour in psalms, his concentration in prayer, his meditation on things divine, his love towards strangers and the poor?'[2] Nor is there any undue bias towards intense asceticism. His life is summed up in the words 'a sufficiency for the body, an abundance for the soul',[3] and there is a definite place for the subordinate, but necessary, human needs. 'What then is the praise due to the saint for his subsidiary works of the hands?' and the answer describes the cultivation of land, the planting of vineyards, and the sowing of vegetables.[4] Dorotheus was evidently on friendly terms with the neighbouring peasants, who assisted him and his monks in the work of rebuilding; when he died he left part of his possessions to the monastery, part to the peasants.[5] And with the end of the saint's life, the monastery, as was so often the case, appears to pass out of history; a small house had little chance of survival unless it enjoyed special imperial protection, and even that was no guarantee against the Turkish invasions of Asia Minor in the eleventh and twelfth centuries, as the story of Christodoulus shows.

The monk Christodoulus was the eleventh-century founder of the monastery of S. John the Evangelist on the island of Patmos. Before the settlement on Patmos at the end of the century he had led a varied life in Asia Minor and Palestine. His short *typicon* and his will tell his own history, and the growth of the monastery is indicated by different imperial bulls, as well as one patriarchal confirmation of the house's independence of

[1] PG, cxx, col. 1064 AB (ch. 10).   [2] Ibid., col. 1065 B (ch. 11).
[3] Ibid., col. 1065 D (ch. 12).
[4] Ibid., cols. 1069 D–1072 A (ch. 16).   [5] Ibid., col. 1072 CD (ch. 17).

outside ecclesiastical jurisdiction.[1] Originally a monk on Mt. Olympus, he left this retreat to travel as a pilgrim in search of solitude to Palestine, where he lived a hermit life in the deserts, which were already peopled with anchorites.[2] Driven westwards by the Turks he found a home in the laura of Stylos on Mt. Latros; he became πρῶτος of the Latros monks,[3] and spoke very highly of their virtues and goodness even in the face of the Turkish danger.[4] From Latros Christodoulus fled to Strobelos, a town near the island of Cos, and there he obtained the help of Arsenius Scenures, a man of property. With Arsenius's aid a house was built and endowed on Cos, and the Emperor's protection gained. Here Christodoulus found that he had temporarily escaped the difficulty of Turkish invasion only to be faced with the problem of protecting his monks from the dangers of intercourse with laymen; he therefore emigrated once more, this time choosing the suitably isolated island of Patmos,[5] where he founded a permanent home.

The history of the house on Patmos, as far as it is known, is that of the normal Byzantine monastery. Throughout the Comnenian period imperial bulls confirmed and increased its privileges of exemption from both taxation and military service. Towards the end of Christodoulus's lifetime he and his monks once again fled from the Turks, this time to Euboea, where he himself died. But this was only a temporary interruption, and the body of the founder with his possessions was taken back to Patmos at his own desire. The house evidently throve in the twelfth century; in 1157 it had seventy-six monks,[6] and by 1196 had as many as a hundred and fifty.[7]

A house of a hundred and fifty was very different from the humble beginning at the end of the eleventh century, and an inventory drawn up in 1201 indicates a corresponding increase in its treasure of beautifully set icons and relics and richly worked vestments, as well as its valuable collection of manuscripts.[8] It is interesting to see which authors were read in a monastery.

---

[1] These documents are in MM, vi.　　[2] MM, vi, p. 60 (chs. 2–3).
[3] Ibid., p. 62 (ch. 5); see also Der Latmos in *Milet*.
[4] Ibid., p. 61 (ch. 4).　　　　　　　　[5] Ibid., pp. 64 ff (chs. 8–9).
[6] Ibid., pp. 108 ff.　　　　　　　　　　[7] Ibid., p. 131.
[8] Ed. Ch. Diehl, BZ, i (1892), pp. 488–525, with an introduction, which is reprinted in *Études Byzantines*, pp. 307–36.

Byzantine monks emphasized abstention from secular learning
as a natural corollary to flight from the world, but, on the other
hand, many of them must have received a normal education
before they became monks, and could not unlearn this training,
even if they tried to forget its more secular elements. Those
who were specially endowed with a love of learning were not
without opportunity for using this in the service of the Church.
They had their theological libraries, and if they were good
copyists they could add to these. Symeon the Young had spent
much of his time as a monk in copying manuscripts, so his
biographer Nicetas notes; Christodoulus says in his *typicon* that
the books in his monastery should be carefully looked after and
copied.[1] The Patmos inventory is excellent evidence for the
kind of books which were likely to be found in a monastery.
Christodoulus had from the beginning shown his love of books,
even to an almost worldly tenacity in retaining them throughout
his forced travels, and in ensuring their ultimate possession to
his Patmos foundation. When he fled from Mt. Latros he took
with him what he could;[2] these volumes were sent for safety to
Constantinople, but after the Patmos house was founded, part
were successfully reclaimed,[3] and went with Christodoulus to
Euboea, to be returned on his death with minute instructions
against their alienation, and safeguards against any future claims
from Mt. Latros, almost as though he had an uneasy conscience
concerning those books which were originally the property of
the Latros communities.[4] The founder's care for books was
evidently respected, and by 1201 the monastery had 330 manuscripts, 267 on parchment, 63 on paper (bombycine). The
contents were in keeping with the aims of monastic life; there
were numerous copies of the Old and New Testaments and the
Church Fathers, of service books and of the lives of the saints.
In the whole collection there were only seventeen secular manuscripts, and of these the more interesting volumes were Josephus,
and a commentary on his Jewish Antiquities, Barlaam and
Joasaph, the history of Scylitzes, and an unnamed volume of
Aristotle.[5] Beyond the library, very little is known about the
life of the Patmos monks in the twelfth century, but if their

[1] MM, vi, p. 74 (ch. 21).   [2] Diehl, op. cit., p. 496, n. 6.
[3] MM, vi, p. 87.   [4] Ibid.   [5] See Diehl, op. cit., pp. 499 ff.

spiritual life was equal to the quality of their manuscripts they more than justified their foundation.

It is noticeable that Christodoulus made no effort to return to the monastery where he had taken his vows. Like many Byzantine monks he had a restlessness that urged him to found a house of his own; in his case he was right. But it is possible that Dorotheus, who was clearly a good monk, would have shown more wisdom had he remained in the monastery at Amisos where he served his novitiate,[1] for if the larger houses were continually losing their better monks, they could not hope to maintain a high standard of life, while the offshoots were often of such a temporary nature that the weakening of the original house scarcely seemed justified. It all leads to the same conclusion: that which really mattered in Byzantium was the individual, the holy man, the saint, who was a man apart and a law unto himself.

Nowhere is this better exemplified than in the story of Symeon the Young. He was the son of a wealthy Paphlagonian family and was destined to appear at court under the auspices of his uncle, and eventually to hold office there. Symeon, however, though he went to Constantinople to be educated, could not be moved from the intense desire which possessed him when he was still a small child. He wished to become a monk, and, as might be expected from the Symeon of later life, he even then had the courage of his convictions. Under the guidance of his confessor and spiritual father, another Symeon and a Studite monk, he made his profession as soon as he reached a reasonable age, and entered the monastery of Studios. Both confessor and novice had exceptionally, perhaps unreasonably, high ideals, and the abbot regarded their criticism as insubordination. Nicetas says that the less worthy of the monks were jealous and therefore instigated the abbot to force the boy to accept him as confessor in the place of the elder Symeon. The attempt failed, and the old man was then ordered to depart.[2] He obeyed, but he took his young follower with him, and they both went to the neighbouring house of S. Mamas, whose abbot was the excellent Antony of well-known virtue.[3]

---

[1] PG, cxx, col. 1056 A (ch. 3).
[2] *Vita Symeonis*, pp. 18–32 (ch. 10–21).   [3] Ibid., p. 32 (ch. 22).

This particular episode shows the difficulty of assessing the quality of Byzantine monasticism. Although Symeon was driven away by an intrigue, the prejudiced Nicetas could impute it only to the abbot and 'the more negligent of the brethren',[1] while Symeon's own conduct was not above reproach; on the other hand, either the good Antony must have been ineffective, or else the monastery had a curiously sudden lapse, if three years after his death it was in the condition described by Nicetas, who says that Symeon as new abbot of S. Mamas was faced by dilapidated buildings, an influx of worldlings, and a paucity of permanent monks.[2]

For more than twenty years Symeon worked at S. Mamas, and then he went into exile, as the result of ecclesiastical opposition to the cult of his spiritual father, the elder Symeon. He crossed the water to Chrysopolis, and there, near the village of Palouciton, he founded a monastery on the site of a ruined chapel of S. Marine. This flourished, and his fame spread, nor did his followers in Constantinople forget him. But, even though pardoned royally by the Patriarch, he refused to return, and died in voluntary exile.

Symeon has a special interest apart from the vicissitudes of his life. In his sermons he shows very clearly the contrast between his own conception of the ideal monk and the life lived by the particular fraternity to whom he addressed his words. Nor is it strange that there should have been such a discrepancy between Symeon's ideal and the practice of his monks. Symeon was an unusual and an uncompromising man, and he found nothing to praise in the pleasant ease which Byzantine monasteries afforded to so many people. His clarity of perception and precision of statement are all the more interesting since there is so little other information to show what life in an eleventh-century monastery meant. Psellus satirizes the monks of Mt. Olympus, John Mauropous describes the life of S. Dorotheus, chronicles mention the imperial use of monastic foundations, Attaleiates outlines the administration he desired, but none give that intimacy of detail which shows exactly how the monks usually lived. This could come only from within, from one who had the unerring eye of an administrator, and yet the

---

[1] *Vita Symeonis*, p. 24 (ch. 16).   [2] Ibid., p. 46 (ch. 34).

experience of a mystic, one who was to himself the greatest of
sinners, but was blessed with that *illuminatio divina* which was
the end of all being, and who was indeed far more human than
would be imagined from Nicetas's life of him.

Symeon had no doubt concerning the aim and course of
monastic life, nor had he failed to notice even the smallest human
weakness which crept in to corrupt it. His twenty-fifth *Oratio*,
which is addressed to novices, gives a clear picture of the everyday life which Symeon's monks led.[1] Rising in the middle of the
night, before daybreak, they prayed, and then assembled for the
doxology. They were to pay due attention to their behaviour
during this service, 'putting aside all sloth, neither lounging,
nor with one foot crossed over the other, nor leaning against the
walls or pillars, but with hands steadfastly clasped, with both
feet firmly planted on the ground, and with head not peering
hither and thither, but bent in front'.[2] This ὀρθρινὴ δοξολογία[3]
evidently consisted of the Six Psalms proper to Mattins, the
verses following them (στιχολογία), and the Lessons, and
Symeon remarks that he hopes that none will approach it without tears. Immediately it is over they are to go out, 'not lingering for the chatter of this or that person or entering into idle
conversation', but entering their cells they are to pray 'with
tears', and to attend to their work (ἐργασία σωματική τις),[4] being
careful never to enter the cell of another, unless it is that
of their spiritual father, or whither they have been sent on
business (εἰ μὴ ἀποσταλῇς, ἢ παρὰ τοῦ διακονιτοῦ τῆς μονῆς).[5]
Always they are to guard their tongues and thoughts, to pass
by, with deeply bowed head, the brother who presumably
might be reproached, since he is engaged in ill-timed gossip
(ὁμιλοῦντα παρὰ καιρόν)[6]. This sounds reminiscent of what
might have been Symeon's own behaviour as a monk, perhaps
muttering to himself as he went by the words which he now

[1] PG, cxx, cols. 440–7; the Greek is still in MS. See p. 204, n. 1.
[2] Ibid., col. 441 (*Or.* 25).
[3] *Cod. gr. monac.* 177, f. 130ᵛ.   [4] Ibid., f. 131ʳ.
[5] Ibid., col. 442; *cod. gr. monac.* 177, f. 131ʳ. But some legitimate conversation must have been allowed, for in his *Capita*, Symeon says that when a
monk is engaged in the biannual wash of his clothes, he should ask a fellow
monk to lend him his garment to wear while his own is drying in the sun
(PG, cxx, col. 673 CD (135)).   [6] *Cod. gr. monac.* 177, f. 131ʳ.

quotes, 'Blessed is the man that walketh not in the counsel of the ungodly, nor standeth in the way of the sinners'—an attitude which would, perhaps, arouse the opposition and resentment of the less worthy.

So the hours pass by in meditation and mourning as befits a pilgrim and a sinner, until the 'hour of the liturgy'.[1] After the liturgy the problem of a meal arises, and Symeon's anxiety for the behaviour of his monks seems to imply that monastic life was frequently lacking in self-restraint. 'Do not rush to the meal which is laid out and stretch an eager hand before the elder brothers have begun to eat, or before the blessing has been said by the priest.'[2] Consume only the modicum of mouthfuls and take 'one or perhaps two drinks', and that at a definite, fixed hour of the day. 'Suppose the brothers sitting round the table urge you to eat or drink more, answer them only by rising up, with clasped hands, bent head, saying in a quiet voice "Excuse me" (συγχώρησον).[3] The length and care with which Symeon warns his novices against the demon of gluttony (ὁ τῆς γαστριμαργίας δαίμων)[4] can only imply that in his experience this was indeed an enemy to be feared in a monastic community. Between the meal and vespers the monk was within his own cell. If it were summer he could read for a short space, no doubt the Bible or Church Fathers, but Symeon nowhere states the extent of the monastic library, nor does he himself ever quote except from the Bible, the Church Fathers, or John Climacus.[5] After this a 'brief sleep' on a straw pallet is permitted, followed by meagre sustenance of bread or vegetables. If it is winter the rest is omitted, and its place taken by manual work. Symeon gives no details about this work, but Nicetas in his Life says that, when Symeon was a monk in S. Mamas, his own manual work was copying MSS. of the Scriptures.[6]

Finally the wooden gong summons all to vespers (ἡ ὑμνῳδία τοῦ λυχνικοῦ).[7] After the blessing the monks again enter their cells in silence, read for a short space, then pray and worship in

[1] PG, cxx, col. 443 (Or. 25).   [2] Ibid.
[3] Cod. gr. monac. 177, f. 134ʳ.
[4] PG, cxx, col. 445 (Or. 25); cod. gr. monac. 177, f. 134ᵛ.
[5] See below on Symeon's attitude to learning and his own education.
[6] Vita Symeonis, p. 38 (ch. 27).
[7] PG, cxx, col. 445 (Or. 25); cod. gr. monac. 177, f. 135ʳ.

silence,[1] again 'with sighs and tears'. When these devotions are finished they read again for a little, and then turn to their work (τοῦ ἐργοχείρου)[2] until the first watch, i.e. the third hour of the night. From this point until the middle of the night sleep is permitted, after which all rise for the morning doxology. In this *Oratio*, which begins with the words 'Whoever, my brothers, has newly renounced the world', the bare framework of the monastic life is set out with a simplicity that would make it readily understood by the novice. But it shows, too, so keen an understanding of the small everyday temptations that it must have conveyed an uncomfortable feeling of insecurity to those of the older brethren who had hoped that their shortcomings had escaped the eye of the abbot.

Symeon stands out as a man of judgement and perception, who could well have been both hated and feared by his monks, nor is it without significance that Nicetas tells the story of the thirty brothers, who could bear his sermons no longer and rose up in a body, and blasphemed like mad dogs.[3] There is something relentless, almost unscrupulous, in the way in which Symeon attacks the weaknesses of his community—the over-eating,[4] the scraps of food snatched for use between meals, the eager curiosity of those who chatted together—'Have you heard about this or that', or, 'Do you know what's happened to that poor fellow . . .' or, 'Do you know what the abbot did to him?'[5] —the irresistible temptation to sleep just a little longer, in order to be the better fortified for prayer—all this and more is described by Symeon in such a way as to make it seem so insignificant and yet so contemptible. Never does he spare or condone: 'You think what good lives you are living, and how like the Holy Fathers you are, but listen to the story of their temptations and wrestlings,'[6] or 'I heard some of you, my fathers and brothers, saying to-day what saints we should have

[1] Sometimes monks must have made considerable noise in singing. Nicetas condemns this: 'If you are singing a song of prayer to God, and a brother comes and knocks at the door of your cell, do not think that the act of prayer is more worth than the act of love, for such would not be well pleasing to God' (PG, cxx, col. 937 A (76)).

[2] *Cod. gr. monac.* 177, f. 136ʳ.

[3] *Vita Symeonis*, pp. 50–2 (chs. 38–9).

[4] PG, cxx, col. 485 B (*Or.* 32).   [5] Ibid., col. 482 BC (*Or.* 32).

[6] Ibid., col. 350 CD (*Or.* 7).

been had we lived in the times of Christ and the apostles, or
the Church Fathers; yet to-day we have to face just as many
difficulties, we may not have such definite heresies to combat,
but we have to overcome the conviction that we cannot lead
saintly lives in the present age'.[1] With such an abbot it was of no
avail to make excuses for personal shortcomings or for lack of
perseverance.

Symeon is equally clear in his definition of the duties of the
heads of monasteries and spiritual fathers. The abbot is the
head of the community, and, though every member has his
functions, he is the most important, and therefore must be
correspondingly careful in his spiritual life, for he is the mediator
between God and man.[2] But in proportion as Symeon perceived
the organic unity of a monastery and the importance of each
individual in the life of the whole, so he realized, no doubt from
personal experience, the necessity for a wise and strong dictator-
ship at its head, more especially as he had probably found that
it was only thus that a high standard could be maintained. To
depend upon outside visitation as a corrective would have been
uncertain, because of the lack of definition in the organization
of Byzantine monasteries, as well as distasteful by reason of the
gulf between the monastic and secular ecclesiastics. The life
of the abbot, then, is one of wise and careful supervision, such
as had been Symeon's own aim, avoiding material excesses in
either food or clothes, putting aside all thought of human praise,
advising and watching the younger members, encouraging in
their pursuit of the *beatus luctus* those who have lived longer in
the religious life, teaching the priests in their study of the Bible
and the apostolic tradition, and finally reproving 'with a moderate
use of rod and staff' those who are turbulent and ill conducted.[3]

In the twenty-fourth *Oratio* which deals especially with the
conduct of the abbot, Symeon speaks of the *pater spiritualis* as
though he were synonymous with the abbot, the *praepositus* and
head of the monastery. Symeon's own experience as a novice
shows that a monk's *pater spiritualis* was not necessarily the head
of the monastery, but could be a member of the community,

---

[1] PG, cxx, cols. 470 Bff (*Or.* 30).   [2] Ibid., col. 434 C (*Or.* 24).
[3] Ibid., cols. 438 C–439 B (*Or.* 24).   Cf. ibid., col. 676 A (*Cap.* 138), where
he insists on obedience to the abbot.

presumably originally chosen by the individual. The difficulty
is that Symeon himself, when he was still a young man, had had
as his own spiritual father another Symeon, a member of the
Studite monastery but not its abbot; and when he himself entered
this house he was clearly very dependent upon Symeon the
Studite, so much so that together they had roused the antagonism
of some of the other monks and the abbot.[1] In any case it seems
unlikely that Symeon would have pressed the impetuous insubordination of his youth against his better judgement as an
administrator. He evidently realized that the choice of a spiritual
father must be subject to the approval of the abbot, otherwise
this would have made for disunity and innumerable other difficulties within the monastery. Symeon was too wise an administrator not to perceive this, and in his twenty-third *Oratio* he
begins by insisting on self-abnegation and obedience. 'After you
have been called to monastic life, my brother, do not criticize the
father who tonsured you, even though he is addicted to harlotry
and carousing, and seems in your opinion to be a poor administrator of the monastery.'[2] On the other hand, he exhorts those
who do not live in a monastery to choose a man who will be
able to guide them, though he admits that a good spiritual
instructor is hard to find, and that many have only the semblance
of piety.[3]

The problem is complicated by Symeon's *Epistola de confessione*,[4] in which he emphasizes the necessity for confessing to
a man of spiritual character. The point under discussion is the
right of an unordained monk to absolve from sin. Symeon
asserts that this sacrament is dependent upon the spiritual
qualities of the absolver, and that, though it was originally a gift
bestowed upon the apostles, from whom it descended to bishops
and priests, it was now exercised by monks because of the unworthiness of the priesthood. The power of binding and loosing
was therefore a prerogative of the monk provided that he led a
good life. Obedience to a wicked abbot and confession to a holy
man were not necessarily incompatible. In the event of the

[1] *Vita Symeonis*, pp. 18–32 (chs. 10–22).
[2] PG, cxx, col. 429 C (*Or.* 23).
[3] Ibid., col. 433 AB (*Or.* 23).
[4] Ed. Holl, *Enthusiasmus und Bussgewalt*, pp. 110–27. Holl, pp. 106–9,
shows that it had been wrongly attributed to John of Damascus.

abbot's forbidding confession to the desired spiritual father the choice of evils could only rest with the individual. When placed in such circumstances Symeon himself had left the Studite house and sought another monastery, at the same time retaining his chosen spiritual father. The problem is only another form of the impossibility of avoiding the inescapable minimum of organization; as an abbot Symeon saw that such discipline must exist, as a man he felt that the only criterion was inward worth which defies both human measure and human organization.

For Symeon to speak so convincingly of the high spiritual vocation of the monk does argue for the existence of monks such as he would have. He himself is an outstanding figure: monasticism may have had its weaknesses, but at its best it produced such men. Even if most monks could not be as Symeon, they could appreciate him, and his writings were widely copied during the Middle Ages; and for lesser men to admire as far as in them lies is as genuine a creativeness as to write a *Liber divinorum amorum*. The explanation of Symeon's power lies neither in his stinging criticisms nor in his stern jurisdiction, but in the spiritual force of his writings. All he did or thought or wrote was part of himself, and his life was a manifestation of that religious experience which is the highest activity. In him Byzantine monasticism finds one of its greatest exponents, and of such a life Basil might well have been thinking when he wrote: 'If thou begin thus and end thus, having trodden the narrow way in the short time of thy ascetic life, by God's grace thou shalt enter Paradise with the splendour of the lamp of the soul, rejoicing with Christ for ever and ever. Amen.'[1]

[1] S. Basil, *De renuntiatione saeculi* (trans. W. K. L. Clarke, *The Ascetic Works of S. Basil* (London, 1925), p. 71).

CHAPTER XI

AN ELEVENTH-CENTURY MYSTIC, SYMEON THE YOUNG

I have said, 'Ye are gods; and all of you are children of the most High.'

Psalm 82, 6.

> His Essence is all Act: He did that He
> An Act might always be.
> His nature burns like fire
> His goodness infinitely does desire
> To be by all possesst;
> It is the glory of His high estate,
> And that which I for evermore admire,
> He is an Act that doth communicate.

T. Traherne, *The Anticipation*.

THE eleventh-century mystic Symeon the Young's capacity for practical affairs was the result of his consuming desire to see God, *vita autem hominis visio Dei*, or, as he might have said, *vita autem hominis Deum fieri*. 'To see' was an inadequate description, for his *Weltanschauung* was the outcome of his longing for, and indeed the very realization of, a far more intimate union. And in his expression of his experiences he shows that he was neither theologian nor philosopher. Maximus the Confessor left weary pages concerning the monothelite controversy, Evagrius and Nicetas are primarily engaged with the setting forth of the psychology of the soul and the Divinity, but Symeon, in a manner that can only attest to the reality of his experience, is interested, not in the intellectual explanation of the divine and human economy, but in the living necessity for the interaction between the two, and so true was the creativeness of his desire and of his experience that it compelled him to write.

The very fact that Symeon is not primarily concerned with teaching or with developing Church doctrine does not lessen his debt to the Church in which he lived; nor does this Church appear to be always at one with the Latin Church, especially on the central point of Symeon's mystical experience, the θέωσις. The editor of Symeon's work in the *Patrologia Graeca* thought it indeed necessary to append a long note of dissent to a certain passage in which Symeon speaks of the essentially corporeal

unity of man with Christ.¹ This is indicative of the difference
in outlook and emphasis between the Greek and the Latin
Churches, and for westerners there is ever the need of thinking
themselves into the Greek Church before they try to understand
a Byzantine mystic.² And so Symeon must be set in his background as far as is possible, for he was not an isolated or an original
figure, save by reason of the reality of his spiritual experiences
and the felicity with which he expressed them. The content of
his thought and its framework owe much to the tradition of
orthodox teaching which formed his heritage and of which he
availed himself, although the joy and vitality of his writings far sur-
pass anything which Maximus or John Climacus or Evagrius ever
wrote. But it is only by a process of relating the part to the whole
that the normality of Symeon's mode of thought is revealed. He
had admittedly read John Climacus, as well as certain of the
Greek Fathers, and he does not attempt, and would, indeed, have
been horrified at, any alteration of the accepted dogma and teaching of the Church. 'For all the glory and blessedness of the saints
was won by these two things—an orthodox faith and a good life.'³

Symeon, in common with other mystics of both western and
eastern Europe, was especially influenced by the writings of
Maximus the Confessor. Now Maximus was perhaps not so
much an original thinker as a skilful collector, and an analysis of
his work reveals the extent to which he was indebted to Evagrius
of Pontus⁴ and, through him, to Origen.⁵ Maximus is therefore
important as providing an unquestionably orthodox channel for
a contribution to Greek theology which might otherwise have
remained suspect among the writings of Evagrius and Origen.
From Evagrius and Origen can be derived (not to the exclusion
or minimizing of other notable influences) Maximus's psychological framework and discipline of the contemplative life, as
well as the hope of deification which animates it. With regard
to this latter, the outstanding characteristic, at least to a westerner,

¹ PG, cxx, col. 531 (19), 'Latinisque auribus non satis dignam censui-
mus . . .'   ² See Lot-Borodine, RHR, cv (1932).
³ PG, cxx, col. 409 B (*Or.* 20); Holl, p. 105, gives the original, ἅπας δὲ ὁ τῶν
ἁγίων ἔπαινος καὶ μακαρισμὸς διὰ τῶν δύο τούτων συνίσταται, διὰ τῆς ὀρθοδόξου
πίστεως καὶ τοῦ ἐπαινετοῦ βίου.
⁴ Evagrius of Pontus was a contemporary of the fourth-century Cappadocian Fathers. Maximus the Confessor lived in the seventh century.
⁵ See W. Bousset and M. Viller.

seems to be the belief in the reality and concreteness of the
process, a heritage perhaps from the Hellenistic mysteries, and
ultimately from Persia.[1] Deification appears to mean nothing
else but the becoming divine of the human being, even though
it may be only temporary. There are, of course, in the Greek
Church interpretations akin to those of the Latin Church. Thus
deification is the immanence of God, the indwelling of Christ in
partnership with a human being. Even so Nicetas, the eleventh-
century follower of Symeon, wrote of 'being made like God *as
far as in us lies* (ὡς ἡμῖν ἐφικτόν)',[2] and he speaks of keeping
this 'likeness to God (τὴν θεοειδῆ ἀφομοίωσιν)'.[3]   And, on the
other hand, the thought of deification does occur among western
mystics, but it is not without significance that it is found
most frequently among those men, John Scotus Erigena, Eck-
hardt, and the kindred school of mystics (as, for instance, Ruys-
broek, and the *Theologica Germanica*) who had been influenced by
Greek theology, especially as seen through the eyes of Maximus
the Confessor. The doctrine of deification was, then, of importance in the Greek Church, and had developed from a heritage
of thought that was not identical with that of the Latin Church.

As far as it is possible to assign a division or discover a water-
shed, this is found at the end of the fourth century: on the one
side is Augustine, whose writings form the basis of the Latin
tradition; on the other the Greeks who followed the Cappadocian school[4] and have nothing that can compare with the subsequent vitality of the western medieval development.[5] But with
regard to the Greeks, it is certainly not true to say that after John
of Damascus 'all thought was blunted and discussion ceased',[6]
although the scholars and heretics who existed later, in the
eleventh century, for instance, were allowed to make no constructive contribution within the Church, or were perhaps not
great enough to do so. The important thing was the maintenance

[1] See G. P. Wetter.   [2] PG, cxx, col. 968 D.   [3] Ibid., col. 969 A.
[4] Gregory of Nazianzus the Theologian, Basil, Bishop of Caesarea, and
Basil's brother, Gregory of Nyssa, were the three famous Cappadocians; they
lived in the fourth century, and, like the Alexandrines, their literary heritage
was Hellenistic, and they naturally wrote in Greek.
[5] See Lot-Borodine, who discusses the difference between the traditions of
the Greek and Latin Churches.
[6] A. J. Macdonald, *Authority and Reason in the Early Middle Ages*, London,
1933, p. 2.

of the traditional doctrine, and as far as there was a real creativeness it was in the realm, not of intellectual thought, but of
religious experience—hence the importance of Symeon.

Symeon was a man who relied on his own personal experience
rather than that of others, and still less did he need to fortify his
position with the authority of the Church Fathers. The *Orationes*
are almost unadorned by literary devices;[1] they are disconcert-
ingly direct, and give the impression of a man who could have
been either a philosopher or a statesman, but never a poet, save
in so far as he did have creative experience through his mystical
life. On the rare occasions when Symeon employs a metaphor
it is usually from political life, as some comparison with the Emperor, or secular administration.[2] Literary references there are
none, save occasionally in passing to the Church Fathers, or
men such as Antony the monk, or Symeon the Studite whom
Symeon loved so well, or John Climacus, whose mystical work
he read when a boy in his father's house,[3] and who probably influenced him more than any. He uses the Bible frequently, he
refers to Gregory the Theologian and John Chrysostom, and
he had read the lives of Anthony, Sabas, Euthymius, and he
mentions Arsenius. But it is difficult to attempt any assessment
of his debt, because whatever he read he made so completely
his own. Nevertheless the debt exists, hence the attempt to give
some account of the outlook of the Greek Church, and the importance of showing how Symeon's position inclines, or otherwise, towards that of Maximus or Evagrius or John Climacus,
his most obvious predecessors in the disavowal of 'the wilderness
of the world' and the construction of that holy way of living
which is the Christian life.

Symeon himself was a man of logic, vigour, and decision, and

[1] The Greek text of the *orationes* and *liber hymnorum divinorum amorum*,
with the exception of four hymns edited by P. Maas, is still in manuscript, and
the edition in the *Patrologia* is the Latin translation of Pontanus. Holl, who
had worked on the MSS., which are numerous, says, 'Pontanus hat treu übersetzt.' Maas has edited Hymns No. 5, 6, 10, 15 (= PG numbering); Hymns
9, 11, 26, and *Oratio* 25 I have transcribed from *cod. gr. monac.* 177. These
writings I have therefore used in the original Greek, which I hope to publish
with an English translation of Symeon's works.

[2] John Climacus does the same, e.g. PG, lxxxviii, col. 640 B.

[3] *Vita Symeonis*, p. 12 (ch. 6). John Climacus was an anchorite who lived
on Mt. Sinai in the sixth century, and who was for a time abbot of Mt. Sinai.

from the time when, scarcely more than a child, he refused to
consider the official life at the imperial court for which he was
destined and turned his face from the pleas of his own father
in Paphlagonia, to the time of his stormy exit with his spiritual
father from the monastery of Studios and his curt rejection many
years later of the Patriarch's offer of peace, his life was a ruthless
pursuit rather than a gradual awakening, and a pursuit that
showed how emphatically the mystic is the supreme man of
action. Thus there was no lack of vitality or conviction in Symeon's
life and words. He chose the monastic life because he thought
that it was only thus that the *best* life was to be found, and his choice
is a reflection upon neither the secular nor the ecclesiastical life
of the Byzantine Empire. It was not because the world was then
particularly evil that he left it, it was not because monastic life
was then especially spiritual that he chose it. In his condemnations he spares neither secular nor ecclesiastic; those who are the
mere hearers of the law, they are *filii tenebrarum*, 'the sons of
darkness, whether they are Emperors, or Patriarchs, or bishops,
or priests, or rulers, or subjects, or laymen, or monks, or
ascetics, or abbots, or poor, or rich, or ill, or well'.[1] Though
perhaps this should be taken as implying the zeal of the spiritual
reformer rather than the unusual vice of the eleventh century.

There was nothing exclusive or private in Symeon's religious
experience—this in itself a proof of its reality. His spiritual
experience was 'an Act that doth communicate', in so much as
Symeon had not only partaken in the divine Act that constitutes
the 'to be' as distinct from the 'to become', but he knew that this,
the only real experience, was for everybody if they so willed. It
was something to be hardly gained, to be counted as the only
real possession, or rather not a possession, but a being possessed.
By reason of the difficulty of approach it followed that only a
few could hope to attain it, though the distinction was not so
much whether a man was *in mundo* or *in statu monachi* as
whether he was spiritually endowed with the courage, and perseverance, and faith, and desire, which alone could bring him into
the presence of God. 'His goodness infinitely does desire To be
by all possesst,' but is this possible if it is so hard to know God?

Symeon would have answered that, as far as the ethics of a

[1] PG, cxx, col. 407 A (*Or.* 20).

good life were concerned, this knowledge was possible for all by
reason of the Incarnation. It would be wrong to think that he
regarded as Christians only those who lived a monastic life; the
emphasis of his sermons is natural in that they must have been
nearly all (if not all) addressed to a monastic community. But
he could speak of Christians 'both monks and seculars',[1] or,
'Some Christians there are who have taken monastic vows, some
do good works while living in the world.'[2] Nor was salvation
only for those who had reached the heights of a mystical
experience, but 'kings, rulers, nobles, wise, unlearned, rich,
poor, beggars, robbers, misers, criminals, lawbreakers, wantons,
homicides, those who have committed every kind of crime', all
these could hope for salvation.[3] He puts the case for eternal
damnation, almost against his will, because it was a logical
possibility, but salvation was clearly for all Christians, and there
is no suggestion that it was only for the monk, 'nobody who
has been baptised in Thy name shall suffer this great and terrible
burden of being separated from Thee'.[4] It is he who lives only
for the world who will find himself beyond the great gulf fixed,
suffering 'in the abyss of punishments, in the chaos of perdition'.[5]

The reason for emphasizing Symeon's attitude towards the
whole body of Christians is that his writings, especially his
orationes, are so monastic in tone, and so clearly the product of
a monk, that it is important to realize that his choice of life was
due not so much to any intolerance of spirit as to a realization
that it was only within a monastic community that he would
find the discipline which would enable him to develop his
spiritual capacity and would provide the quiet detachment in
which this could function. For that experience of God which
was the crowning spiritual experience was not for all. It was in a
way a foretaste of life after death, the result of a long and difficult
and solitary wrestling, and those conditions under which it could
best be achieved were found in the monastery or the hermit's cell.
It is, indeed, possible for all who wish, wrote Symeon, *but* they
must lead a life free from the agitations of all disturbances, a life

[1] PG, cxx, col. 338 c (*Or.* 4).   [2] Ibid., col. 336 c (*Or.* 4).
[3] Ibid., col. 359 B (*Or.* 8). Cf. ibid., col. 497 A (*Or.* 33) 'universis enim,
etiam laicis, non monachis tantum . . .'
[4] Ibid., col. 511 D (*Div.* 2).   [5] Ibid., col. 512 B (*Div.* 2).

of calm.[1] So Symeon assumes monasticism as the background of his writings because it was the natural thing for him to do.

Nor was there anything rigid or repressive about Symeon's way of life, and once its preliminary discipline was recognized it became inevitable, inescapable, the only desirable life. All the negations, that which a monk might not do, this was only a minor part of Symeon's work, and, like Evagrius or John Climacus, his *orationes* are full of those things which a monk must do. 'To do' was as essential to Symeon as 'to be'. Maximus emphasized that 'the commandments of God are light, and he clearly lacks divine light who does not practice the divine commandments'.[2] So thought Symeon, and his most noticeable characteristic is his passionate activity. His striving for the *divina illuminatio* and longing for experience of God did not mean negation or in-activity: it meant a more sincere religious life, an elimination of mechanical psalm-singing or fasting, and the most scrupulous self-searching and penitence. It was essentially a real thing, and there could be no compromise. Compare Evagrius's *Sententiae ad eos qui in coenobiis et xenodochiis habitant fratres*,[3] or Maximus's *Liber asceticus*,[4] with any one of Symeon's sermons, and the difference is apparent. Evagrius produces something terse but cold and bare, Maximus joins together a collection of suitable passages, but Symeon's words possess a vitality that could only come from genuine personal experience; this was the secret of his influence. There was no difference between Symeon's own experience and that for which he urged his monks to hope, there was no reserve or holding back, save only in so far as a measured discipline was necessary for the purpose of life. Even so, when really speaking about discipline Symeon frequently breaks the bonds of restraint, and inspired by a lyrical passion he attempts to describe that mystical experience which defies all definition and illuminates 'with a radiance beyond all words'.[5]

As in the daily routine all reliance on material well-being, or even appreciation of the beauty of the world, must be eliminated, so in spiritual development Symeon considered knowledge of human sciences to be only a hindrance. 'Possess God, and you

[1] PG, cxx, col. 544 C (*Div.* 18).
[2] Ibid., xc, col. 1280 B (*Cent.*, iii. 45).   [3] Ibid., xl, cols. 1277 ff.
[4] Ibid., xc, cols. 911 ff.   [5] Ibid., cxx, col. 516 B (*Div.* 4).

will need no book.'¹ To read was, within limits, permissible,
but any concentration on humanist studies was fruitless.² The
spirit of God is revealed 'not to the rhetoricians and philosophers, not to those learned in the writings of the Greeks, not
to those studying foreign works . . . but to the poor in spirit and
in life, to the pure in heart and in body'.³ Nicetas definitely
minimizes Symeon's own education as a boy, thus reflecting his
master's attitude towards learning. 'He was entrusted to a
grammarian and was taught the elements (προπαιδεία) . . .
when he was older he zealously attacked other subjects.'⁴ But
he had sufficient sense, so Nicetas relates, if not completely to
abandon these, at least to acquire a knowledge only of grammar.
Nicetas clearly was torn between a desire to emphasize Symeon's
later distaste for worldly knowledge and to give him due credit
for his very obvious intelligence. For, in spite of definite rejection of secular learning, he was a man of marked intellectual
ability. He may have despised knowledge, but he undoubtedly
demanded clear logical thought from all with whom he came in
contact. His monks were exhorted to realize what they were
doing; 'What point is there in praying "Deliver us from evil"
if you do not know the precise nature of the evil from which you
need deliverance?' he asked.⁵

So if Symeon placed no faith in the technique of secular logic,
it is nevertheless with the utmost clarity that he taught his
monks not only how to live an orderly external life but how to
develop the spiritual life which was the point of their existence.
Within the monastic framework, the outward discipline which
Symeon sets forth with a statesmanlike emphasis, there was an
inner, but no less distinct, discipline. Symeon is extraordinarily
normal and balanced in the life he would have his monks lead,
and this is because of his insistence on *doing*⁶ as the essential
corollary of *believing*. No doubt existed in his mind concerning

---

¹ PG, cxx, col. 353 D (*Or.* 7).

² Holl, pp. 37–8, shows Symeon's inaccuracy in quoting from the Bible,
confusing S. Paul with S. James, but the editor of the *Patrologia Graeca*
corrects without noting the inaccuracy.

³ Symeon, Letter to Stephen of Nicomedia, ed. Hausherr, *Vie de Syméon
le Nouveau Théologien*, introd., p. lxv.

⁴ *Vita Symeonis*, pp. 2–4 (ch. 2).   ⁵ PG, cxx, col. 337 C (*Or.* 4).

⁶ On the nature of this *doing* cf. the monastic life described in Chapter X.

the path by which they are to travel; the foundations of a good
life are love and humility, the hope of the Christian is found in
Christ, and the end is the *divina illuminatio*, the knowledge of
God. What was the point of the praying, and meditation, and
mourning, and psalm-singing, which filled the life of the monk?
To know God, but this would in itself have been an inadequate
answer, and Symeon's merit is that his *orationes* present simply
and clearly the means which any monks could understand and
employ. Without reading the *orationes* it is difficult to appreciate
their normality and universality, for Symeon always makes the
discipline of a spiritual life appear to be the natural and inevitable conduct which indeed it is. 'No one would presume
to interrupt a conversation with an earthly king, and still less
will any demon dare to attack you while you are speaking to
the heavenly King,' he says, when he is talking of singing
psalms.[1] Symeon knew his people, as his psychological penetration shows, and he loved them as he could not help doing,
but, in spite of his sincerity and his anxiety, there is something
detached, and perhaps inhuman, about his attitude. He saw too
clearly, and, suffering from the disadvantage of an intense
critical faculty, he condemned human weaknesses and never
sympathized with them, nor did he possess the capacity for
criticism of a more kindly nature, such as John Mauropous
would have given. But his clarity of vision had, too, its strength,
for it was to this that Symeon owed the reality and depth of his
own spiritual experiences. It would be interesting to know how
many of Symeon's monks were ever blessed with even a measure
of the spiritual development for which their abbot taught them
to long. The only evidence is that of Nicetas, whose life of
Symeon bears so plainly the imprint of his love for his abbot.
His writings about the conduct of this earthly life can bear no
comparison with Symeon's, and they show that without rare
endowment of intellectual understanding, without a genuine
gift for spiritual creativeness, it was not possible to write as
Symeon wrote of the *divina illuminatio*. Nicetas had not these
gifts, and in tracing out the stages in a soul's progress he relies
completely on the framework of Maximus and Evagrius. Still,
there are echoes of his master, though whether from intercourse

[1] PG, cxx, col. 386 B (*Or.* 15).

with Symeon or from an experience which Symeon had taught
him to know it is impossible to say. 'When you descend [from
your contemplation of God] speak to your brothers of the Eternal
Life and of the mystery of the Kingdom of God,' wrote Nicetas,[1]
and he surely had in his mind Symeon, who certainly shared all
he had. To estimate the effect of such a man is perhaps impossible, for so often the greatest debts remain unchronicled. And
in any case, Symeon would have said that the thing that mattered
was the reality, rather than the measure, of any spiritual experience; nor was there any such thing as uniformity of insight,
for to each was given in varying degree, and to each was his
appointed function. What Symeon did emphasize was that the
possibility of life in its fullest meaning was offered to all.

Symeon's theology follows logically from his view of life. He
is no theologian as such, and his sermons are never learned
expositions of doctrinal questions. He studied the Bible, and
the works of the Fathers, only because of the help which they
gave in matters of practical action and spiritual development.
In this there is a striking contrast with Maximus, who quotes
as a commentator and expositor for the sake of proving his
argument, while Symeon quotes because the words have become
part of him and his experience and are the most natural ones to
use.[2] Compare, for instance, Symeon's *orationes de poenitentia*[3]
with Maximus's on penitence and the hope of salvation.[4] The
latter consists of thirteen quotations from the Old and New
Testaments, while in the former there are in proportion just as
many illustrations from the Bible, but the difference is arresting.
Maximus's runs like this:

'The old man replied: For men to save themselves is impossible, but
with God all things are possible . . . we hear Him speaking through
Isaiah saying . . . and again . . . therefore Isaiah said . . . and again
the prophesy of Joel . . . but Ezechiel . . . but the third book of Kings
[apropos of Naboth and Jezebel] . . . but David said . . . meanwhile
the Lord announced in the Gospel . . . wherefore Peter asked . . .
and was answered. . . . What can [the old man at last] equal such
bounty, or rival so great a love of mankind (φιλανθρωπία)?'

---

[1] PG, cxx, col. 885 c (*Cap.* 74).   [2] Cf. p. 208, note 2.
[3] Especially *orationes* 26, 32, and 33.
[4] PG, xc, cols. 948–50 (*Cap.* 40). The *Liber Asceticus* is a dialogue between
an old and a young man.

Thus closes Chapter 40, but the conception of penitence is continued by the old man in five more chapters in which he repeats in his own words the thoughts of Chapter 40. Now Symeon, if he is writing for his monks, both uses his Bible and gives them some help for the activity of their own penitence.[1] He quotes as freely, though not at such length, as Maximus, but with a point, 'What is true penitence, what should be the attitude of the sinner, and what is our evidence of God's attitude as revealed through Christ?' Then the quotations from the New Testament, eleven on end, but occupying only half a column, and conveying in their cumulative effect a striking emphasis, after which Symeon proceeds to examine the nature of humility and the nature of the spiritual attainment which follows genuine repentance. But never does he lose the sense of the relation of action to spiritual experience; it is only the genuinely spiritual life that can know the revelations of so great a mystery. Maximus ends thus:

'And so, brothers, let us avoid the world and its rulers; let us renounce the flesh and the things of the flesh; let us strive towards the heavens, where is our city; let us imitate the divine Apostle; let us comprehend the Lord of life; let us drink the living waters; let us join the heavenly choirs; let us praise our Lord Jesus Christ, with the Archangels of the Lord, to Whom be glory and kingdom, with the Father, and Holy Spirit, now and for ever to all eternity. Amen.'

It sounds good, but what did it mean to a monk who found goodness difficult to attain? Symeon knew that eternity is now, and the divine in the present. So he ends:

'Wherefore I beseech you, my brothers in Christ, not to wish to describe the ineffable things only by words, which is an impossibility, both for those who teach and for those who learn. For neither can they who teach the divine things which are perceived by the mind alone demonstrate these things clearly by obvious examples, and represent their truth as though busying themselves with some business transaction, nor can those who are taught discern the truth only from the spoken word; *but* let us be zealous in understanding, and contemplate such matters by activity, toil and fatigue. So that, if in this way we shall have been taught the meaning of such things as the sacred mysteries, God may be glorified thereby, and we glorify Him in learning these things, and He glorify

[1] PG, cxx, cols. 447–51 (*Or.* 26).

us in Christ Himself, our God, to Whom be all glory, honour and worship, with the Father, and the most holy and lifegiving Spirit, now and ever to all eternity. Amen.'[1]

Both of them end with the same words, but the difference in approach and in experience is significant.

As might be deduced from these contrasted passages, the theology which lay behind Symeon's thought and action was of a simple and orthodox character. But it must indeed be emphasized that Symeon's reluctance to enter into the arena of intellectual analysis and discussion of theological matters was in no way due to any deficiency of capacity, but was the result of another and a definitely selected mode of approach. That Symeon himself was more than able to hold his ground in his quarrel with Stephen of Nicomedia is apparent from his letter on the relation of the Father to the Son.[2] This was not due to any miraculous assistance, but was the natural product of a mind that was accustomed to think clearly and readily, as any reader of his *orationes* would admit. Sometimes Symeon almost guards himself against his natural capacity for thought. 'There are five *genera* or *modi* of knowing God,'[3] he begins, and then, very much as Psellus in his *Omnifaria Doctrina*, he attempts to give some reasoned explanation of the Godhead. But this is not for long: 'It is only necessary to know that God is, and to inquire into the nature of His being is not only rash, but, indeed, exceedingly stupid,'[4] for, as the potter and the vase he fashions are both made from clay, and yet both totally different, so is God as widely removed from man, and is to be adored and worshipped in silence, the God Whom no man has seen or can see. Again and again Symeon shows that he values theology, or perhaps more simply, the teaching of the Bible and the Fathers, in so far as it provides him with the framework within which the one great experiment, the essay to realize God, may be made. So he speaks of the Trinity, of angels, of demons, in terms which were familiar to any Christian, and by his stress of certain things, as faith, grace, works, he shows the manner in which he thought

[1] PG, cxx, col. 451 AB (*Or.* 26).

[2] *Vita Symeonis*, pp. 100-8 (chs. 74-8), and pp. lxiii-lxv, where the text of the letter is given.

[3] PG, cxx, col. 331 A (*Or.* 3).   [4] Ibid., col. 332 A (*Or.* 3).

divine goodness should find its response in human beings. It is always a living relationship, and unhampered by the difficulties which encompass even the most faithful of those Christians who allow themselves to be beset by philosophical problems; Symeon's interpretation has therefore an affinity with that perfect simplicity of Christ's life, and as such he is, like S. Francis of Assisi, akin to the 'doers' of all generations.

Every aspect of the Godhead plays a definite part in Symeon's life. It is God the Father who is the providence behind human existence, 'whether corporeal or incorporeal, it was God who made all things which are in heaven, or earth, or the void';[1] it is through the Incarnation that Christians may hope to atone for the Fall and to gain salvation, and may have a living example of that practice, or doing, without which there is no spiritual progress; it is by means of the indwelling of the Holy Spirit, through grace, that human beings are able consciously to become more and more aware of the presence of God, and finally even to attain in this life to a knowledge of Him, who is *et extra mundum et intra nos*. But everything that Symeon wrote emphasizes his especial faith in Christ. Even so he never forgets Christ in the Godhead, 'God was undivided in substance before Christ, my God, took upon Him human limbs. For when He assumed the form of a human body, He bestowed His Holy Spirit, and by this means is united in substance to all the faithful; and this unity is inseparable and indissoluble.'[2] The reason for his frequent appeal to Christ as a friend was that it was only through Christ that the perfect human life could be seen, and Symeon, with all his longing for goodness, always attempted its present realization. That perfection eluded him he never denied, but he knew his solution, and returned again and again to his model, 'Alas . . . why is it that we do not trust in Christ? Why do not we follow Him?'[3] Sometimes Symeon writes as the author of the *De imitatione* in addressing Christ, and being answered by Him, 'Speak, O Christ, to Thy servant . . .'.[4] 'Alas, my Christ, tell me what to do. . . . Write, He replied, those things which I say unto you, and have no fear.'[5] Sometimes he

---

[1] PG, cxx, col. 515 D (*Div.* 3).   [2] Ibid., col. 591 C (*Div.* 36).
[3] Ibid., col. 591 C (*Div.* 36).   [4] Ibid., col. 575 C (*Div.* 30).
[5] Ibid., col. 558 C (*Div.* 22).

writes as S. Bernard of Clairvaux in glorifying the Christ who was the centre of his religion. 'Unbelievable is Thy beauty, O Lord Jesus, incomparable is Thy splendour, indescribable is Thy grace, and far beyond all word and expectation. Thy ways, Thy goodness, Thy gentleness, exceed all mortal thoughts. Longing for Thee and love of Thee is far greater than any love or longing for men.'[1] Symeon and Bernard have much in common, above all their devotion to God through Christ, their approach to him in love and humility, their stress on the reality of their religious experience, their lack of desire for theological emphasis. But Symeon rarely has those human details which Bernard loved; he wished not so much to give Christ the attributes of a human being as to think of an upward process of Christ teaching men to know Him in His divinity.

It is difficult to discover any consistency in Symeon's attitude towards the Godhead. He regarded Christ, not only as the Redeemer of the world, but as the living force deriving its power from God the Father, whereby the world existed, and knew the eternal *pronoia*. In one passage he thus distinguishes between God the Father and God the Son, 'O Lord Jesus Christ, O Lord Saviour of souls. . . . Thou art God and Lord God, Thou holdest in Thy hand all creation since Thou controllest the whole universe; Thy hand, O Lord, is that great power which, fulfilling the will of the Father, constructs, builds, creates and administers our affairs in a way that is indescribable.'[2] Holl discusses how far Symeon overstressed the importance of Christ, and how far he saw in Christ both the Holy Spirit and God the Father, as opposed to the Greek Church's tendency towards tritheism; but he concludes that this was unintentional.[3] It was, indeed, the obvious result of Symeon's striving for means whereby every one might realize that there is a link between God and mankind, and of his own spiritual communion with God which could only be, as it were, with a single Person. There seem to be two sides to Symeon's Christology, first the conception, which was at one with the teaching of the Greek Church, of Christ as the Logos, the force whereby mankind knows divinity, and secondly the great love of Christ as a personal friend,

---

[1] PG, cxx, col. 563 D (*Div.* 26).
[2] Ibid., col. 560 D (*Div.* 24).   [3] Holl, pp. 104-5.

which is not so usual in the writers of the Orthodox Church, and certainly not in Maximus or John Climacus.

Symeon, then, finds that it is in knowledge of Christ, through grace, that man can hope to lead a true life. To him the first step in the attainment of this is the renunciation of the world. He admits that God made the world, and that God could do no evil, but there is in his writings nothing to point to an appreciation of the beauty of the natural world. Here we have no abiding city, but we seek one to come, and sin, as Symeon saw it, was too great a love of the world. Perhaps if Symeon had been taught by a man like John Mauropous he would have learnt that it is no weakness to love much that he ruthlessly sweeps aside, but that it can be weakness to need so to renounce it. 'He who is a monk keeps himself apart from the world and walks for ever with God alone';[1] that God may be seen in the world, and through the world, does not seem possible to Symeon. Perhaps this is because he would have attacked the foundation of monastic life had he preached other than he did, and it must be remembered that he says very little about the nature of individual relationships or the nature of those works on which he insists. The brothers were occupied not only with fasting and praying, but with almsgiving, and this last must have brought them into relation with people outside their community, but Symeon is silent on this point. He does make it quite clear that there should be no intercourse between the monks themselves, except in so far as the abbot, or spiritual father, allows this. Though even Symeon admits that it is of the greatest help, and even essential, to have the wise guidance of an older man. Spiritual development, then, was something in which ordinary human fellowship had little part; it was a solitary process with which the individual alone was concerned.

The point of this stand against the world was the attainment of perfect control over bodily desires, in so far as they meant carnal self-indulgence. It was not mortification for the sake of mortification, it was the throwing off of certain impediments. Maximus, and Evagrius, and, indeed, Nicetas,[2] speak of the different stages in the process whereby the soul ascends towards its participation in the being of God, the *practica*, the *theoretica*

[1] PG, cxx, col. 516 B (*Div.* 4).   [2] Ibid., col. 941 c (85).

or *physica*, and the *theologica*. Thus, having attained *apatheia* or the purification of the soul, the mystic proceeds to true knowledge through the grace of God, and thence to the summit of all, the participation in the Godhead. Nicetas, who relies far more on Maximus and Evagrius than Symeon did, symbolizes this threefold development in words from the Song of Songs:

'Rise up, come to me, my fair dove, δι' ἐμπράκτου φιλοσοφίας. For lo! the winter of lusts is past, the rain of unworthy thoughts is over and gone; the flowers of virtue appear with sweet scented thoughts on the earth of thy heart. Rise up, come to me ἐν γνώσει φυσικῆς θεωρίας; come, my dove, freely shelter in the protection and shades μυστικῆς θεολογίας, and by faith in the immovable rock, which is thy God.'[1]

Symeon was certainly in agreement with the end which Evagrius or Maximus sought, but his means were less definitely stated, because he never inclined to academic explanations. Consequently there is in him far less clearly cut demarcation between the different stages, which Maximus, for example, so stresses. He does speak of *apatheia*, but not frequently; *theologia*, the final consummation or knowledge, he knows, not only as a distant attainment, but as a privilege which he himself had realized. Perhaps the difference between a theoretical and detached analysis of the soul's spiritual progress, and the actual practical development with which Symeon was concerned, can best be seen in a comparison of the respective presentations of Maximus, Evagrius, and Symeon. 'The wise monk', wrote Evagrius, 'will be ἀπαθής . . . knowledge of the Trinity is better than the knowledge of the incorporeal, and meditation on it than the reasoning of the world.'[2] Evagrius's own *Capita* begin, 'Christianity is the doctrine of our Saviour Jesus Christ, as worked out through the πρακτική and φυσική and θεολογική.'[3] Maximus's stages are the same, except that he is much more lengthy. Symeon, on the contrary, shows his usual preference for the more concrete, and less theoretical, expression. His *Capita* begin with a discussion of the practical meaning of faith, and he has throughout his writings a vivid conception of the relation between θεωρία and πρᾶξις. 'In proportion as we daily fulfil the commandments of God, shall we be purified,

[1] PG, cxx, col. 924 C (50).   [2] Ibid., xl, cols. 1281 CD.
[3] Ibid., col. 1221 D (1).

grow radiant, become illumined, be counted worthy of the revelations of the great mysteries.'[1]

It naturally follows that to Symeon it is the avoiding of evil, rather than its origin, which is important; and he is not always very clear on the way in which evil came into the world, for he says in one passage that evil results from the demons,[2] and in another that evil comes from our own will, 'a man is good or evil not according to nature, as some think, but from his own free will'.[3] Perhaps he meant that evil originated with the fall of the angels, who then became demons His world was peopled with *daemones*; the reality of the symbolism, and indeed it was a concrete fact to the Byzantine world, is evident from his remark that freedom consists in 'security from demons'.[4] Read Evagrius's *Capita practica ad Anatolium*[5] to understand how sinister a place the world could become, for to him, as to Symeon, temptations were the attacks of the demons 'who, like unseen enemies, with perfect tactics, are always besieging us through ourselves'.[6]

It was by reason of the sin which the demons wrought that there arose imperfections, and blindness of vision, thus necessitating that vigilant watch to guard against the unceasing assaults. But at least Christians were capable of realizing this, 'for there remains in us just the knowledge that we are evil',[7] a self-knowledge which Symeon often emphasized, and even demanded, 'but as long as a Christian cannot plainly and clearly realize what is evil, he is no true Christian'.[8] Symeon demanded a high standard from his Christian, for the quality of discerning *perspicue ac limpide* was not one that monastic life would always foster, but on the other hand, as Symeon shows, any great spiritual experience required outstanding qualities of thought and intellect. Not that this individual effort was in itself sufficient, but it had to be made. 'It is of no avail to be instructed unless the soul retains that which has been taught. He who knows how to read, and reading, does not understand what he has read, is unlearned . . . there is in us

[1] PG, cxx, col. 449 c (*Or.* 26). [2] Ibid., cxx, col. 382 c (*Or.* 14).
[3] Ibid., col. 482 A (*Or.* 32). [4] Ibid., col. 388 c (*Or.* 15).
[5] Ibid., xl, cols. 1220–52. Cf. S. Athanasius's *Vita S. Antonii*, trans. J. B. McLaughlin, London, 1924, chaps. ix–x, pp. 50–61, on how to distinguish good from bad visions. [6] Ibid., cxx, col. 365 A (*Or.* 10).
[7] Ibid., cols. 382 D–383 A (*Or.* 14). [8] Ibid., col. 366 B (*Or.* 10).

the capacity for study, but to understand comes from the grace of God.'[1]

Whatever Symeon may have said about the importance of grace, he realized that there was no such thing as mystical experience unaccompanied by a long mental discipline and a severe spiritual wrestling. For Symeon the problem was like that which Augustine had to face, but he assumes the free will of men. The gift of grace was the underlying reason why it was possible for a human being ever to hope to know God, but any permanent condition of inactivity, or of despair, was unknown to Symeon, because the point was not so much speculation as to whether grace was present or not, but the knowledge that grace was unavailing without a continual striving towards a more perfect life. It was the bestowal of grace which was the point of the sacrament of baptism, it was a further gift of grace which came from the laying on of hands which Symeon describes,[2] it was grace which lay behind all change and conversion, and it was communicated by means of the Church's sacraments. Symeon accepted this as the normal means of approach, oddly at variance with his very individual teaching with regard to the illumination, through which a man may most nearly approach, and perhaps know, God. Grace depends on the attitude of the individual. God is good and desires the salvation of all, *if* they indicate by their actions that they so wish. Grace is then the foundation of the spiritual life, 'without the illumination of the Holy Spirit, those things which are divine and beneficial can be neither understood nor preserved'.[3] But it is not arbitrarily bestowed, it comes to all who show the Christian disposition, it is dependent upon human choice, 'for those who believe in Christ have eternal life, which is the grace of our Lord Jesus Christ'.[4] And this *vita aeterna* comes through faith.

Now the act of faith is, as Symeon said, simply belief in Christ, and this is the irreducible minimum of a Christian creed, it is the point to which Symeon in his *orationes* again and again returns; he seems to realize, perhaps in despair, that here was

---

[1] PG, cxx, col. 385 BC (*Or.* 15).

[2] Cf. ibid., col. 330 AB (*Or.* 2), where Symeon speaks of laying on of hands after absolution for sin. Holl, pp. 58 ff., discusses whether Symeon is referring to a sacrament, such as confirmation in the Latin Church.

[3] Ibid., col. 385 CD (*Or.* 15).   [4] Ibid., col. 350 B (*Or.* 6).

one thing which surely his monks could understand, and the
key to a spiritual inheritance which was theirs if they would
take it. For, with all Symeon's stress on works, he knew that
these were the inevitable corollary of faith, and had no life apart
from their source.

Grace, faith, evil, these were forces within and without, working for better or for worse. *How* did they manifest themselves in
the action of the Christian, what was the *praxis* whose other
side was the *illuminatio*? It is mourning, and penitence, and
tears which are the foundation of Symeon's inner discipline,
and it is necessary to realize how very real a place was given to
tears. Nor was Symeon alone in this, for Evagrius speaks to
monks or nuns just as normally as Symeon concerning the in-
evitability of tears. Sorrow was not, as Aquinas says, due to
considering Christ's Passion, nor were tears shed 'through a
certain tenderness of the affections', nor would Symeon have
agreed that 'the first and direct effect of devotion is joy, while
the secondary and accidental effect is sorrow which is according
to God'.[1] The Eastern Church had a definite discipline of tears,
and the Latin Church, whether it gives it a place or not as such,
did produce mystics who evidently found such practice of assistance. Within its cell 'the soul finds floods of tears, wherewith
it nightly washes and cleanses itself, that it may become the
more familiar with its Maker, the more remote from all the
turmoil of the world',[2] wrote à Kempis. This was indeed a
condition well known to the mystics, and it was part of the
beatus luctus that Symeon taught his monks to seek.

Without mourning there could be no humility, the foundation
of a right understanding, 'for humility brings forth mourning,
and mourning nourishes its mother'.[3] 'Blessed are the poor
in spirit for theirs is the kingdom of heaven,' and, 'Blessed are
they that mourn for they shall be comforted,' but why mourn
if there is hope of the kingdom of heaven? 'Give your minds,
I ask you, to the things which I shall say, and lay hold on the
point of this question, as well as its solution'[4] (were Symeon's

[1] *Summa Theologica*, ii (2), Q. 82, Art. 4 (vol. xi (1922), p. 29, English
translation of the English Dominicans).
[2] *De imitatione*, i. 20, p. 37, ed. M. J. Pohl, 1904, Freiburg, vol. ii, *opera
omnia*.
[3] PG, cxx, col. 448 c (*Or.* 26).   [4] Ibid., col. 413 B (*Or.* 21).

monks not attending to him?). Consolation, Symeon explains, can only come to the man who is humble, 'where there is humility, there is the light of the Spirit',[1] and humility means of necessity a self-dissatisfaction, and penitence, accompanied by tears, which purge the soul. 'Where there is a flow of tears, brothers, with true understanding, there is the splendour of the divine light, and where there is the splendour of this light, there is an abundant supply of all good, and the sign of the Holy Spirit is planted in the heart, whence arise all the fruits of life.'[2]

This humility and penitence were the foundation of Symeon's own life, and, like Augustine in his Confessions, he is sometimes overpowered by the breadth and depth and height of the love of God. This only served to increase his sense of his own worthlessness and unhappiness, for Symeon's difficulties were perhaps greater than his monks could have realized. He very rarely allows his personal circumstances to intrude, but in one passage he reveals the extent to which external circumstances did affect his self-discipline. 'I long for tears, the tears of salvation, the tears which will wash away the blackness of my soul . . . for my heart has been filled with the evils of this life, with many afflictions, with the envy of those who contrived my exile . . .'[3] As he urges his monks when they are beset by temptations, perhaps at meals, or when going about their daily round, to turn their thoughts inwards, and reflect on their inadequacy and inability and impurity, so he himself does likewise and does not spare himself, rather condemning himself the more in that he has been so blessed in his spiritual life. 'Why am I so downcast and oppressed?' he asks; though perhaps it is a natural reaction after a period of spiritual joy such as a vision must have been. 'Allurements and human praises dull and enervate my soul. . . . I imagine myself greater than all, and free from any disturbing influences, a holy man, wise, and an excellent theologian, and rightly to be venerated by all mortals.'[4] So, in spite of his pride and impatience of criticism, Symeon recognizes his failings, and asks:

'But why should I, a lost soul, a fornicator, be a ruler of brothers,

---

[1] PG, cxx, col. 413 D (Or. 21).   [2] Ibid., col. 414 D (Or. 21).
[3] Ibid., cols. 517 D–518 A (Div. 5); Maas, p. 333 (= No. 4 in Maas).
[4] Ibid., col. 524 AB (Div. 12).

a priest of the divine sacraments, and a servant of the sinless Trinity?[1]
. . . But blessed Saviour, pitiful and pitying, grant me to partake in
the divine virtue that in word and in prudence I may guide the
brothers, whom Thou hast entrusted to me, and may lead them to the
pastures of Thy divine laws, and restore them to the heavenly mansions
of the Kingdom, whole, unharmed, radiant in the beauty of virtue,
worthy to adore at Thy dread judgement.'[2]

Symeon's monks might have understood him better, and
loved him more, had they heard his private meditations as well
as the *orationes* which were prepared for them. For, in his over-
anxiety for them, perhaps he did not understand that unconscious influence is more effective than the most forcible of
sermons, and that encouragement is not necessarily followed by
spiritual deterioration.

If right humility was the basis of all virtue, the crown or head
of it was *love*: 'Pedes virtutum sunt humilitas, caput charitas.
Absque his duabus virtutibus omnis alia virtus vana et inanis
est.'[3] Neither Maximus nor Evagrius nor John Climacus make
this very definite emphasis, again because they order, arrange,
catalogue, while Symeon thrusts forth his own conviction and
experience, not lists of virtues or vices. 'These are the virtues
of the soul,' wrote Maximus, and gives eighteen of them, followed
by the virtues of the body, six in number.[4] 'Here', said Evagrius,
'are the different methods of combating vice,' and he gives five,
ranging from pure prayer to manual labour.[5] It is not that they
did not give practical advice, it is not in the content of their
writings that they are so very different from Symeon, but in
spirit. Read any of those who tried to write about the best possible
life, and then read Symeon. It is as though they say, 'Here are
the instructions, follow them if you can,' while Symeon says:
'Know the incomprehensible joy of the divine experience, I
know it, so can you; let us live together this life which has no
beginning, no end, but is a continual struggle.'

Nowhere is this irresistible enthusiasm and compellingness
and vitality more apparent, nowhere is the contrast between the
mystic and the ecclesiastic more striking, than when Symeon

---

[1] PG, cxx, col. 528 B (*Div.* 14).   [2] Ibid., col. 529 B (*Div.* 14).
[3] Ibid., col. 383 B (*Or.* 14).   [4] Ibid., xc, col. 785 C (*Inter.* 1).
[5] Ibid., xl, col. 1275 B (*De octo vitiosis cogitationibus*).

writes of love. None would have denied the place he assigns to
it, but few could speak as he spoke. Love is the fulfilment of a
spiritual life, its τέλος, that which makes possible a knowledge
of God. Love is not the experience itself, but it is that which is
the link between God and man, 'O blessed bond, O indescribable strength, O heavenly disposition, how excellent is the soul
which is animated by the divine inspiration and perfected in
exceeding love of God and man.'[1] It is love which makes a
soul divine and not earthly, which lifts it above all worldly
desires and selfish thoughts; the *divina illuminatio* is a rare gift,
a temporary knowledge, as it were, of what is eternal, but love is
a permanent possession, that which enables human beings to
know the reality of their divinity.

'O most longed for love, blessed is the man who lays hold of thee,
for henceforth he shall be enthralled by no disquieting desire for
earthly beauty . . . he who comprehends thee, or is comprehended
by thee, is indeed unerring, since thou art the fulfilment of the law.
For thou art the leader of the prophets, the friend of the company of
apostles, the courage of the martyrs, the inspiration of the Fathers
and doctors.'[2]

Love is the true knowledge of God, the doorway which bears
the name of the Word Himself.

But beyond love itself there is a special manifestation of it,
and this Symeon calls the *divina illuminatio*. As perfection of
soul is his hope, both for himself and for all men, so this perfection is only made possible by the belief in one perfect incomprehensible God. It was a belief based on faith, but that belief
carried with it a confident assurance that an active faith could,
if the soul strove sufficiently to purge itself of evil, be rewarded
by a knowledge of God, which would reveal itself in a vision.
This was, as Symeon's writings and life show, no miraculous
consummation of any state of inactivity; it was a hardly gained
experience, to be won and then lost, only to be regained and lost
anew. How it came and why it came remained inexplicable, but
Symeon does give many descriptions of that vision which he
himself must often have known. He does not stress any definite

---

[1] PG, cxx, col. 425 B (*Or.* 22). This is one of Symeon's finest sermons.
[2] Ibid., cols. 422 C–423 C (*Or.* 22); *cod. gr. monac.* 177, f. 108ʳ–109ʳ.

stages by which he approached the presence of God, but he often speaks of the effect of it on both body and soul.

It is here that the θέωσις, or deification, occurs, a process alien to a western mind. Aquinas's position[1] is that it is possible for created intellect to see God, and that therefore 'it must be absolutely granted that the blessed see the essence of God',[2] but he proceeds in Article 8 of the same question (How God is known by us), 'No created intellect in seeing God can know all that God does or can do, for this would be to comprehend His power.'[3] To comprehend God is to be God, and it is this that the Greeks admitted, the Latins denied. Maximus and Evagrius speak quite naturally of becoming God. As man attains through ἀπάθεια to γνῶσις he acquires a σῶμα πνευματικόν, and finally becomes as God in his knowledge of God 'ἐν τῇ Μονάδι οὔκ εἰσιν οἳ ἄρχουσιν οὐδὲ οἱ ὑπ' ἀρχάς, ἀλλὰ πάντες θεοί εἰσιν (iv. 51).[4] Maximus explains that he means by deification a sharing in the essence of God, through grace.[5] 'There is one ἐνέργεια of God and of the saints,'[6] and, in commenting on Dionysius the Areopagite, he says, 'We are made gods and sons and the body and limbs and part of God,'[7] and further on he uses in the same way the passage from Ephesians iv. 11–16.[8] Symeon takes a similar passage from 1 Corinthians xii. 27, and makes it clear that it is not a symbolical use of the body of Christ, 'And we shall become as gods, joined in intimacy to God, showing no stain in our body but all being in likeness to the whole body of Christ, each one of us having as our limb the complete Christ. For the one is made many, and the one yet remains undivided, but each part is indeed the whole Christ.'[9]

The moment of this deification is, as far as it is realized in a

---

[1] *Summa Theologica*, i, Q. 12, Art. 1. But cf. K. E. Kirk, p. 548, Note S, on Aquinas's mystical experience. Would the problems of the beatitude and of the relation of *delectatio* to *beatitudo* arise if the doctrine of deification were admitted? (Cf. Kirk, pp. 551–2.)

[2] *Summa Theologica*, i, Q. 12, Art. 1, p. 122 (vol. i (1920), 2nd ed., translation of the English Dominicans).

[3] Ibid., p. 138.   [4] Evagrius, quoted by Bousset, p. 321.

[5] PG, xci, cols. 33 A–36 A (*Opuscula theologica et polemica*).

[6] Ibid., col. 33 A.

[7] Ibid., col. 1092 C (*Ambiguorum liber*).

[8] Ibid., cols. 1096 B ff.

[9] Ibid., cxx, col. 532 BC (*Div.* 15). Cf. ibid., cols. 592 D–593 A (*Div.* 37); and the passages in *Div.* 15 omitted in the PG, but published by Maas.

temporal life, the moment of that experience, which, for want of better words, is called *visio Dei*.

'Do you say there can be no vision, no knowledge of Him Who is unseen and incomprehensible?' asked Symeon, 'for He Himself, Who is above all being, and before all time, uncreated, became incarnate, and appeared to me as a created being, and miraculously deified me, whom He had received. Surely you believe this and have no doubts? If, then, God, Who was made man, as you believe, adopted me, a human being, and deified me, then I, a god by adoption, perceive Him, Who is God by nature.'[1]

This explanation may, or may not, appear to be the true explanation of that experience which has come to those who are called mystics, but it was reality to Symeon and to others of the Greek Church. It is interesting that they, in common with some western mystics, use the word 'light', φῶς, to describe the means by which God became known to man.[2] As such He always appeared to Symeon, 'ἁπλοῦν μὲν καὶ ἀνείδεον, πλὴν ὡς φῶς.'[3] At such times Symeon is unconscious of his body, 'ubi autem hoc corpus tum sit, nescio,'[4] and his experience is preluded by an absence of all disturbing thoughts; but at its climax it is not a condition of apathy or inactivity, it is creative in the way that any consummation of love is creative; and it is accompanied by the most complete feeling of joy, 'ἡ γὰρ ἡδονή, τῆς καλῆς ἀπαθείας',[5] such as could only be known by participation in the Godhead.

To his monks Symeon gives an unusually restrained account of this knowledge which may be theirs.

'The virtue of the Holy Spirit shall suddenly come upon you, appearing not in the likeness of fire which can be perceived by the sense, . . . but in the likeness of light, which shall open the mind, with all peace and joyfulness of soul, thus, that you may comprehend, it shall appear to you—that which is the beginning of that eternal first light, and the splendour and glory of everlasting happiness—and, while this light is shining, all restless and unquiet thoughts shall

---

[1] PG, cxx, cols. 592 c–593 A (*Div.* 37).

[2] Cf. Wetter, on the use of the word *light* in the Hellenistic mystery religions to indicate a very real and physical transmutation of man into God.

[3] PG, cxx, col. 688 A (*Cap.* 152).

[4] Ibid., col. 526 c (*Div.* 13).

[5] Ibid., col. 521 B (*Div.* 9); *cod. gr. monac.* 177, f. 222ᵛ.

disappear, and every movement that might disturb the soul vanish, every evil of the body be healed. Then the eyes of the heart are purged, and they see God as it is written in the beatitudes. Then, as in a mirror, the soul sees its errors, and is cast into an abyss of humility, and, having perceived the greatness of the glory, is filled with all joy and satisfaction, and, amazed at the miracle which is beyond expectation, sheds an abundance of tears. And thus the whole man is changed, and knows God, and is known by Him.'[1]

[1] PG, cxx, cols. 432 AB (*Or.* 23).

APPENDIX

Michael Psellus's περὶ τῶν ἰδεῶν ἃς ὁ Πλάτων λέγει [1]

'THE Ideas of Reality, of which Plato maintains the existence, constitute the Intelligible World, which he generally calls "the ideal living being". As to this world, all very wise men are agreed as to its existence, but as to its nature[2] few seem to me to have apprehended this. For I have come across books of writers of repute, who supposed that the Ideas were thoughts in the mind of the Creator, intelligible wisdoms, after the manner of which the patterns of the physical world were created, so that these issue like radii from the centre,[3] in the likeness of which the Father has made this Universe. For with God[4] thoughts are not mere moulds or insubstantial first principles, but substantial entities and realities. For they say that There (i.e. in the other world) nothing is accidental and foreign to the main purpose.[5] Therefore those who speak thus first posit the Creator of all, and then the Ideas, i.e. his creative thoughts, and after them the physical universe, composed of heaven and earth and the intermediate heavenly bodies. For There (i.e. in the real world), the things which exist are simply and really archetypal, Here, complex and imitative. This is the way they talk in interpretation of the Platonic doctrine, but to me they seem not to have laid hold of the precise point of his teaching.[6] If I am to set forth something more than has been already said, I will not set forth my own thinking, but, as though divining the mind of the first expounder,[7] make my exposition more accurate than the rest. For Plato, with this fair thought in mind, sought to discover the forms[8] of the bodies here acquired, and who embodied them in underlying moulds. For instance, as in the Forms created by Art, thinking the Idea of the bed adventitious, he finds that on the one hand Art, and on the other the artist, has put something into the bed, and that Art has drawn its definitions from the Soul, and the Soul,

---

[1] Ed. C. G. Linder, P, xvi (1860), pp. 523–6. The whole second half of the passage is very difficult and probably has many corruptions. It is difficult with one badly transcribed manuscript to know what the original can have been. In translating this passage I owe a great deal to the help of Mr. W. D. Ross, who also suggested possible textual emendations.

[2] τί ⟨δέ⟩ ποτέ ἐστιν οὗτος.   [3] [νοητὰς γραμμάς].

[4] εἶναι γὰρ [καί].   [5] Reading ἐπεισοδιῶδες for ἐπεισιῶδες.

[6] This is the neo-Platonic division of the Universe, and is set forth in the *Enneads*. One of Plotinus's most characteristic distinctions is between ἐκεῖ and ἐνθάδε.

[7] i.e. Plato.   [8] ἐνταῦθα ⟨μορφάς⟩.

not from itself, but from some other source still;[1] and so too in the physical world, while Nature[2] directly presents one set of Forms, and others the Soul embodies by putting definitions into Nature, and the Mind has first furnished the Soul with the starting-point for the Form.[3] And we may not go further lest we seek first principles of first principles *ad infinitum*. For physical Form is not like intelligible Form, but is acquired, and enters the body as a stranger, whence it is changed to a good physical shape, and finally to formlessness.[4] Wherefore in the Body the Form is not pure. For otherwise it would not change and assume an opposite character. Not even the Soul is the Form in itself and nothing else, for then were every Soul a stable and unchanging thing. Yet we see some Souls enter into that which is beyond and above Reason. But it is otherwise with the perfectly unchanging and perfectly pure Form. What then is that but the immaterial and creative Mind? For the Mind is twofold, on the one hand, like the Form of the Soul, giving it an eternal shape, on the other, altogether apart[5] and surpassing all Minds, which is Mind pure, in respect both of being and function, on the threshold of the Good, and itself Intelligible Beauty. And therefore this is identical with its own objects, and He is the First Thinker.[6] The first Ideas are then in his mind, and are simple first principles of Reality, and what He, the First Thinker is, so, too, are they which are in the full sense his Thoughts. For they spring of themselves, and not from other sources.[7] But the second class of Form, and the third, are shapes and moulds of the first. And, in a sense, existing things and Ideas are of the same kind. For the Idea is the Real World, original and arche-

---

[1] This is the argument of Plato, *Republic*, x.

[2] φύσις is the intermediary between the World Soul and Matter (ὕλη), deriving its activity from the Soul. It is through the medium of Nature that the Sensible World is created, and it is Nature that gives Form to Matter, and there is in it an element of reason (cf. *Enn*. iii. 8. 2 (i, p. 333)), 'there is an unmoved element in Nature which is reason (ὁ λόγος)'.

[3] Cf. Psellus, περὶ νοῦ, ed. Ruelle, p. 249, who says here that Mind is intelligible, Soul only in so far as it partakes of Mind; Plotinus, *Enn*. v. 9. 6–7 (ii, pp. 253–5).

[4] καὶ τελευταῖον εἰς τὸ ἀνείδεον, i.e. finally dies. Psellus is discussing here the degradation of Form.

[5] ὁ δὲ ὁ παντάπασι χωριστός. . . . Cf. Aristotle.

[6] Cf. Plotinus, *Enn*. iii. 8. 9 (i, pp. 341–2), 'Mind, then, is not the First Principle, but there must be something beyond it . . . and this, since it is not νοῦς and not a duality, must be beyond both νοῦς and νοητόν.'

[7] Cf. Plotinus, *Enn*. v. 5. 9 (ii, p. 216), 'The First Principle does not stand apart, distant from all things, and, although it is not contained in anything, it is not true to say that it possesses nothing, because it is the sum of all things.'

typal, and is a creative Idea. Realities seem in the first place to consist of the Ideas.[1] For these[2] we divide, and we declare them to be
set forth for Reason from the Good through the action of the Intelligible World. For sensible things are what they are said to be by
participation, the underlying nature (i.e. matter) receiving Form
from above, Art passing into sensible Things by means of an image,
Art itself remaining absent from Matter in detachment, and having
the true statue. But Mind is Realities themselves, having all things
in itself, not as in a place, but in the sense that it itself possesses them.
And everything in the Real World is both together and separate none
the less, yet again not together, for each is a peculiar potentiality. The
capacities of the seeds bear an image of rational order.[3] For in the
Whole all things are confounded, and, as it were, in one centre, and
Soul impinges on them, as not being in possession of them, or
acquires them or finds a way through them to the end, but Mind on
the other hand stands firm, being the apprehension of all Realities
alike. And Mind as a whole is all the Forms, and the several mani-
festations of Mind are the several Forms, as the whole of knowledge
contains all arts and sciences ($\theta\epsilon\omega\rho\dot{\eta}\mu\alpha\tau\alpha$), on the ground that each
is a part of the whole, not separate, but having each a function within
the whole. We must consider Reality before Mind,[4] because it is
Realities that must be placed in the knowing Mind; but the actuality
($\dot{\epsilon}\nu\dot{\epsilon}\rho\gamma\epsilon\iota\alpha$)[5] of both is the same.[6] The dividing Mind is something
different. That which is itself undivided, and does not divide, is
the one and the All. The archetype must be in the Mind, and the
Mind must take this Intelligible Universe as the pattern of the visible.
For as, when there is the Form of a living being and a Matter which
receives the seminal Form,[7] a living being must come into existence,
so, when there is intelligent and all-powerful Nature, and nothing
hinders its operation, the Matter must be shaped and the Form
must shape it; and the created world has the Form split into parts,
here men, here the sun, but in the One are all Forms alike. As many
things, then, as are Form in the Sensible World, these are from the

[1] The Greek of this passage seems to be corrupt, and the translation is
therefore queried.
[2] i.e. $\tau\dot{\alpha}$ $\check{o}\nu\tau\alpha$ (realities), not $\alpha\dot{\iota}$ $\dot{\iota}\delta\dot{\epsilon}\alpha\iota$.
[3] Cf. the Stoic $\lambda\dot{o}\gamma o\iota$ $\sigma\pi\epsilon\rho\mu\alpha\tau\iota\kappa o\dot{\iota}$.
[4] Reading $\pi\rho o\epsilon\pi\iota\nu o\epsilon\dot{\iota}\nu$ instead of $\pi\rho o\sigma\epsilon\pi\iota\nu o\epsilon\dot{\iota}\nu$.
[5] Note the contrast of $\dot{\epsilon}\nu\dot{\epsilon}\rho\gamma\epsilon\iota\alpha$ and $\delta\dot{\upsilon}\nu\alpha\mu\iota s$.
[6] The text of this sentence is probably corrupt, but no satisfactory emenda-
tion suggests itself.
[7] $\check{\upsilon}\lambda\eta$ is that which provides a receptacle for Form, which $\phi\dot{\upsilon}\sigma\iota s$ gives it.
Cf. the view that the male parent contributes the form, the female parent the
matter.

Real World, and those not of the nature of Form have not come from Beyond. In the Beyond Eternity takes the place of the Time which we have in this world, and whichever of the things in that world you take is substance, and there is not even a Form of evil there. For the evil in this world comes from want, defect, and privation. There are no patterns of the imitative Arts there, while the creative Arts, in so far as they make use of proportions, would derive thence their principles. The Forms of universals alone are there; the differentiae of particular things come from Matter. And we must not think that all things which are images here are archetypal. So much for the Platonic theory of Ideas, worked out by him at length, but summarised in brief and in a clearer form for you in our essay.'

BIBLIOGRAPHY

The details given in the bibliography are not repeated in the notes of the text. Where there is more than one edition I have either given first that which I have used, or else stated in the text which edition is cited. I have not always given all editions of an author, but the best, and the most accessible.

This is not a complete bibliography, but will, I hope, give the general reader some idea of the available sources for the period.

I. ABBREVIATIONS

AB	*Analecta Bollandiana*, Paris and Brussels, 1882– .
AEG	*Annuaire de l'association pour l'encouragement des études grecques en France*, Paris and Brussels, 1867–87.
AGP	*Archiv für Geschichte der Philosophie*, Berlin, 1912– .
ASS	*Acta sanctorum*, Antwerp, 1643– .
B	*Byzantion*, Paris, 1924– .
BNJ	*Byzantinisch-neugriechische Jahrbücher*, Berlin, 1920– .
BZ	*Byzantinische Zeitschrift*, Leipzig, 1892– .
CB	*Corpus scriptorum historiae byzantinae*, Bonn, 1828–97.
CMH	*Cambridge Medieval History*, Cambridge, 1911–36.
Dölger	F. Dölger, *Corpus der griechischen Urkunden des Mittelalters und der neueren Zeit*, Reihe A, Abt. I, 1. Teil, Regesten von 565–1025, 2. Teil, Regesten von 1025–1204, Munich and Berlin, 1924–5.
EHR	*English Historical Review*, London, 1886– .
EO	*Échos d'orient*, Paris, 1897– .
Freh	J. Leunclavius, *Juris graeco-romani tam canonici quam civilis tomi duo . . . cura M. Freheri . . .*, Frankfurt, 1596.
GBL	*Geschichte der byzantinischen Litteratur*, ed. K. Krumbacher, 2nd ed., Munich, 1897 (=Handbuch d. klass. Altertums-Wissenschaft, ed. I. von Müller, ix, 1).
H	*Hermes*, Berlin, 1866– .
HZ	*Historische Zeitschrift*, Munich, 1859– .
IRAIC	*Izvêstiya russkago archeologicheskago instituta v Konstantinopolê* (Transactions of the Russian Archeological Institute at Constantinople), Odessa, 1896– .
JA	*Journal asiatique*, Paris, 1822– .
JHS	*Journal of Hellenic Studies*, London, 1880– .
Jus	C. E. Zachariae von Lingenthal, *Jus graeco-romanum*, 7 vols., Leipzig, 1856–84 (c. = collatio, n. = novel).
K	K. N. Kanellakes, Χιακὰ ἀνάλεκτα, Athens, 1890.
MAT	*Mémoires de l'académie des sciences, inscriptions, et belles-lettres de Toulouse*, dixième série, Toulouse, 1901–12.

MM   F. Miklosich et J. Müller, *Acta et diplomata graeca medii aevi sacra et profana*, 6 vols., Vienna, 1860–90.

NJ   *Neue Jahrbücher für das klassische Altertum*, Leipzig, 1898– .

Notices et extraits. . . . *Notices et extraits des manuscrits de la bibliothèque nationale et autres bibliothèques publiés par l'institut national de France*, v–xxxiv, Paris, 7th year of the Republic (1798–9)–1895.

OC   *Orientalia christiana*, Rome, 1923– .

P   *Philologus, Zeitschrift für das klassische Altertum*, Stolberg, 1846– .

Pauly-Wissowa   A. F. von Pauly's *Real-encyclopädie der klassischen Altertumswissenschaft*. Neue Bearbeitung . . . herausgegeben von Georg Wissowa, i–vii (1), Stuttgart, 1894–1910. Continued by W. Kroll and others, 1912– .

PG   J. P. Migne, *Patrologiae cursus completus*, . . . *series graeco-latina*, Paris, 1857–66.

PL   *Patrologiae cursus completus*, . . . *Series latina*, Paris, 1844–55.

PO   *Patrologia orientalis*, Paris, 1907– .

PW   *Philologische Wochenschrift*, Leipzig, 1921– .

REG   *Revue des études grecques*, Paris, 1888– .

RH   *Revue historique*, Paris, 1876– .

RHR   *Revue de l'histoire des religions*, Paris, 1880– .

RHS   *Revue historique du sud-est européen*, Bucharest and Paris, 1924– .

RO   *Revue de l'orient latin*, Paris, 1893– .

ROC   *Revue de l'orient chrétien*, Paris, 1896– .

RP   *Revue de philologie, de littérature et d'histoire anciennes*, Paris, 1845– .

Sathas *Bibliotheca graeca medii aevi*, ed. K. N. Sathas, 7 vols., Venice and Paris, 1872–94.

SML   *Stimmen aus Maria–Laach*, Freiburg i. Breisgau, 1871– .

T   *Teubner* edition.

TLZ   *Theologische Literaturzeitung*, Leipzig, 1876– .

Usp Vost P. Uspensky, Istoriya Afona (pt. 3), *Vostok khristianskiy*, Kiev, 1877.

VV   *Vizantiyskiy Vremennik* (Byzantina chronica), St. Petersburg, 1894– .

ZMNP   *Zhurnal ministerstva narodnago prosvêshcheniya* (Journal of the Ministry of Public Instruction), St. Petersburg, 1834–?1923.

ZWT   *Zeitschrift für wissenschaftliche Theologie*, Jena, 1858– .

II. ORIGINAL AUTHORITIES AND COLLECTIONS OF SOURCES

ALLATIUS, L. *De ecclesiae occidentalis atque orientalis perpetua concensione*, Cologne, 1648. (This contains a report of the synod's action in the suppression of the Bogomile heresy in Manuel Comnenus's reign.)

ANNA COMNENA. *Alexias*, ed. A. Reifferscheid, 2 vols., Leipzig, 1884 (T). Also ed. L. Schopenus, 2 vols., CB, 1839–78, and PG, cxxxi. Translated by E. A. S. Dawes, *The Alexiad of the Princess Anna Comnena*, London, 1928; I have sometimes used this translation, sometimes made my own from Reifferscheid's text; my references are to the book and chapter of the *Alexias*; the volume and page of Reifferscheid follows in brackets.

Anthologia Palatina, ed. H. Stadtmüller, 3 vols., Leipzig, 1894–1906 (T); for other editions *see* GBL, p. 728.

Anonymou Synopsis Chronice, ed. Sathas, vii, 1894.

ARETHAS of Caesarea. PG, cvi, *Commentarius in Apocalypsin*. 2 *Orationes*.

ATTALEIATES, Michael. *Historia*, ed. I. Bekker, CB, 1853. *Diataxis*, MM, v. Also Sathas, I.

BALSAMON, Theodore. PG, cxxxvii–cxxxviii, *In canones SS. apostolorum, conciliorum, et in epistolas canonicas SS. patrum*.

BASIL I. PG, cvii, *Kephalaia ad Leonem filium*.

BRYENNIUS, Nicephorus. *Historiarum libri IV*, ed. A. Meineke, CB, 1836. Also PG, cxxvii.

CECAUMENUS. *Strategicon*, ed. B. Wassiliewsky and V. Jernstedt, St. Petersburg, 1896.

CEDRENUS, George. *Synopsis historiarum*, ed. I. Bekker, 2 vols., CB, 1838–9. Also PG, cxxi–cxxii, where the numbers in the Latin translation correspond to the pages in Bekker.

CERULARIUS, Michael. PG, cxx, one sermon, and a ruling on adultery, otherwise concerned with the schism of 1054. *See* A. MICHEL on the schism.

CHRISTODOULUS. *Diataxis*, MM, vi, pp. 59–80. *See also* MILET.

CHRISTOPHORUS MYTILENAEUS. *Die Gedichte des Christophoros Mytilenaios*, ed. E. Kurtz, Leipzig, 1903.

CONSTANTINE VII. *De cerimoniis aulae Byzantinae*, ed. J. J. Reiske, 2 vols., CB, 1829–30. Also in PG, cxii. This is being re-edited by A. Vogt, and chapters 1–46 (1–37 Reiske), with a commentary, have been published, Paris, 1935.

De thematibus, and *De administrando*, ed. I. Bekker, CB, 1840. Also in PG, cxiii.

Vita Basilii, ed. I. Bekker, CB, 1838 (= Theophanes Continuatus, Bk. V).

Narratio de Imagine Edessena, PG, cxiii.

CONSTANTINE CEPHALAS. See *Anthologia Palatina*.

CONSTANTINE the Rhodian. REG, ix (1896), ed. E. Legrand, Description des œuvres d'art et de l'église des Saints-Apôtres de Constantinople, poème en vers ïambiques par Constantin le Rhodien, pp. 32–65. With an archaeological commentary by Theodore Reinach, pp. 66–103.

COSMAS VESTITOR. PG, cvi, *Oratio et canon acrostichus*.

DIMITRIEVSKY, A. *Opisanie liturgicheskikh rukopisey, khranyashchikhsya v bibliotekakh pravoslavnago vostoka* (The liturgical manuscripts in the libraries of the Orthodox East). I. *Typica*, pt. i, Kiev, 1895. II. *Euchologia*, Kiev, 1901. III. *Typica*, pt. ii, St. Petersburg, 1917.

DÖLGER, F. *Corpus der griechischen Urkunden des Mittelalters und der neueren Zeit*, Reihe A, Abt. I, 1. Teil, Regesten von 565–1025; 2. Teil, Regesten von 1025–1204, Munich and Berlin, 1924–5.

EUSTATHIUS of Thessalonica. *Opuscula*, ed. G. L. F. Tafel, Frankfurt, 1832; this contains various sermons, addresses, and letters.

    2 *Orationes*, ed. G. L. F. Tafel, *De Thessalonica eiusque agro*, Berlin, 1839, pp. 401–39.

    7 *Orationes*, ed. W. Regel, *Fontes rerum Byzantinarum*, i, fasc. 1, St. Petersburg, 1892.

    PG, cxxxv–cxxxvi contain nearly all Eustathius's writings, other than the commentaries, for which see Cohn's article in Pauly-Wissowa, vi. 1.

EUSTRATIUS of Nicaea. Ed. A. K. Demetracopoulos, *Bibliotheca ecclesiastica*, Leipzig; 1866. (These are writings on theological controversies.)

    Ed. G. Heylbut, *Berliner Aristoteleskommentare*, xx, Berlin, 1892. (His commentaries on the *Ethics*.)

EUTHYMIUS, Patriarch of Constantinople. 2 *Orationes*, PO, xvi, pp. 499–514.

EUTHYMIUS MALACES, Metropolitan of Neae-Patrae. Ed. G. L. F. Tafel, *De Thessalonica eiusque agro*, Berlin, 1839, pp. 394–400 (funeral oration on Eustathius).

    Ed. M. Treu, Δελτίον τῆς Ἱστορικῆς καὶ Ἐθνολογικῆς Ἐταιρείας τῆς Ἑλλάδος, v (1896–1900), pp. 197–218.

    Ed. A. Papadopoulos-Kerameus, *Noctes Petropolitanae*, St. Petersburg, 1913, pp. 89–102, 115–25.

    See also Stadtmüller, *Michael Choniates . . .*, pp. 306 ff.

EUTHYMIUS ZIGABENUS. PG, cxxviii, *Commentarius in Psalterium*.

    PG, cxxix, *Commentarius in quattuor Evangelia*.

    PG, cxxx, *Panoplia dogmatica*.

    PG, cxxxi, *Expositio symboli. Disputatio de fide. Dialogus de fide Christianorum. Confutatio Massalianorum. Adversus Phundagiatas.*

EVAGRIUS of Pontus. PG, xl.

GENESIUS, Joseph. *Historia,* ed. C. Lachmann, CB, 1834; and PG, cix.

GEORGE of Nicomedia. PG, c, 10 *Orationes.*

GEORGIUS MONACHUS. *Vitae recentiorum Imperatorum,* ed. I. Bekker, CB, 1838 (with Theophanes Continuatus).

GLYCAS, Michael. *Annales,* ed. I. Bekker, CB, 1836. *Letters and Annales,* PG, clviii.

GREGORIUS MAGISTER. See V. Langlois, Mémoire sur la vie et les écrits du Prince Grégoire Magistros, JA, 6me série, xiii (1869), pp. 5–64.

GREGORY PARCOURIANUS. *Typicon,* ed. L. Petit, VV, xi (1904), Supplement No. 1, pp. i–xxxii, 1–63, Typicon de Grégoire Parcourianos pour le monastère de Pétritzos (Bačkovo) en Bulgarie.

IRENE DUCAS. *Typicon,* ed. MM, v, pp. 327–91. Also PG, cxxvii.

ISAAC COMNENUS (brother of John II Comnenus). *Typicon,* ed. L. Petit, IRAIC, xiii (1908), pp. 17–77.

JOHN of Antioch. PG, cxxxii, *Oratio de disciplina monastica et de monasteriis laicis non tradendis.*

JOHN CAMENIATES. *De excidio Thessalonicensi,* ed. I. Bekker, CB, 1838, after Theophanes Continuatus.

JOHN CINNAMUS. *Historia,* ed. A. Meineke, CB, 1836; also PG, cxxxiii.

JOHN CLIMACUS. PG, lxxxviii.

JOHN II COMNENUS. *Typicon,* ed. A. Dimitrievsky, *Typica,* i, pp. 656–702.

JOHN CURIOTES (or GEOMETRES). PG, cvi (sermons, hymns, and poetry), and ed. J. Sajdak, *Ioannis Kyriotis Geometrae hymni in SS. Deiparam,* Posen, 1931 (*Analecta byzantina edita cura societatis litterarum Posnaniensis,* fasc. 1).

JOHN ITALUS. *Opuscula selecta,* ed. G. Cereteli, 2 vols., Tiphlis, 1924–6.

JOHN MAUROPOUS. Archbishop of Euchaita.

De legum custode et athenaeo Constantinopolitano. Decretum seu novella imp. Constantini Monomachi descripta a Ioanne Euchaitensi et ab Angelo Card. Mai latine versa, ed. J. Cozza-Luzi, *Studi e documenti di storia e diritto,* Anno V, pp. 289–316. Rome, 1884.

Iohannis Euchaitorum metropolitae quae in codice vaticano graeco 676 supersunt, ed. P. de Lagarde (Abh. d. König. Gesell. d. Wiss. zu Göttingen, xxviii), Göttingen, 1882. Also PG, cxx. The more complete edition is that of Lagarde, although this gives only the text and makes no attempt at chronological arrangement of the letters. See the review of Neumann, TLZ, 1886, Nr. 24, cols. 565 ff., and Nr. 25, cols. 594 ff.; also Sternbach, *De Ioanne Psello,* concerning the authenticity of poems 13–17 in Lagarde. The etymological poem which Lagarde gives in his preface is published in a more complete form by Reitzenstein, who uses Cod. 296 of the library of the Alexandrian Patriarch at Cairo.

Canones. These are almost all in manuscript. One of the most important MSS. is *Vindob. cod. th. gr.* 78 (Nessel, i, pp. 161–2 = the *Vindob. cod. th. gr.* 299 mentioned by J. Draeseke, BZ, ii (1893), p. 463). *Vindob. cod. th. gr.* 146 (Nessel, i, p. 224 = the *Vindob. cod. th. gr.* 309 mentioned by J. Draeseke, op. cit., p. 464) contains more of John's canons, but this codex is at present almost illegible, because the centre of each folio has been obliterated, probably by damp.

KANELLAKES, K. N. Χιακὰ ἀνάλεκτα, Athens, 1890.

LEO DIACONUS. *Historia*, ed. C. B. Hase, CB, 1828. Also PG, cxvii.

LEO GRAMMATICUS. *Chronographia*, ed. I. Bekker, CB, 1842. Also PG, cviii.

LEO VI, the Wise. PG, cvii (sermons, polemic, hymns, poems, and the *Tactica*).
See also *Sylloge Tacticorum Graecorum*, ed. R. Vári, *Leonis Imperatoris Tactica*, i, Budapest, 1917; ii, fasc. 1, Budapest, 1922.

LEUNCLAVIUS, J. *Juris graeco-romani tam canonici quam civilis tomi II . . . cura M. Freheri . . .*, Frankfurt, 1596.

LIUDPRAND, Bishop of Cremona. *Antapodosis*, and *Relatio de legatione Constantinopolitana*, ed. I. Bekker, 1915 (Scriptores rerum Germanicarum in usum scholarum); PL, cxxxvi; and the *Relatio* in CB after Leo Diaconus. Translated by F. A. Wright, *The Works of Liudprand of Cremona*, London, 1930.

MANASSES, Constantine. *Synopsis historica*, ed. I. Bekker, CB, 1837 (with Joel and George Acropolites). Also PG, cxxvii.

MANSI, J. D. *Sacrorum conciliorum nova et amplissima collectio*, xv–xxii, Venice, 1770–8.

MATTHEW of Edessa. *History*, ed. and trans. E. Dulaurier, Paris, 1858 (*Bibliothèque historique arménienne*).

MAXIMUS the Confessor. PG, xc and xci.

MICHAEL CHONIATES (ACOMINATUS). *Opera*, ed. S. P. Lampros, 2 vols., Athens, 1879–80; PG, cxl, containing some letters, 2 sermons, the *orationes* on Eustathius and Nicetas, and a poem on Athens.

MICHAEL ITALICUS. *Letters*, ed. J. A. Cramer, *Anecdota graeca e codicibus manuscriptis bibliothecarum Oxoniensium*, iii, Oxford, 1836, pp. 158–203.

MIKLOSICH, F., and MÜLLER, J. *Acta et diplomata graeca medii aevi sacra et profana*, 6 vols., Vienna, 1860–90.

Milet. Ergebnisse der Ausgrabungen und Untersuchungen seit dem Jahre 1899, ed. T. Wiegand (Königliche Museen zu Berlin), iii, pt. 1, Berlin, 1913: *Der Latmos*. Note *Monumenta Latrensia Hagiographica*, ed. H. Delehaye, pp. 97 ff. (especially on Christodoulus).

Νεαμονησία, ed. Gregorius Photeinus (Γρηγορίος Φωτεῖνος), Chios, 1865.

NICEPHORUS II PHOCAS. *De velitatione bellica*, ed. C. B. Hase, CB, 1828 (with Leo the Deacon).

NICETAS BYZANTINUS. PG, cv, *Refutatio epistolae regis Armeniae. Refutatio Mohamedis.*

NICETAS CHONIATES (ACOMINATUS). *Chronicle*, ed. I. Bekker, CB, 1835; PG, cxxxix.
Thesaurus orthodoxae fidei, PG, cxxxix–cxl.

NICETAS DAVID PAPHLAGO. PG, cv, 20 *Orationes, Vita S. Ignatii.*

NICETAS STETHATUS. PG, cxx, *Tres centuriae asceticae. De salutatione manuale. Libellus contra Latinos* (Latin only, the Greek is given by Michel, ii, pp. 322 ff.).
Dialexis, ed. A. Michel, ii, pp. 320-1.
De azymis et sabbatorum jejuniis, et nuptiis sacerdotum (Antidialogue), ed. A. Michel, ii, pp. 322-42.
Altera synthesis contra Latinos de Filioque, ed. A. Michel, ii, pp. 371-409.
Vita Symeonis junioris, ed. I. Hausherr and G. Horn, OC, xii (July and September, 1928), Nr. 45.

NICHOLAS of Methone. *Orationes duae contra haeresim dicentium sacrificium pro nobis salutare non trishypostatae divinitati, sed patri soli esse . . .*, Leipzig, 1865.
Other theological *orationes*, ed. A. K. Demetracopoulos, *Bibliotheca ecclesiastica*, Leipzig, 1864.
Refutation of Proclus's *Elements of Theology*, ed. J. T. Vomel, Frankfurt, 1825.

NICHOLAS MUZALON. Abdication poem, ed. S. J. Doanidu, Ἑλληνικά, vii (1934), pp. 109-50.

NICHOLAS MYSTICUS. PG, cxi, *Epistolae.*

NICOULITZA. *De officiis regiis libellus*, ed. B. Wassiliewsky and V. Jernstedt, St. Petersburg, 1896.

PARTHEY, G. F. C. *Hieroclis synecdemus et notitiae Graecae episcopatuum. Accedunt Nili Doxopatrii notitia patriarchatuum et locorum nomina immutata*, Berlin, 1866. There is the later edition of E. Gerland, but only the first volume has been published. *See* B, vii (1932), pp. 512-26.

PETIT, L. Documents inédits sur le concile de 1166 et ses derniers adversaires, VV, xi, 1904, pp. 465-93.

PHILIPPUS SOLITARIUS. *Dioptra*, PG, cxxvii.

Philopatris seu qui docetur dialogus, ed. C. B. Hase, CB, 1828 (with Leo Diaconus).

PHOTIUS. *Opera*, PG, ci–civ. See also *Monumenta graeca ad Photium eiusque historiam pertinentia*, ed. J. Hergenröther, Regensburg, 1869.

PLOTINUS. *Enneads*, ed. R. Volkmann, 2 vols., Leipzig, 1883-4 (T); ed. E. Bréhier, 5 vols., Paris, 1924-31, with a translation.

PSELLUS, Michael. (The fullest bibliography of Psellus's works is found in E. Renauld, *Étude de la langue et du style de Michel Psellos*: only those of his writings which are more important for this book are given here.)

Chronographia, ed. Sathas, iv, Paris, 1874. This was republished with emendations by J. B. Bury in the *Byzantine Texts*, London, 1899. A third edition with a French translation has been published by E. Renauld, 2 vols., Paris, 1926–8. A number of errors in text and translation are noted in the reviews of J. Sykutres, BZ, xxvii (1927), pp. 99–105, xxix (1929), pp. 40–8, and H. Grégoire, B, ii (1925), pp. 550–67, iv (1927–8), pp. 716–28. My references are throughout to Renauld's edition, the figures in brackets referring to volume and page.

Funeral orations and panegyrics, Sathas, vols. iv and v.

Accusation du Patriarche Michel Cérulaire devant le Synode, ed. L. Bréhier, REG, xvi (1903), pp. 375–416, and xvii (1904), pp. 35–76. Parts of the *Accusation* are translated by J. Draeseke, *Psellos und seine Anklageschrift*. . . .

Rede über den rhetorischen Charakter des Gregorios von Nazianz, ed. A. Mayer, BZ, xx (1911), pp. 27–100.

Περὶ τῶν ἰδεῶν ἃς ὁ Πλάτων λέγει, ed. C. G. Linder, P, xvi (1860), pp. 523–6.

XLII chapitres inédits et complémentaires du recueil de Michel Psellus, intitulé διδασκαλία παντοδαπή *ou notions variées*, ed. C. E. Ruelle, AEG, xiii (1879), pp. 230–78.

Ἐξήγησις τῆς Πλατωνικῆς ἐν τῷ Φαίδρῳ διφρείας τῶν ψυχῶν καὶ στρατείας τῶν θεῶν, ed. A. Jahn, H, xxxiv (1899), pp. 315–19.

PG, cxxii, *Omnifaria doctrina*.

Questionum naturalium solutiones.

Dialogus de operatione daemonum (French translation by E. Renauld, REG, xxxiii (1920), pp. 56–95).

Graecorum opiniones de daemonibus.

De anima celebres opiniones.

Commentarius in psychogoniam Platonicam.

Expositio in oracula Chaldaica.

Expositio brevis dogmatum Chaldaicorum.

De operatione daemonum. Accedunt inedita opuscula Pselli, ed. J. F. Boissonade, Ψελλός, Nuremberg, 1838.

Épître sur la Chrysopée. Opuscules et extraits sur l'alchimie, la météorologie et la démonologie. Choix de dissertations inédites (= passages on Gregory Nazianzus, John Climacus, book of Job, and an account of the miracle at the church of S. Mary of Blachernae). Ed. J. Bidez, *Catalogue des manuscrits alchimiques grecs*, vi, Brussels, 1928.

Oratio in salutationem, ed. M. Jugie, PO, xvi (1922), pp. 515–25.

Orationes et dissertationes, ed. E. Kurtz and F. Drexl, Milan, 1936 (= *Michaelis Pselli scripta minora, magnam partem adhuc inedita*, vol. i), Orbis Romanus, V.

Epistolae. These are edited in various collections, and there is no complete edition (vol. ii of the Kurtz–Drexl edition is to contain unedited letters).

Sathas, v, 208 letters; 20 of these are also published in the *Recueil des historiens des croisades*, i, pp. 8–97, but Sathas says that they should be addressed to Isaac Comnenus and not Alexius.

PG, cxxii, 9 letters = Boissonade, $\Psi\epsilon\lambda\lambda\acute{o}s$, pp. 170–88.

3 letters = Tafel, *De Thessalonica eiusque agro*, 1839, pp. 361–7.

Miscellanea maximam partem critica, ed. F. T. Friedemann and J. B. G. Seebode, Wittenberg, 1827, ii, pp. 601–23. Zervos, p. 33, says that this contains 21 letters published by F. Creuzer, but there are more than this, although Nos. 32–5 are perhaps too short to be called letters.

Néa Σιών, 1908, pp. 497–516, ed. Papadopoulos-Kerameus. 17 letters. This edition is not given by Renauld, but is mentioned by Zervos, p. 34.

Archives des missions scientifiques et littéraires, 3rd series, ii (1873), pp. 612–19, ed. C. E. Ruelle. 3 letters on music.

AEG, viii (1874), pp. 193–221. 2 letters ed. by Sathas, with a French translation.

See Zervos, p. 34, for bibliography concerning these letters.

SCYLITZES, John. *See* CEDRENUS.

Sententiae synodales et sanctiones pontificiae archiepiscoporum et patri-archarum Constantinopolis, PG, cxix, cxxvii, cxxxvii-cxxxviii, and cxl. *See also* L. ALLATIUS, J. D. MANSI, and L. PETIT.

SUIDAE *Lexicon*, ed. A. Adler, 4 vols., Leipzig, 1928–35 (Lexicographi graeci, i). Also G. Bernhardy, Halis and Brunswicke, 1853.

SYMEON the Young. PG, cxx, *Orationes* (Latin only).

Liber divinorum amorum (Latin only). German translation by K. Kirchhoff, Hellerau, 1930. The Greek text of four of these hymns is edited by P. Maas, Aus der Poesie des Mystikers Symeon, in *Festgabe Albert Ehrhard*, ed. A. M. Königer, Bonn, 1927, pp. 327–41.

Capita practica et theologica.

De alterationibus animae et corporis (Latin only).

Duae orationes.

Epistola de confessione, ed. K. Holl, *Enthusiasmus und Bussgewalt*, Leipzig, 1898, pp. 110–27. Also PG, xcv, where it is wrongly attributed to John of Damascus.

Letter to Stephen, Archbishop of Nicomedia, ed. I. Hausherr and G. Horn, OC, xii (July–Sept. 1928), Nr. 45, pp. lxiii-lxv.

SYMEON LOGOTHETE (or MAGISTER). *Chronicle*, ed. V. Sreznevsky, St. Petersburg, 1905 (this is the Slavonic version).

SYMEON MAGISTER. *Chronographia*, ed. I. Bekker, CB, 1838 (with Theophanes Continuatus).

SYMEON METAPHRASTES. *Vitae sanctorum*, PG, cxiv-cxvi.

Synodicon for the first Sunday in Lent, ed. Th. Uspensky, *Zapiski imperatorskogo novorossiyskogo universiteta*, vol. 59, Odessa, 1893.

THEODORUS DAPHNOPATES. PG, lxiii (under John Chrysostom's name, cols. 567–902) and cxi. *Orationes, see* GBL, p. 170.

THEODORUS PRODROMUS. PG, cxxxiii (poetry and letters). Ed. E. Miller and E. Legrand, *Trois poèmes vulgaires de Théodore Prodrome,* Paris, 1875. Ed. E. Legrand, *Bibliothèque grecque vulgaire,* i, Paris, 1880 (6 poems, including the 3 edited by Miller and Legrand). Ed. E. Miller, *Mélanges de philologie et d'épigraphie,* pt. i, Paris, 1876 (poems, including the 3 edited by Miller and Legrand). Ed. D–C. Hesseling and H. Pernot, *Poèmes prodromiques en grec vulgaire,* Amsterdam, 1910. See also *Notices et extraits . . .,* vi–ix.

THEODOSIUS the Deacon. *De expugnatione Cretae,* ed. C. B. Hase, CB, 1828 (with Leo Diaconus). Also PG, cxiii.

THEOPHANES CONTINUATUS. *Chronographia,* ed. I. Bekker, CB, 1838.

THEOPHYLACTUS of Achrida, Archbishop of Bulgaria. PG, cxxiii–cxxvi (letters and exegesis).

Timarion, ed. B. Hase, *Notices et extraits,* ix (1813), 2, pp. 163–246. Also ed. A. Ellissen, *Analekten der mittel- und neugriechischen Literatur,* pt. 4, Leipzig, 1860 (with translation).

Trial of John Italus for Heresy, ed. Th. Uspensky, IRAIC, ii (1897), pp. 1–66.

Vita S. Antonii Cauleae, PG, cvi.

S. Eustratii, ed. A. Papadopoulos-Kerameus, *Ἀνάλεκτα Ἱερο-σολυμιτικῆς σταχυολογίας,* St. Petersburg, IV, 1897.

S. Euthymii, ed. C. de Boor, Berlin, 1888.

S. Georgii hagioritae, AB, xxxvi (1917–19, published in 1922), pp. 69–159.

S. Ignatii, PG, cv.

S. Lazari Galesiotae, ASS, Nov., iii, pp. 502–608.

S. Lucae junioris, ASS, Feb., ii, pp. 83–100.

S. Lucae stylitae, ed. I. Vogt, AB, xxviii (1909), pp. 5–56; and in Delehaye, *Les Saints stylites.*

S. Nicolai studitae, PG, cv.

Sae. Theophano, ed. E. Kurtz, Zwei griechische Texte über die hl. Theophano, die Gemahlin Kaisers Leo VI, St. Petersburg, 1898 (*Mémoires de l'académie impériale des sciences de St. Petersburg,* VIII série, classe historico-philologique, iii, no. 2).

Symeonis junioris, see NICETAS STETHATUS.

XIPHILINUS, John. PG, cxx, *Orationes.*

ZACHARIAE VON LINGENTHAL, C. E. *Jus graeco-romanum,* 7 vols., Leipzig, 1856–84. There is a later edition by J. Zepos and P. Zepos, Athens, 1931; *see* F. Dölger's review, BZ, xxxii (1932), pp. 245–6. My references are to the 1856–84 edition.

ZONARAS, John. *Epitome historiarum,* i–ii, ed. M. Pinder, iii, ed. T. Büttner-Wobst, CB, 1841–97. Also ed. L. Dindorf, 6 vols., Leipzig, 1868–75 (T); and PG, cxxxiv–cxxxv.

240   BIBLIOGRAPHY

III. SECONDARY AUTHORITIES

BANDINI, A. M. *Catalogus codicum graecorum bibliothecae laurentianae,*
3 vols., Florence, 1764–70.
BARBIER, E. Le. *St. Christodule et la réforme des couvents grecs*, Paris,
1863.
BAYNES, N. H. *The Byzantine Empire*, London, 1925.
BERNDT, A. *Joannes Mauropus', Erzbischofs von Euchaita, Gedichte,
ausgewählt und metrisch übersetzt* (Wissenschaftliche Beilage zu
dem Programme des Gymnasiums und Realgymnasiums zu
Plauen i. V., Ostern, 1887, Progr. Nr. 507), Plauen, 1887.
BEVAN, E. R. *Later Greek Religion*, London, 1927.
BEZOBRAZOV, P. Materiali dlya istorii vizantiyskoy imperii. I. (Monas-
tic records), ZMNP, Nov. 1887, ccliv, pp. 65–78. II. (Psellus's
writings), ibid., March 1889, cclxii, pp. 72–91. III. (Michael
VII and Robert Guiscard), ibid., May 1889, cclxv, pp. 23–31.
IV. (Michael Cerularius), ibid., pp. 32–84.
BIDEZ, J. *Michel Psellus, Épître sur la Chrysopée. Opuscules et extraits
sur l'alchimie, la météorologie et la démonologie. En appendice,
Proclus, Sur l'art hiératique; Psellus, Choix de dissertations inédites*
(Catalogue des manuscrits alchimiques grecs, vi), Brussels, 1928.
See review of H. Grégoire, B, iv (1927–8, published in 1929),
pp. 728–34.
Psellus et le commentaire du Timée de Proclus, RP, xxix (1905), pp.
321–7.
Vie de Porphyre (Univ. de Gand. Recueil de travaux, publ. par la
Faculté de Philosophie et Lettres, Fasc. 43), Gand, 1913.
BIGG, C. *The Christian Platonists of Alexandria*, Oxford, 1886.
BOLLANDISTS, Society of. *Bibliotheca hagiographica graeca*, 2nd ed.,
Brussels, 1909.
BOUSSET, W. *Apophthegmata. Textüberlieferung und Charakter der
Apophthegmata patrum. Untersuchungen zur Vita Pachomii.
Euagriosstudien*, Tübingen, 1923.
BRÉHIER, E. *La Philosophie de Plotin*, Paris, 1928.
BRÉHIER, L. *Le Schisme oriental du XIᵉ siècle*, Paris, 1899.
BRÉHIER, L. L'enseignement supérieur à Constantinople dans la der-
nière moitié du XIᵉ siècle, *Revue internationale de l'enseignement*,
xxxviii (1899, Aug.), Nr. 8, pp. 97–112.
Notes sur l'histoire de l'enseignement supérieur à Constantinople,
B, iii (1926), pp. 73–94, iv (1927–8), pp. 13–28.
BROCKHAUS, H. *Die Kunst in den Athos-Klöstern*, Leipzig, 1891.
BROSSET, M. F. *Les ruines d'Ani, capitale de l'Arménie sous les rois bagra-
tides, aux Xᵉ et XIᵉ siècles. Histoire et description*, St. Petersburg,
1860.
BUCKLER, G. G. *Anna Comnena*, Oxford, 1929.
BULGAKOV, S. *The Orthodox Church*, London, 1935.

BURY, J. B. *History of the Eastern Roman Empire*, London, 1912.
History of the Later Roman Empire, 2 vols., London, 1923.
Roman Emperors from Basil II to Isaac Komnenos, EHR, iv (1889),
    pp. 41–64, 251–85.
The Imperial Administrative System in the Ninth Century (British
    Academy Supplemental Papers, I), London, 1911.
The Ceremonial Book of Constantine Porphyrogennetos, EHR,
    xxii (1907), pp. 209–27, 417–39. See also *Selected Essays*.
Selected Essays, ed. H. W. V. Temperley, Cambridge, 1930.
BUSSELL, F. W. *The Roman Empire. Essays on the Constitutional His-
    tory from the Accession of Domitian (A.D. 81) to the Retirement of
    Nicephorus III (A.D. 1081)*, 2 vols., London, 1910.
Cambridge Medieval History, ii–v.
CATOIRE, A. Deux anomalies du droit d'appel dans l'église orthodoxe,
    EO, xiii (1910), pp. 219–24.
CHALANDON, F. *Essai sur le règne d'Alexis Ier Comnène* (1081–1118),
    Paris, 1900.
Jean II Comnène (1118–43) et Manuel I Comnène (1143–80), Paris,
    1912.
COXE, H. O. *Catalogi codicum manuscriptorum bibliothecae Bodleianae:
    pars tertia codices Graecos et Latinos canonicianos complectens*,
    Oxford, 1854.
DAWKINS, R. M. *The Monks of Athos*, London, 1936.
DELEHAYE, H. *Les légendes grecques des saints militaires*, Paris, 1909.
Les Saints stylites, Paris and Brussels, 1923 (Subsidia hagiographia,14).
Deux typica byzantins de l'époque des Paléologues, Brussels, 1921 (this
    contains some discussion of the earlier *typica*).
DESLANDES, S. Une question de droit canonique — De quelle autorité
    relèvent les monastères orientaux? EO, xxi (1922), pp. 308–22.
DIEHL, C. De la signification du titre de 'proèdre' à Byzance, *Mélanges
    Schlumberger*, i, pp. 105–17.
La Société byzantine à l'époque des Comnènes, RHS, vi (1929, nos.
    7–9), pp. 197–280.
Le trésor et la bibliothèque de Patmos au commencement du 13^e
    siècle, *Études byzantines*, Paris, 1905, and BZ, i (1892), pp. 488–525.
Mélanges offerts à, 2 vols., Paris, 1930.
DÖLGER, F., and MAAS, P. Zu dem Abdankungsgedicht des Nikolaos
    Muzalon, BZ, xxxv (1935), pp. 2–14.
DRAESEKE, J. Johannes Mauropus, BZ, ii (1893), pp. 461–93.
Michael Psellos im 'Timarion', BZ, vi (1897), pp. 483–90.
Psellos und seine Anklageschrift gegen den Patriarchen Michael
    Kerullarios, ZWT, xlviii (1905), Heft II, pp. 194–259, Heft III,
    pp. 362–409.
Zu Michael Psellos, ZWT, xxxii (1889), pp. 303–30.
Zu Eustratios von Nikäa, BZ, v (1896), pp. 319–36.
DREVES, G. Johannes Mauropus, SML, xxvi (1884), Heft II, pp. 159–79.

Du Cange, C. du F. *Historia byzantina*, Paris, 1680.

Dunlap, J. E. *The Office of the Grand Chamberlain in the Later Roman and Byzantine Empires* (University of Michigan Studies, Humanist Series, xiv, pt. ii), New York, 1924.

Ebersolt, J. *Orient et occident: Recherches sur les influences byzantines et orientales en France avant les croisades*, Paris and Brussels, 1928.

Ferradou, A. *Des biens des monastères à Byzance*, Bordeaux, 1896.

Finlay, G. *History of Greece*, vols. 1–4, Oxford, 1877.

Fischer, W. *Studien zur byzantinischen Geschichte des elften Jahrhunderts* (Wissenschaftliche Beilage zu dem Programme der Gymnasial- und Realschul-Anstalt zu Plauen i. V., Progr. Nr. 495), Plauen i. V., 1883.

Fuchs, F. *Die höheren Schulen von Konstantinopel im Mittelalter* (Byzantinisches Archiv, 8), Leipzig, 1926.

Gasquet, A. *De l'autorité impériale en matière religieuse à Byzance*, Paris, 1879.

De l'emploi du mot βασιλεύς dans les actes de la chancellerie byzantine, RH, xxvi (1884, Nov.–Dec.), pp. 281–302.

Gelzer, H. *Ausgewählte kleine Schriften* (II. Das Verhältnis von Staat und Kirche in Byzanz), Leipzig, 1907.

Gerland, E. *Corpus notitiarum episcopatuum ecclesiae orientalis graecae.* Band i, Die Genesis der Notitia episcopatuum. Heft I, Einleitung, Constantinople, 1931.

Gfrörer, A. F. *Byzantinische Geschichten*, ed. J. B. Weiss, 3 vols., Graz, 1872–7.

Gibbon, E. *The Decline and Fall of the Roman Empire*, ed. J. B. Bury, 4th ed., 7 vols., London, 1909–14.

Grumel, V. Le 'miracle habituel' de Notre-Dame des Blachernes à Constantinople, EO, xxx (1931), pp. 129–46.

Hapgood, I. F. *Service Book of the Holy-Orthodox Catholic Apostolic Church*, 2nd ed., New York, 1922.

Hasluck, F. W. *Athos and its Monasteries*, London, 1924.

Hausherr, I. *La méthode d'oraison hésychaste* (OC, ix (June and July 1927), 2, Nr. 36).

Hausherr,, I., and Horn, G. *Un Grand Mystique byzantin. Vie de Syméon le Nouveau Théologien par Nicétas Stéthatos* (OC, xii (July and Sept. 1928), Nr. 45). *See* V. Laurent's review in EO, xxviii (1929), pp. 431–43.

Hergenröther, I. *Photius, Patriarch von Constantinopel*, 3 vols., Regensburg, 1867–9.

Hergès, A. Le Monastère du Pantocrator à Constantinople, EO, ii (1898–9), pp. 70–88.

Hirsch, F. *Byzantinische Studien*, Leipzig, 1876.

Holl, K. *Enthusiasmus und Bussgewalt beim griechischen Mönchtum. Eine Studie zu Symeon dem Neuen Theologen*, Leipzig, 1898.

Inge, W. R. *The Philosophy of Plotinus*, 2 vols., London, 3rd ed., 1929.

JANIN, R. Un Ministre byzantin: Jean l'Orphanotrophe, EO, xxx (1931, Oct.–Dec.), pp. 431–43.

JUGIE, M. Deux nouvelles homélies mariales inédites de Saint Euthyme, patriarche de Constantinople (†917), EO, xxiii (1924), pp. 286–8.

La vie et les œuvres d'Euthyme, patriarche de Constantinople (IXᵉ–Xᵉ siècle), EO, xvi (1913), pp. 385–95, 481–92.

La vie et les œuvres d'Euthyme Zigabène, EO, xv (1912), pp. 215–25.

KIRK, K. E. The Vision of God, 2nd ed., London, 1932.

KOUKOULES, Ph. Λαογραφικαὶ εἰδήσεις παρὰ τῷ Θεσσαλονίκης Εὐσταθίῳ, 'Επετηρὶς 'Εταιρείας Βυζαντινῶν Σπουδῶν, i (1924), Athens, pp. 5–40.

KRETIKIDES, E. Περίβασις εἰς τὰς μονὰς καὶ μετόχια τῆς Σάμου, ἔκδοσις β΄, 'Ερμουπόλει, 1873.

KRUMBACHER, K. Geschichte der byzantinischen Litteratur (527–1453), 2nd ed., Munich, 1897 (= Handbuch d. klass. Altertums-Wissenschaft, ed. I. von Müller, ix, 1).

KURTZ, E. Zu Michael Psellos, BZ, xv (1906), pp. 590–8.

LABORDE, L. Les écoles de droit dans l'empire d'orient, Bordeaux, 1912.

LAKE, K. The Early Days of Monasticism on Mt. Athos, Oxford, 1909.

LAMPROS, S. P. Collection de romans grecs en langue vulgaire et en vers, Paris, 1880.

LANGLOIS, V. Mémoire sur la vie et les écrits du Prince Grégoire Magistros, JA, 6ᵐᵉ série, xiii (1869), pp. 5–64.

LAURENT, V. Les sources à consulter pour l'établissement des listes épiscopales du patriarcat byzantin, EO, xxx (1931), pp. 65–83.

Réponses canoniques inédites du patriarcat byzantin, EO, xxxiii (1934), pp. 298–315.

LIEBERICH, H. Studien zu den Proömien in der griechischen und byzantinischen Geschichtsschreibung, Munich, 1898–1900.

LOT-BORODINE, M. La Doctrine de la 'déification' dans l'Église grecque jusqu'au XIᵉ siècle, RHR, cv (1932, Nr. 1, Jan.–Feb.), pp. 5–43; cvi (1932, Nr. 2–3, Sept.–Dec.), pp. 525–74; cvii (1933, Nr. 1, Jan.–Feb.), pp. 8–55.

MÄDLER, H. Theodora, Michael Stratiotikos, Isaac Komnenos. Ein Stück byzantinischer Kaisergeschichte (Wissensch. Beilage zu dem Progr. des königlichen Gymnasiums zu Plauen i. V., Progr. Nr. 545), Plauen i. V., 1894.

MAAS, P. Literarisches zu der Vita Euthymii, BZ, xxi (1912), pp. 436–40. See also DÖLGER.

MARIN, E. Les Moines de Constantinople depuis la fondation de la ville jusqu'à la mort de Photius (330–898), Paris, 1897. See Diehl's review, BZ, viii (1899), pp. 193–6.

MEYER, P. Die Haupturkunden für die Geschichte der Athosklöster, Leipzig, 1894.

MICHEL, A. *Humbert und Kerularios. Quellen und Studien zum Schisma des XI. Jahrhunderts* (Quellen und Forschungen aus dem Gebiete der Geschichte der Görresgesellschaft, xxi and xxiii), 2 vols., Paderborn, 1924–30. *See* reviews of M. Viller, B, ii (1925, published in 1926), pp. 615–19, and M. Jugie, B, viii (1933), fasc. 1, pp. 321–6.

MORDTMANN, J. *Esquisse topographique de Constantinople*, Lille, 1892. *See* BZ, ii (1893), pp. 145–8 for C. Diehl's review.

MORTREUIL, J. A. B. *Histoire du droit byzantin*, 3 vols., Paris, 1843–6.

MÜLLER, H. F. *Dionysios, Proclos, Plotinos*, Münster, 1918.

NESSEL, D. de. *Breviarium et supplementum commentariorum Lambecianorum sive catalogus aut recensio specialis codicum mss. graecorum, nec non linguarum orientalium augustissimae bibliothecae caesareae Vindobonensis*, 2 vols., Vienna, 1690.

NEUMANN, K. *Byzantinische Kultur und Renaissancekultur*, HZ, xci (1903), pp. 215 ff.

Die Weltstellung des byzantinischen Reiches vor den Kreuzzügen, Leipzig, 1894. French translation in RO, x (1903–4), pp. 56–171.

Griechische Geschichtsschreiber und Geschichtsquellen im zwölften Jahrhundert, Leipzig, 1888.

NISSEN, W. *Die Diataxis des Michael Attaliates von 1077*, Jena, 1894.

Die Regelung des Klosterwesens im Romäerreiche bis zum Ende des 9. Jahrhunderts, Hamburg, 1897.

NORDEN, W. *Das Papsttum und Byzanz. Die Trennung der beiden Mächte und das Problem ihrer Wiedervereinigung bis zum Untergange des byzantinischen Reiches (1453)*, Berlin, 1903.

OECONOMOS, L. *La vie religieuse dans l'empire byzantin au temps des Comnènes et des Anges*, Paris, 1918.

PARGOIRE, J. Les Saint-Mamas de Constantinople, IRAIC, ix (1904), fasc. 1–2, pp. 261–316.

PETIT, L. La vie et les œuvres de Syméon le nouveau théologien, EO xxvii (1928), pp. 163–7.

PÉTRIDÈS, S. Le chrysobulle de Manuel Comnène (1148) sur les biens de l'église, ROC, iv (xiv), 1909, pp. 203–8.

PITRA, J. B. *Hymnographie de l'église grecque*, Rome, 1867.

PRAECHTER, K. Michael von Ephesos und Psellos, BZ, xxxi (1931), pp. 1–12.

RAMBAUD, A. *L'Empire grec au Xème siècle: Constantin Porphyrogénète*, Paris, 1870.

Michel Psellos, RH, iii (1877), pt. 2, pp. 241–82. And in *Études sur l'histoire byzantine*, Paris, 1912.

REITZENSTEIN, R. *M. Terentius Varro und Johannes Mauropus von Euchaita—eine Studie zur Geschichte der Sprachwissenschaft*, Leipzig, 1901.

RENAULD, E. *Étude de la langue et du style de Michel Psellos*, Paris, 1920.

Les mots latins dans la 'Synopsis legum' et le 'De legum nomini-
bus' de Michel Psellos, MAT, viii (1908), pp. 77–96.
Lexique choisi de Psellos, Paris, 1920.
Quelques termes médicaux de Psellos, REG, xxii (1909), pp.
251–6.
Syntaxe des verbes composés dans Psellos, MAT, ix (1909), pp.
17–64; x (1910), pp. 1–56.
Syntaxe des verbes simples dans Psellos, MAT, xi (1911), pp. 1–16;
xii (1912), pp. 1–16.
RHODIUS, B. *Beiträge zur Lebensgeschichte und zu den Briefen des
Psellos* (Wissenschaftliche Beilage zu dem Programme des könig-
lichen Gymnasiums zu Plauen i. V.), Plauen i. V., 1892. See
review of J. Seger in BZ, ii (1893), pp. 148–51.
RUELLE, C. E. La Chrysopée de Psellos, REG, ii (1889), pp. 260–6.
Traduction de quelques textes grecs inédits. Lettres de Psellus, AEG,
viii (1874), pp. 130–42.
RUNCIMAN, S. *The Emperor Romanus Lecapenus and his Reign. A
Study of Tenth-Century Byzantium*, Cambridge, 1929.
SALAVILLE, S. Philosophie et théologie ou épisodes scolastiques à
Byzance de 1059 à 1117, EO, xxix (1930), pp. 132–56.
SANDYS, J. E. *A History of Classical Scholarship*, 3 vols., 3rd ed., Cam-
bridge, 1921.
SCABALANOVITCH, N. *Vizantiyskoe gosudarstvo i tserkov v XI. vêkê*
(Byzantine State and Church in the eleventh century), St. Peters-
burg, 1884.
SCHEMMEL, F. Die Schulen von Konstantinopel vom 12.–15. Jahrhun-
dert, PW, 1925, cols. 236–9.
SCHLUMBERGER, G. *L'épopée byzantine à la fin du Xe siècle*, 3 vols.,
Paris, 1896–1905.
Mélanges offerts à, 2 vols., Paris, 1924.
Un Empereur byzantin au Xe siècle, Nicéphore Phocas, Paris, 1890.
SOLOVIEV, A. Histoire du monastère russe au Mont Athos, B, viii
(1933), fasc. 1, pp. 213–38.
SOPHOCLES, E. A. *Greek Lexicon of the Roman and Byzantine Periods*,
3rd ed., New York, 1900.
STADTMÜLLER, G. *Michael Choniates Metropolit von Athen (ca. 1138–
ca. 1222)*. OC, xxxiii (2), Feb.–March, 1934, N^r 91.
STEIN, E. Untersuchungen zur spätbyzantinischen Verfassungs- und
Wirtschaftsgeschichte, *Mitteilungen zur osmanischen Geschichte*,
Bd. ii (1923–5), 1–2, Hanover, 1925, pp. 1–62.
STEIN, L. Die Kontinuität der griechischen Philosophie in der Gedan-
kenwelt der Byzantiner, AGP, ix (1896), pp. 225–46.
STEMPLINGER, E. *Das Plagiat in der griechischen Literatur*, Leipzig
and Berlin, 1912.
STEPHANIDES, B. K. Οἱ κώδικες τῆς 'Αδριανουπόλεως, BZ, xiv
(1905), pp. 588–611.

STÉPHANOU, E. Jean Italos: L'immortalité de l'âme et la résurrection, EO, xxxii (1933), pp. 413-28.

STERNBACH, L. De Ioanne Psello, Eos, ix (1903), pp. 5-10.

STRZYGOWSKI, J. Nea Moni auf Chios, BZ, v (1896), pp. 140-57.

SUVOROV, N. Vizantiyskiy papa. Iz istorii tserkovno-gosudarstvenych otnosheniy v Vizantii (A Byzantine Pope. From the history of the relation between Church and State in Byzantium), Moscow, 1902.

SVOBODA, V. La Démonologie de Michael Psellos, Brno, 1927.

TAFEL, G. L. F. Betrachtungen über den Mönchsstand. Eine Stimme des zwölften Jahrhunderts, Berlin, 1847 (a translation of Eustathius of Thessalonica's De emendanda vita monachica, with an introduction on Eustathius's life).

TAYLOR, A. E. Platonism and its Influence, London, 1927.

TODE, H. De Timarione dialogo byzantino, Greifswald, 1912.

TOZER, H. F. Byzantine Satire, JHS, ii (1881), pp. 233-70.

TREU, M. Ein byzantinisches Schulgespräch, BZ, ii (1893), pp. 96-105.

— Michael Italikos, BZ, iv (1895), pp. 1-22.

UBERWEG, F. Grundriss der Geschichte der Philosophie. Zweiter Teil, Die patristische und scholastische Philosophie, ed. B. Geyer, 11th ed., Berlin, 1928.

USPENSKY, F. Notes sur l'histoire des études byzantines en Russie, B, ii (1925), pp. 1-53.

USPENSKY, P. Istoria Athona (pt. 3), Vostok khristianskiy, Kiev, 1877.

USPENSKY, Th. Mnêniya i postanovleniya konstantinopolskikh pomêstnykh soborov XI i XII vv. o razdachê tserkovnykh imushchestv (kharistikarii) (Decisions and rulings of the local councils at Constantinople in the eleventh and twelfth centuries concerning the granting of ecclesiastical property). IRAIC, v (1900), pp. 1-48.

— Ocherki po istorii vizantiyskoy obrazovannosti (Notes on the history of Byzantine civilization), St. Petersburg, 1892. Part of this is in ZMNP, pt. 277 (1891, Sept. and Oct.), pp. 102-59, 283-324.

VALDENBERG, V. Nikoulitza et les historiens byzantins contemporains, B, iii (1926), pp. 95-121.

VANDERSTUYF, S. Étude sur Saint Luc le Stylite (879-979), EO, xii (1909), pp. 138-44, 215-21, 271-81; xiii (1910), pp. 13-19, 140-8, 224-32.

VAN MILLINGEN, A. Byzantine Churches in Constantinople, London, 1912.

— Byzantine Constantinople: the Walls of the City and Adjoining Historical Sites, London, 1899.

VASILIEV, A. A. Histoire de l'empire byzantin, traduit du russe par P. Brodin et A. Bourguina, 2 vols., Paris, 1932.

VILLER, M. *Aux sources de la spiritualité de Saint Maxime. Les Œuvres d'Évagre le Pontique* (Extrait de la Revue d'Ascétique et de Mystique, xi, Avril–Juillet, 1930), Toulouse, 1930.

VOGT, A. *Basile Ier, empereur de Byzance (867–886) et la civilisation byzantine à la fin du IXe siècle*, Paris, 1908.

La jeunesse de Léon VI le sage, RH, clxxiv (1934), pp. 389–428.

WELLNHOFER, M. Die thrakischen Euchiten und ihr Satanskult im Dialoge des Psellos Τιμόθεος ἢ περὶ τῶν δαιμόνων, BZ, xxx (1929–30), pp. 477–84.

WETTER, G. P. *Phos* (Φῶs). *Eine Untersuchung über hellenistische Frömmigkeit; zugleich ein Beitrag zum Verständnis des Manichäismus* (Skrifter utgifna af K. Humanistiska Vetenskaps-Samfundet i Uppsala), Uppsala and Leipzig, 1915.

WEYMANN, C. *The Neo-Platonists*, Cambridge, 1901.

WROTH, W. *Catalogue of the Imperial Byzantine Coins in the British Museum*, 2 vols., London, 1908.

YAKOVENKO, P. A. Izslêdovaniya v oblasti vizantiyskikh gramot. Gramoty Novago Monastyrya na ostrovê Khiosê (Research in Byzantine records. Records of Nea Monê on the island of Chios), *Ucheniya zapiski yurevskago universiteta (Acta et commentationes universitatis jurievensis, olim dorpatensis)*, vi (1917), pp. i–viii, 1–96, Juriev, 1917.

K istorii immuniteta v Vizantii (Contributions towards the history of the *immunitas* in Byzantium), Juriev, 1908.

ZACHARIAE VON LINGENTHAL, C. E. *Geschichte des griechisch-römischen Rechts*, 3rd ed., Berlin, 1892.

ZERVOS, C. *Un philosophe néoplatonicien du XIe siècle: Michel Psellos*, Paris, 1919.

ZHISHMAN, J. *Die Synoden und die Episkopalämter in der morgenländischen Kirche*, Vienna, 1867.

Das Stifterrecht (τὸ κτητορικὸν δίκαιον) *in der morgenländischen Kirche*, Vienna, 1888.

ADDENDA

While this book was in the press the first volume of a new edition of Michael Psellus appeared (*Orationes et dissertationes*, ed. E. Kurtz and F. Drexl, Milan, 1936. *See* Bibliography under PSELLUS). It was too late for me to use this, but it should be consulted. It contains a good deal which is now published for the first time, and also makes more accessible certain writings which were previously only to be found in periodicals, notably, the *Accusation* against the Patriarch Michael Cerularius, and the essay on the Platonic Ideas.

INDEX

1. GENERAL

* Placed *before* the figures to which it refers indicates the more important references.

2. AUTHORITIES CITED

Acominatus. *See* Michael *and* Nicetas Choniates.
Akty russkago . . ., 177.
Allatius, L.
   De ecclesiae . . . concensione, 98, 99.
   Diatriba de Psello, 78.
Andréadès, A., 173.
Anna Comnena, 10, 14, 19, 37, 71, 88–91, 93, 95–7, 103–4, 110, 142–3, 152, 161.
Anonymou Synopsis Chronice, 146, 161.
Aquinas, Thomas, 219, 223.
Arethas of Caesarea, 31, 34.
Athanasius, Archbishop of Corinth, 30.
Athanasius, Bishop of Alexandria, *Vita S. Antonii*, 217.
Attaleiates, Michael.
   Diataxis, 168, 179, 183–4.

History, 46, 50–1, 53, 59, 123, 129, 146–7, 154–7, 160–2, 175.
Augustine, Bishop of Hippo, 77.

Balsamon, Theodore, 98, 121, 127, 130, 169.
Bandini, A. M., 86.
Basil I, 24.
Basil the Great, 200.
Basilica, 120.
Bevan, E. R., 77.
Bezobrazov, P., *Materials* . . . *II*, 59, 69, 78–9.
Bidez, J., *Catalogue* . . . , 81–3, 87–8.
Bousset, W., 223.
Bréhier, L., *Le schisme oriental* . . . , 146, 155.
Brockhaus, H., 167.
Brosset, M. F., 128.
Bryennius, Nicephorus, 164.

3. GREEK WORDS

[169] MARMONT DU HAUTCHAMP ((Barthélemi), *Mizirida, princesse du Firando,* vol. I-III, Paris, Veuve Musier, 1738 ; vol. IV-VI, Paris, Rouy & Damonneville, 1743.

[170] MARMONTEL (Jean-François), *Contes moraux,* La Haye, s. n., 2 vol., 1761.

[171] — *Nouveaux contes moraux,* Paris, Merlin, 3 vol., 1765.

[172] — *Bélisaire,* Paris, Merlin, 1767.

[173] MILON DE LAVALLE, *Mémoires de la comtesse Linska, histoire polonaise,* Paris, Mesnier, 2 vol., 1739.

[174] MONCRIF (François-Augustin PARADIS DE), *Essais sur la nécessité et sur les moyens de plaire,* Paris, Prault fils, 1738.

[175] MOUHY (Charles de FIEUX, chevalier de), *Lamekis, ou les Voyages extraordinaires d'un Égyptien dans la terre intérieure, avec la découverte de l'île des Sylphides,* vol. I-II, Paris, L. Dupuis, 1735-1736 ; vol. III-IV, Paris, Poilly, 1737, vol. V-VIII, La Haye, Néaulme, 1738.

[176] — *Mémoires de M. le marquis de Fieux,* vol. I, Paris, Prault fils, 1735 ; vol. II-IV, Paris, Dupuis, 1736.

[177] — *Mémoires posthumes du comte de D... B... avant son retour à Dieu, fondé sur l'expérience des vanités humaines,* vol. I, Paris, P. Ribou, 1735 ; vol. II-III, Paris, G.-A. Dupuis, 1737 ; vol. IV, La Haye, J. Néaulme, 1741.

[178] — *Paris, ou le Mentor à la mode,* Paris, P. Ribou, 2 vol., 1735-1736.

[179] — *La Paysanne parvenue, ou les Mémoires de Mme la marquise de L. V.,* Paris, Prault fils, 7 vol., 1735-1736.

[180] — *Le Répertoire, ouvrage périodique,* t. Ier, Paris, frères Dupuis, 1735.

[181] — *La Mouche, ou les Aventures de M. Bigand,* Paris, L. Dupuis, 2 vol., 1736.

[182] — *La vie de Chimène Spinelli, histoire véritable,* Paris, Ribou, 6 vol., 1737.

[183] PERRIN (Jean-Antoine-René), *les Égarements de Julie,* Londres, s. n., 3 vol., 1756.

[184] PRÉVOST (Antoine-François), *Mémoires et aventures d'un homme de qualité qui s'est retiré du monde,* vol. I-IV, Paris, G. Martin, 1728-1729 ; vol. V-VI, Amsterdam, s. n., 1731 ; vol. VII *(Histoire du chevalier Des Grieux et de Manon Lescaut),* Amsterdam, s. n., 1733. (1731 ?).

[185] — *Le philosophe anglais, ou Histoire de M. Cleveland, fils naturel de Cromwell, écrite par lui-même...,* vol. I-II, Paris, Didot, 1731 ; vol. III-V, Paris, Didot (ou J. Guérin), 1732 ; vol. VI, Utrecht, E. Néaulme, 1738 ; vol. VII, Utrecht, E. Néaulme, 1739 ; vol. VIII, s. l., s. n., 1739.

[186] — *Le Doyen de Killerine, histoire morale composée sur les mémoires d'une illustre famille d'Irlande, et ornée de tout ce qui peut rendre une lecture utile et agréable,* vol. I, Paris, Didot, 1735 ; vol. II, La Haye, P. Poppy, 1739 ; vol. III-VI, s. l., s. n., 1739-1740.

[187] — *Histoire d'une Grecque moderne*, Amsterdam, Desbordes, 2 vol., 1740.

[188] — *Histoire de Marguerite d'Anjou, reine d'Angleterre*, Amsterdam, F. Desbordes, 4 vol., 1740.

[189] — *Campagnes philosophiques, ou Mémoires de M. de Montcal, aide-de-camp de M. le maréchal de Schomberg, contenant l'histoire de la guerre d'Irlande*, Amsterdam, Desbordes, 4 vol., 1741.

[190] — *Mémoires pour servir à l'histoire de Malte, ou Histoire de la jeunesse du commandeur de ****, Amsterdam, F. Desbordes, 2 vol., 1741.

[191] — *Histoire de Guillaume le Conquérant, duc de Normandie et roi d'Angleterre*, Paris, Prault fils, 2 vol., 1742.

[192] — *Voyages du capitaine Robert Lade en différentes parties de l'Afrique, de l'Asie et de l'Amérique ; contenant l'histoire de sa fortune, et ses observations sur les colonies et le commerce des Espagnols, des Anglais, des Hollandais, etc.*, Paris, Didot, 2 vol., 1744.

[193] — *Mémoires d'un honnête homme*, Amsterdam, s. n., 2 vol., 1745.

[194] — *Le Monde moral, ou Mémoires pour servir à l'histoire du cœur humain, par M...*, ancien résident de France, dans plusieurs cours étrangères, Genève, s. n., 2 vol., 1760.

[195] RAMSAY (Andrew Michael), *les Voyages de Cyrus, avec un discours sur la mythologie*, Paris, Quillau, 3 vol., 1727.

[196] RICCOBONI (Marie-Jeanne LABORAS DE MÉZIÈRES, dame), *Lettres de Mistress Fanni Butlerd à Milord Charles Alfred de Caitombridge*, Amsterdam, s. n., 1757.

[197] — *Histoire de M. le marquis de Cressy*, Amsterdam, s. n., 1758.

[198] — *Lettres de Milady Juliette Catesby à Milady Henriette Campley, son amie*, Amsterdam, s. n., 1759.

[199] — *Les Vrais caractères du sentiment, ou Histoire d'Ernestine*, Liège, Boubers, 1765.

[200] RICHARDSON (Samuel), *Pamela, ou la Vertu récompensée* (traduit par l'abbé PRÉVOST de l'anglais : *Pamela, or Virtue Rewarded*), Londres, Osborne, 2 vol., 1742.

[201] — *Lettre anglaise, ou Histoire de Miss Clarisse Harlove* (traduit par l'abbé PRÉVOST de l'anglais : *Clarissa, or The History of a Young Lady*), Londres, Nourse, 6 vol., 1751.

[202] — *Nouvelles lettres anglaises, ou Histoire du Chevalier Grandisson* (traduit par l'abbé PRÉVOST de l'anglais : *The History of Sir Charles Grandison*), Amsterdam, s. n., 4 vol., 1755-1756.

[203] ROUSSEAU (Jean-Jacques), *Julie, ou la Nouvelle Héloïse. Lettres de deux amants, habitants d'une petite ville au pied des Alpes*, Amsterdam, Marc-Michel Rey, 6 vol., 1761. Cf. éd. D. Mornet (ci-dessus n° 106) ; et éd. Bernard Guyon et Henri Coulet, « Bibliothèque de la Pléiade », *Œuvres complètes* de J.-J. ROUSSEAU, t. II, Paris, Gallimard, 1961.

[204] SADE (Donatien-Aldonse-François, marquis de), *Justine, ou les Malheurs de la vertu*, en Hollande, Libraires associés, 1791.

[205] — *Histoire de Juliette, ou les Prospérités du vice*, en Hollande, s. n., 1797.

[206] — *La Philosophie dans le boudoir*, Londres, s. n., 1795.

[207] SMOLLETT (Tobias), *Aventures de Roderik Random* (traduites par P. HERNANDEZ et P.-F. PUISIEUX de l'anglais : *The Adventures of Roderick Random*), Londres, Nourse, 3 vol., 1761.

[208] — *Histoire et aventures de Sir Williams Pickle* (traduit par François-Vincent TOUSSAINT de l'anglais : *The Adventures of Peregrine Pickle, in Which Are Included Memoirs of a Lady of Quality*), Amsterdam, s. n., 4 vol., 1753.

[209] — *Fathom et Melvil* (traduit par T.-P. BERTIN de l'anglais : *The Adventures of Ferdinand Count Fathom*), Paris, Gueffier, 4 vol., an VI [1798].

[210] TENCIN (Claudine-Alexandrine de), *Mémoires du comte de Comminge*, La Haye, J. Néaulme, 1735.

[211] VADÉ (Jean-Joseph), *Lettres de La Grenouillère, entre M. Jérosme Dubois, pêcheux du Gros-Caillou, et Mlle Nanette Dubut, blanchisseuse de linge fin*, La Grenouillère, s. d., [1749], cf. *Œuvres de Vadé*, éd. Julien Lemer, Paris, Garnier, 1875 (?).

[212] VOLTAIRE, *Candide ou l'Optimisme, traduit de l'allemand de M. le Dr Ralph*, s. l., s. n., 1759, cf. éd. A. Morize, « Société des textes français modernes », Paris, Droz, 1913.

[213] — *L'Ingénu, Histoire véritable, tirée des manuscrits du P. Quesnel*, Utrecht, s. n., 1767, cf. éd. William R. Jones, « Textes Littéraires français », Genève, Droz, 1957.

III

ÉTUDES MODERNES (XIXᵉ ET XXᵉ SIÈCLES)

[214] ABENSOUR (Léon), *la Femme et le féminisme avant la Révolution*, Paris, Leroux, 1923.

[215] ADAM (Antoine), *Histoire de la littérature française au XVIIᵉ siècle*, Paris, Domat, 5 vol., 1948-1956.

[216] ASCOLI (Georges), Essai sur l'histoire des idées féministes en France du XVIᵉ siècle à la Révolution, *Revue de Synthèse historique*, XIII (1906), pp. 25-57, 99-106 et 161-184.

[217] BACHMAN (Albert), *Censorship in France from 1715 to 1750 : Voltaire's Opposition*, New York, Publications of the Institute of French Studies, Inc., 1934.

[218] BARRAS (Moses), *The Stage Controversy in France from Corneille to Rousseau*, New York, Publications of the Institute of French Studies, Inc., 1933.

[219] BEAUVOIR (Simone de), *le Deuxième sexe*, Paris, Gallimard, 2 vol., 1949.

[220] BIRNBAUM (Johanna, geb. Göhr), *Die « Memoirs » um 1700 ; eine Studie zur Entwicklung der realistischen Romankunst vor Richardson*, Halle, Niemeyer, 1934.

[221] BLANCHARD (Frederic T.), *Fielding the Novelist; a Study in Historical Criticism*, New Haven, Yale University Press, 1926.

[222] BONNO (Gabriel), Liste chronologique des périodiques de langue française du XVIIIe siècle, *Modern Language Quarterly*, V (1944), pp. 3-35.

[223] BOULLÉE (Auguste Aimé), *Histoire de la vie et des ouvrages du chancelier d'Aguesseau*, Paris, Desenne, 2 vol., 1835.

[224] BRAY (René), *la Formation de la doctrine classique en France*, Paris, Hachette, 1927.

[225] BRUNETIÈRE (Ferdinand), Le Sage (1883), in *Études critiques sur l'histoire de la littérature française*, 3e série, Paris, Hachette, 1890, pp. 63-120.

[226] — Marivaux (1884), *ibid.*, pp. 121-187.

[227] — L'abbé Prévost (1885), *ibid.*, pp. 189-258.

[228] — Le roman français au XVIIe siècle (1890), in *Études critiques sur l'histoire de la littérature française*, 4e série, Paris, Hachette, 1891, pp. 27-50.

[229] — L'influence des femmes dans la littérature française (1886), in *Questions de critique*, Paris, Calmann-Lévy, 1889, pp. 23-61.

[229 A] BUNDY (Jean), Fréron and the English Novel, *Revue de littérature comparée*, XXXVI (1962), pp. 258-265.

[229 B] BUSSON (Henri), La théologie de l'abbé Prévost, in *Littérature et théologie*, Paris, Presses Universitaires de France, 1962, pp. 195-242. *Publications de la Faculté des Lettres et des Sciences humaines d'Alger*, XLII.

[230] CABOCHE (Charles), *les Mémoires et l'histoire en France*, Paris, Charpentier, 2 vol. 1863.

[231] CAHEN (Albert), Introduction à son édition de *Télémaque*, Paris, Hachette, 1920.

[232] CALVERTON (Victor Francis), *Sex Expression in Literature*, New York, Boni & Liveright, 1926.

[233] CAMUS (Albert), Roman et révolte, in *l'Homme révolté*, Paris, Gallimard, 1951, pp. 319-331.

[234] CHASLES (Philarète), Du roman et de ses sources dans l'Europe moderne, *Revue des Deux Mondes*, XXX (1842²), pp. 550-574. Réimprimé sous le double titre de « Sources germaniques du roman moderne » et « Naissance du roman au Moyen Age », in *Études sur les premiers temps du christianisme et sur le Moyen Age*, Paris, Amyot, 1847, pp. 340-376.

[235] CHERBULIEZ (Victor), *l'Idéal romanesque en France (1610-1816)*, Paris, Hachette, 1911.

[236] CHÉREL (Albert), *Fénelon au XVIIIe en France (1715-1820) son prestige, son influence*, Paris, Hachette, 1918.

[236 A] CHERPACK (Clifton), *An Essay on Crébillon Fils*, Durham (North Carolina), Duke University Press, 1962.

[237] CLAPP (John M.), An 18th century attempt at a critical view of the novel : the *Bibliothèque Universelle des Romans*, *Publications of the Modern Language Association*, XXV (1910), pp. 60-96.

[238] CLARETIE (Léo), *Essai sur Lesage romancier*, Paris, Colin, 1890.

[239] CLARK (Ruth), *Anthony Hamilton (Author of Memoirs of Count Grammont), His Life and Works and His Family*, Londres et New York, John Lane, 1921.

[240] CROSBY (Emily A.), *Une romancière oubliée : Mme Riccoboni ; sa vie, ses œuvres, sa place dans la littérature anglaise et française du XVIIIe siècle*, Paris, Rieder, 1924.

[241] DALLAS (Dorothy Frances), *le Roman français de 1660 à 1680*, Paris, J. Gamber, 1932.

[242] DELOFFRE (Frédéric), *Marivaux et le marivaudage ; étude de langue et de style*, Paris, Belles-Lettres, 1955.

[243] — Le problème de l'illusion romanesque et le renouvellement des techniques narratives de 1700 à 1715, in *La Littérature narrative d'imagination ; des genres littéraires aux techniques d'expression* (colloque de Strasbourg, 23-25 avril 1959), Paris, Presses Universitaires de France, 1961, pp. 115-133.

[243 A] — Un morceau de critique en quête d'auteur : le jugement du *Pour et Contre* sur *Manon Lescaut*. *Revue des Sciences humaines*, fasc. 106 (avril-juin 1962), pp. 203-212.

[244] DUCARRE (Joseph), Une « supercherie littéraire » de l'abbé Prévost : *Les Voyages de Robert Lade, Revue de littérature comparée*, XVI (1936), pp. 465-476.

[245] DULONG (Gustave), *L'abbé de Saint-Réal ; étude sur les rapports de l'histoire et du roman au XVIIe siècle*, Paris, Champion, 2 vol., 1921.

[246] ENGEL (Claire-Éliane), *le Véritable abbé Prévost*, Monaco, Éditions du Rocher, 1958.

[247] ESTRÉE (Paul d'), Un journaliste policier : le chevalier de Mouhy, *Revue d'Histoire littéraire de la France*, IV (1897), pp. 195-238.

[248] ÉTIEMBLE (René), Textes critiques accompagnant son édition des *Romanciers français du XVIIIe siècle*, « Bibliothèque de la Pléiade », Paris, Gallimard, t. I (1960).

[249] ÉTIENNE (Servais), *le Genre romanesque en France depuis l'apparition de la Nouvelle Héloïse jusqu'aux approches de la Révolution*, Bruxelles, Lamartin, 1922, in *Mémoires de l'Académie royale de Belgique*, 2e série, t. XVII, premier mémoire.

[250] FOSTER (James R.), *History of the Pre-Romantic Novel in England*, New York, The Modern Language Association of America, 1949.

[251] GENLIS (Félicité Stéphanie, comtesse de BRUSBART DE), *De l'influence des femmes sur la littérature française, comme protectrices des lettres et comme auteurs, ou Précis de l'histoire des femmes françaises les plus célèbres*, Paris, Maradan, 1811.

[252] GONCOURT (Edmond et Jules de), *la Femme au XVIIIe siècle*, Paris, Charpentier, 1862.

[253] GREEN (Frederick Charles), A forgotten novel of manners of the eighteenth century : *la Paysanne parvenue* by le Chevalier de Mouhy, *Modern Language Review*, XVIII (1923), pp. 309-316.

[254] — Realism in the French novel of the first half of the 18th century *Modern Language Notes*, XXXVIII (1923), pp. 321-329.

[255] — *La Peinture des mœurs de la bonne société dans le roman français de 1715 à 1761*, Paris, Presses Universitaires de France, 1924.

[256] — The Chevalier de Mouhy, an eighteenth century French novelist, *Modern Philology*, XXII (1924-1925), pp. 225-237.

[257] — Further evidence of realism in the French novel of the 18th century, *Modern Language Notes*, XL (1925), pp. 257-270.

[258] — The critic of the seventeenth century and his attitude toward the French novel, *Modern Philology*, XXIV (1927), pp. 285-295.

[259] — The eighteenth century French critic and the contemporary novel, *Modern Language Review*, XXIII (1928), pp. 174-187.

[260] — *French Novelists, Manners and Ideas ; From the Renaissance to the Revolution*, Londres et Toronto, J. M. Dent & Sons, 1928.

[261] — *Minuet; a Critical Survey of French and English Literary Ideas in the Eighteenth Century*, Londres, J. M. Dent & Sons, 1935.

[261 A] HAAC (Oscar A.), L'amour dans les collèges jésuites : une satire anonyme du dix-huitième siècle, *Studies on Voltaire and the Eighteenth Century*, t. XVIII, pp. 95-111, Genève, Institut et Musée Voltaire, 1961.

[262] HAZARD (Paul), *la Pensée européenne au XVIII⁰ siècle*, Paris, Boivin, 3 vol., 1946.

[263] HEINZ (Hans), Gil Blas und das zeitgenössische Leben in Frankreich, *Romanische Forschungen*, XXXVII (1916), pp. 778-953.

[264] HORNER (Joyce), *The English Women Novelists and their Connection with the Feminist Movement (1688-1797)*. Smith College Studies in Modern Languages (Northampton, Massachusetts), XI (1929-1930).

[265] JOLIAT (Eugène), *Smollett et la France*, Paris, Champion, 1935.

[266] JONES (Claude E.), The English novel : a critical view, 1756-1785, *Modern Language Quaterly*, XIX (1958), pp. 147-159 et 213-224.

[267] JONES (Silas Paul), *A List of French Prose Fiction from 1700 to 1750*, New York, H. W. Wilson Co., 1939.

[268] LANCASTER (Henry Carrington), *French Tragedy in the Time of Louis XV and Voltaire (1715-1774)*, Baltimore, Johns Hopkins Press, 2 vol., 1957.

[269] LANSON (Gustave), Étude sur *Gil Blas*, in *Hommes et livres*, *études morales et littéraires*, Paris, Lecène et Oudin, 1895, pp. 185-214.

[270] LARNAC (Jean), *Histoire de la littérature féminine en France*, Paris, Kra, 1929.

[271] LEAVIS (Queenie D.), *Fiction and the Reading Public*, Londres, Chatto & Windus, 1932.

[272] LE BRETON (André), *le Roman français au XVII⁰ siècle*, Paris, Boivin, 1890.

[273] — *Le Roman français au XVIII⁰ siècle*, Paris, Boivin, 1898.

[274] LELY (Gilbert), *Vie du marquis de Sade*, Paris, Gallimard, 2 vol., 1952-1957.

[275] — Une supercherie littéraire de Sade : *Isabelle de Bavière, Mercure de France*, CCCXL (Novembre 1960), pp. 476-488.

[276] LEVESQUE (Eugène), cf. Urbain, Charles.

[277] MAGENDIE (Maurice), *le Roman français au XVIIᵉ siècle, de l'Astrée au Grand Cyrus*, Paris, Droz, 1932.

[278] MASSON (Pierre-Maurice), *Une vie de femme au XVIIIᵉ siècle : Mme de Tencin (1682-1749)*, Paris, Hachette, 1909.

[279] MAURY (Fernand), *Étude sur la vie et les œuvres de Bernardin de Saint-Pierre*, Paris, Hachette, 1892.

[280] MAUZI (Robert), *l'Idée de bonheur au XVIIIᵉ siècle*, Paris, Colin, 1960.

[281] MAY (Georges), Racine et *les Liaisons dangereuses, French Review*, XXIII (1949-1950), pp. 452-461.

[282] — *Quatre Visages de Denis Diderot*, Paris, Boivin, 1951.

[283] — L'histoire a-t-elle engendré le roman ? Aspects français de la question au seuil du Siècle des Lumières *Revue d'Histoire Littéraire de la France*, LV (1955), pp. 155-176.

[284] MEAD (William), *Les Liaisons dangereuses* and moral « usefulness », *PMLA*, LXXV (1960), pp. 563-570.

[285] MEISTER (Paul), *Charles Duclos (1704-1772)*, Genève, Droz, 1956.

[286] MILLE (Pierre), *le Roman français*, « Librairie de Paris », Paris, Didot, 1930.

[287] MONGLOND (André), *le Préromantisme français*, Grenoble, Arthaud, 2 vol., 1930.

[288] MONNIER (Francis), *Le Chancelier d'Aguesseau, sa conduite et ses idées politiques, et son influence sur le mouvement des esprits pendant la première moitié du XVIIIᵉ siècle*, Paris, Didier, 1860.

[289] MOOIJ (Anne Louis Anton), *Caractères principaux et tendances des romans psychologiques chez quelques femmes-auteurs, de Mme Riccoboni à Mme de Souza (1757-1826)*, Groningue, de Waal, 1949.

[290] MOORE (Alexander P.), *The « Genre poissard » and the French Stage of the Eighteenth Century*, New York, Publications of the Institute of French Studies, Inc., 1935.

[291] MORILLOT (Paul), *le Roman en France de 1610 jusqu'à nos jours*, Paris, Masson, 1893.

[292] MORNET (Daniel), Les enseignements des bibliothèques privées (1750-1780), *Revue d'Histoire littéraire de la France*, XVII (1910), pp. 449-496.

[293] — Introduction à son édition de *la Nouvelle Héloïse*, Paris Hachette, t. I (1925).

[294] — *Les Origines intellectuelles de la Révolution française (1715-1787)*, Paris, Colin, 1933.

[295] MORRIS (Thelma), *L'abbé Desfontaines et son rôle dans la littérature de son temps (Studies on Voltaire and the Eighteenth Century*, t. XIX), Genève, Institut et Musée Voltaire, 1961.

[296] MORRISSETTE (Bruce Archer), *The Life and Works of Marie-Catherine Desjardins (Mme de Villedieu) 1632-1683*, Saint-Louis, Washington University, 1947.

[297] PHELPS (William Lyon), *The Advance of the English Novel*, New York, Dodd, Mead & Co., 1916.

[298] PICARD (Raymond), L'univers de *Manon Lescaut, Mercure de France*, CCXLI (avril 1961), pp. 606-622 ; et CCXLII (mai 1961), pp. 87-105.

[299] POTTINGER (David T.), *The French Book Trade in the Ancien Régime (1500-1791)*, Cambridge, Harvard University Press, 1958.

[300] RATNER (Moses), *Theory and Criticism of the Novel in France from l' « Astrée » to 1750*, New York, thèse de doctorat de New York University, 1938.

[301] REYNIER (Gustave), *le Roman réaliste au XVII⁰ siècle*, Paris, Hachette, 1914.

[302] — *La Femme au XVII⁰ siècle ; ses ennemis et ses défenseurs*, Paris, Plon, 1933.

[303] RICHARD (Pierre), *La Bruyère et ses « Caractères »*, Amiens, Malfère, 1946.

[304] ROCHEBLAVE (Samuel), *Essai sur le comte de Caylus, l'homme, l'artiste, l'antiquaire*, Paris, Hachette, 1889.

[305] RODDIER (Henri), *l'Abbé Prévost, l'homme et l'œuvre*, Paris, Hatier-Boivin, 1955.

[306] ROUGEMONT (Denis de), *l'Amour et l'Occident*, Paris, Plon, 1939.

[307] RUTHERFORD (Marie-Rose), Un inédit sur l'abbé Prévost, *French Studies*, IX (1955), pp. 227-237.

[307 A] — (LABRIOLLE-RUTHERFORD, M.-R. de), Le Pour et Contre et les romans de l'abbé Prévost (1733-1740), *Revue d'Histoire littéraire de la France*, LXII (1962), pp. 28-40.

[308] SAINTE-BEUVE (Charles Augustin de), *Portraits littéraires* (1844), éd. Maxime Leroy, « Bibliothèque de la Pléiade », Paris, Gallimard, 2 vol., 1949-1951.

[309] — *Causeries du lundi* (1851-1862).

[310] SAINT-RENÉ TAILLANDIER (René-Gaspard-Ernest), Un poète comique du temps de Molière : Boursault, sa vie et ses œuvres, in *Études littéraires*, Paris, Plon, 1881, pp. 1-197.

[311] SAINTSBURY (George), *A History of the French Novel*, t. I : *From the Beginning to 1800*, Londres, McMillan, 1917.

[312] SCHMIDT (Albert-Marie), Duclos, Sade et la littérature féroce, *Revue des Sciences humaines*, fasc. 62-63 (avril-septembre 1951), pp. 146-155.

[313] SEILLIÈRE (Ernest), *le Péril mystique dans l'inspiration des démocraties contemporaines*, Paris, Renaissances du Livre, 1918.

[314] — *Les Étapes du mysticisme passionné (de Saint-Preux à Manfred)* Paris, Renaissance du Livre, 1919.

[315] — *Les Origines romanesques de la morale et de la politique romantiques*, Paris, Renaissance du Livre, 1920.

[316] SHAW (E. P.), A Note on the temporary suppression of *Tom Jones* in France, *Modern Language Notes*, LXXII (1957), p. 41.

[317] SPITZER (Leo), A propos de *la Vie de Marianne*, *Romanic Review*, XLIV (1953), pp. 102-126.